Serial Selves

Serial Selves

• • • • • • • • • • • • • • • • •

Identity and Representation in Autobiographical Comics

FREDERIK BYRN KØHLERT

Rutgers University Press

New Brunswick, Camden, and Newark, New Jersey, and London

Library of Congress Cataloging-in-Publication Data

Names: Køhlert, Frederik Byrn, author.
Title: Serial selves : identity and representation in autobiographical comics
    / Frederik Byrn Køhlert.
Description: New Brunswick : Rutgers University Press, [2019] | Includes
    bibliographical references and index.
Identifiers: LCCN 2018025365 | ISBN 9780813592251 (pbk.) | ISBN 9780813592299 (cloth)
Subjects: LCSH: Autobiographical comic books, strips, etc.—History and
    criticism. | Self-perception in art. | Narrative art—Themes, motives.
Classification: LCC PN6714 .K64 2019 | DDC 741.5/35—dc23
LC record available at https://lccn.loc.gov/2018025365

A British Cataloging-in-Publication record for this book is available from the British Library.

♾ The paper used in this publication meets the requirements of the American National
Standard for Information Sciences—Permanence of Paper for Printed Library Materials,
ANSI Z39.48-1992.

www.rutgersuniversitypress.org

Manufactured in the United States of America

Contents

Serial Selves

Introduction

● ● ● ● ● ● ● ● ● ● ● ● ●

Serial Selves

In "Di(e)ary Comic," a one-page autobiographical comic published by cartoonist Gabby Schulz on his website in 2012, the artist depicts what is for him a seemingly ordinary day. "Today I drew some comics," Schulz innocuously begins, above an image of himself bent over his drawing desk in which he looks both tired and slightly disheveled (see fig. I.1). While this panel initially seems to be a fairly standard depiction of the artist at work, Schulz introduces a metalevel in the next panel, which shows the cartoonist turning away from his desk to finish the drawing from the first panel while informing the reader that "Then I drew a comic about drawing that comic." Drawing himself drawing himself is only the beginning of Schulz's satire of the navel-gazing he associates with certain autobiographical comics, however, and the comic continues to play with the form by repeatedly blurring the line between the cartoonist's lived and drawn lives. Explaining that "Then I drank some tea while thinking about comics within comics (then drew a comic about it)," followed by "Then I took a break from all that to draw *this* diary comic in an unconscious attempt to nest myself in yet another layer of meta-self-absorption," Schulz depicts himself with his head halfway into a

1

FIG. I.1. Gabby Schulz sees the whole universe in "Di(e)ary Comic," from *Gabby's Playhouse* (www.gabbysplayhouse.com); original in author's collection.

page he is drawing—and from which a detached arm emerges in order to draw yet *another* comic. At this point even his comics are drawing more comics, and the proliferation of metalayers seems potentially endless. After noting that "Then I hung out with some cartoonists" and asking the reader to "Guess what we talked about," Schulz concludes the brief piece with a panel that visually literalizes his apparent belief that the genre has its metaphorical head up its ass—a vantage point, he assures us, that constitutes a "blessed gift" allowing him to "see the whole universe."

Despite its lighthearted and self-deprecating tone, Schulz's comic is itself also a formally adventurous example of the genre it lampoons, and as such touches upon many of the concerns prompted by the question of what happens when you draw yourself in comics form, including issues of auto-biographical subjectivity, proliferating self-representation across and between words and images, and the relationship between the self and the outside social "universe" as mediated visually through comics. If, as Schulz suggests, making autobiographical comics allows you to see and negotiate your relationship with the world through the form's self-reflective engagement with autobiographical representations, then the nature and tenor of those representations (as well as their status as visual objects designed to be looked at by others) might matter politically, especially for people on the social and cultural margins.

This book examines autobiographical self-expression by marginalized authors in the comics form. Compared to traditional literary autobiography, the visuality of the comics form adds a level of expression that allows artists to engage with issues of representation in different and sometimes unexpected ways through the embodiment of the self on the page. Such representation is never straightforward or self-contained, however, but is in implicit conversation with an extended history of, for example, misogynist, racist, or ableist visual traditions that artists working in the form must contend with in various ways. Moreover, in a culture increasingly dominated by the visual—a tendency that is only growing with the online world's reliance on images in the form of easily shared memes, infographics, and, of course, web comics—autobiographical comics offer a way of taking control of representation in a direct and politically loaded engagement with the visual self. Through detailed formal analysis, I argue that because comics rely on both highly personal hand-drawn aesthetics and a serially networked approach to narrative, the form can challenge conventional representational schemes in a complex dance of appropriation and resignification that is always open to the creation of new meanings. Further, the multimodal hybridity of the comics form—consisting, as it does, of multiple overlapping, interdependent, and often competing verbal and visual codes—creates a distinctively unstable and decentered reading experience that enables the drawn performance of the autobiographical self as a site of ideological struggle.

Returning for a moment to Schulz (who is, to be clear, a white male, although his comics consistently engage with issues regarding illness, masculinity, and the nonstandard body that are similar to those of the artists studied here), then perhaps one of the most extraordinary things about "Di(e)ary Comic" is that there is a tradition of autobiographical comics—along with, of course, a set of attendant conventions (and possibly even clichés)—for him to both draw upon and satirize. For most people, the word *comics* probably does not bring to mind a short story about a sleepy-looking man drawing himself, but instead the fantastic world of superheroes, especially as expressed through the dozens of films released since the current wave of superhero comics adaptations began in the early 2000s. Since then, figures such as Batman, Iron Man, and Spider-Man—followed, belatedly, by Wonder Woman in 2017—have dominated both the global movie theater box office and the general public's conception of what the comics form is capable of expressing. This is understandable for both historical and culturally hegemonic reasons, since the superhero genre has played (and continues to play) a central role in the comics world, with its plot devices and instantly recognizable aesthetics being perhaps the form's most noticeable contribution to American as well as world culture.

Alongside the glossy and lucrative realm of superheroes and other mainstream comics inflected by the fantastic, however, a different tradition of comics began to appear in the 1960s and 1970s, centered in San Francisco and inspired by the irreverent attitude of the counterculture. After the comics publishing industry's introduction of the regulatory Comics Code Authority in 1954—occasioned by what David Hajdu has called "the Great Comic-Book Scare" of the early 1950s, during which concerned politicians, social reformers, and parent groups threatened the industry with boycott unless it agreed to self-police and exclude objectionable content such as "excessive violence" and "sex perversion"—comic books had become increasingly tame and lost most of their onetime subversive appeal. Seizing upon the sanitized and culturally harmless form of comics with rebellious zeal, the artists associated with the "underground comix" movement (with the *x* used to indicate an alternative slant), including Robert Crumb, Justin Green, and Aline Kominsky (later, after her marriage to Crumb, known as Aline Kominsky Crumb), broke new ground regarding the kinds of experience typically portrayed in the form. Crumb, for example, produced countless short comics depicting his various (and often disturbing) sexual fantasies, and Green, in *Binky Brown Meets the Holy Virgin Mary* from 1972—often considered the first long-form autobiographical comic—told the story of his struggles with Catholic guilt and obsessive-compulsive disorder, the combination of which led him to believe that invisible "penis-rays" were emanating from his various body parts and contaminating nearby religious iconography. Adding a welcome female perspective, Kominsky Crumb invented an alter ego named The Bunch, who featured in comics about such personal matters as early sexual experiences and a troubled relationship with an overbearing mother. Meanwhile, in Cleveland, music collector and hospital file clerk Harvey Pekar wrote stories about his everyday life and work, illustrated by others (Crumb among them) and published in a series ironically entitled *American Splendor* beginning in 1976. Confrontational, intimate, and often taboo-breaking, these and many other comics associated with the underground greatly expanded the potential of the form to depict lived experience and tell autobiographical stories in words and pictures.

Directly inspired by Green's radical use of comics to produce a highly personal and emotionally challenging story, fellow underground cartoonist Art Spiegelman continued this line of experimentation by drawing a three-page autobiographical comic entitled "Maus" about his parents' experiences during the Holocaust. Despite its inconspicuous first publication in a 1972 one-off comic book called *Funny Aminals*—which also featured contributions by Crumb and Green, among others—Spiegelman's brief comic provided its author with the inspiration for the longer two-volume *Maus*, which in most conceptualizations of American comics history is almost single-handedly responsible for definitively demonstrating the possibilities of the form for serious and reality-based work. Originally serialized in *Raw*, an ambitious comics anthology magazine edited by Spiegelman and his wife Françoise Mouly, *Maus* was collected in stand-alone volumes published in 1986 and 1991. In addition to glowing reviews, the collected work was eventually awarded a special Pulitzer Prize in 1992—a watershed event that also helped legitimize the historically maligned comics form as an object worthy of critical as well as scholarly attention.

Seizing on the new space established by the countercultural underground and confirmed by the highbrow success of *Maus*, a new generation of cartoonists started drawing autobiographical comics in the late 1980s and early 1990s. Most influentially, perhaps, a trio of Toronto-based artists consisting of Chester Brown, Joe Matt, and Seth created comics depicting events from their lives, such as Brown's inability, as a teenager, to connect emotionally with his mother and Matt's obsession with pornography. Drawn and sometimes self-published as photocopied zines or mini-comics in the do-it-yourself aesthetic of the punk- and grunge-inflected alternative culture of the time, autobiographical comics soon acquired the reputation of being a lo-fi delivery system for the exposure of their authors' most private thoughts and desires, sometimes to an unflattering degree. While exceptions have, of course, appeared regularly, the stereotype nevertheless quickly became so entrenched that the *Comics Journal*, on the cover of a 1993 special issue, could ask its readers, "How much longer are we going to be able to stand all those damn autobiographical cartoonists?" (*Comics Journal*, vol. 162, cover). As the issue's half-mocking cover image also suggests, the often self-absorbed nature of many autobiographical comics was ripe for parody around the time when the genre reached its preliminary peak in the early 1990s.

Of the eleven autobiographical characters portrayed on the *Comics Journal* cover, nine are male, two are female, and all are white. Although this selection perhaps reveals the somewhat limited viewpoint of the artist behind the satirical image, it is also not an entirely inaccurate reflection of the demographic breakdown of creators making autobiographical comics in the early 1990s. But while the genre could perhaps be accused of being exceedingly white and male (in addition to straight and able-bodied) for its first few decades, such a criticism would be significantly more difficult to level today. Instead of further compounding the tendency to tell a narrow range of stories by demographically similar authors, autobiographical comics have in the last few decades experienced a virtual explosion of diversity in both subject matter and authorial perspective.

As Hillary Chute has amply demonstrated, women creators of autobiographical comics have especially been at the vanguard of the genre—as well as the form itself—for the past few decades. In *Graphic Women*, her study of women's life writing in comics form, Chute closely examines the work of Lynda Barry, Alison Bechdel, Aline Kominsky Crumb, Phoebe Gloeckner, and Marjane Satrapi, all of whom have published influential long-form autobiographical narratives. Most famously, perhaps, Bechdel's *Fun Home* and Satrapi's *Persepolis* have continued where Spiegelman's *Maus* left off in terms of bringing autobiographical comics into bookstores and the popular consciousness—not least because of their successful and award-winning adaptations as, respectively, a Broadway musical and an animated film. Chute argues that "against a valorization of absence and aporia, graphic narrative asserts the value of presence, however complex and contingent" (*Graphic Women* 2), and her analysis makes clear that a central attraction of the form for women creators is its ability to show and make visual that which is either silenced or otherwise effaced in contemporary culture, especially as it pertains to gendered experience. As such, Chute neatly points to comics' potential for "autobiography as re-facement" (*Graphic Women* 80–81), a perspective that this study continues, but with a more inclusive focus on several different experiences of marginality.

In addition to the female perspective examined by Chute, the aforementioned explosion of diverse perspectives in contemporary autobiographical comics has resulted in deeply personal stories about such matters as sexuality (including, for example, Meags Fitzgerald's *Long Red Hair*, Nicole J. George's *Calling Dr. Laura*, Ariel Schrag's four volumes of *High School Comic Chronicles*, and Howard Cruse's *Stuck Rubber Baby*, a fictionalized account of growing up gay in the American South during the civil rights era) and ethnoracial difference (Toufic El Rassi's *Arab in America*, Lila Quintero Weaver's *Darkroom*, Gene Luen Yang's semiautobiographical *American Born Chinese*, and John Lewis's *March*, written with Andrew Aydin and drawn by Nate Powell), as well as a large and ever-expanding number of comics depicting lives marked by such challenges as illness, trauma, depression, and disability, including David B's *Epileptic*; Jeffrey Brown's *Funny Misshapen Body*; Al Davison's *The Spiral Cage*; Peter Dunlap-Shohl's *My Degeneration*; Brian Fies's *Mom's Cancer*; Ellen Forney's *Marbles*; Tom Hart's *Rosalie Lightning*; Jennifer Hayden's *The Story of My Tits*; Sarah Leavitt's *Tangles*; Frederik Peeters's *Blue Pills*; Harvey Pekar and his wife Joyce Brabner's *Our Cancer Year*, illustrated by Frank Stack; John Porcellino's *The Hospital Suite*; Gabby Schulz's three books *Monsters*, *Sick*, and *A Process of Drastically Reducing One's Expectations*; David Small's *Stitches*; Georgia Webber's *Dumb*; and Julia Wertz's *The Infinite Wait*, among many others. Of course, these themes rarely appear in isolation, and most of the titles listed productively engage with the authors' navigation of multiple intersecting identities, such as Schrag's extensive four-volume consideration of what it meant to be young, queer, and female in the very specific cultural moment of 1990s California.

As this list suggests, there is much more to explore in autobiographical comics than questions of gender, and although the present study begins with two chapters that build on the insights of Chute and others in order to focus on alternative representations of femininity in the comics of Julie Doucet and the depiction and working through of sexual trauma in Gloeckner's work, it also broadens the scope and examines autobiographical comics by authors writing from and against other positions of marginality. It does so across five thematically organized chapters, which in addition to gender and trauma investigate the productive potential of representing lives marked by issues of homosexuality, disability, and ethnoracial difference in autobiographical comics. Instead of attempting an exhaustive overview of comics invested in these perspectives, each chapter consists of an extensive case study of a single artist's work, which in addition to Doucet's various stories published in her serialized comic book *Dirty Plotte* and Gloeckner's *A Child's Life* and *The Diary of a Teenage Girl* include, in order, Schrag's *High School Comic Chronicles*, Davison's *The Spiral Cage*, and El Rassi's *Arab in America*.

Together, the chapters that follow broaden the scope of contemporary studies of autobiographical comics by opening the conversation to other, differently marginalized subject positions. While the study of autobiographical comics created by women constitutes a particularly important strand in the existing scholarship—and one to which this study owes an obvious debt—my discussion of the central role played by the visual in the construction of various exclusionary categories starts from the assumption that the cultural mechanisms that serve to marginalize women are both historically and structurally different from those establishing for example disability as a social category. The book therefore departs from approaches that theorize marginality as a single, unified category. Instead, I consider the concept of marginality from several different perspectives—those of gender, trauma, homosexuality, disability, and race/ethnicity—and argue that only by examining the specificities of each subject position's relation to visuality and the history of representation can we arrive at a more comprehensive understanding of the opportunities and challenges the comics form offers for self-representation and the production of autobiographical subjectivity.

Autobiographical Selves

The promise of all autobiography, of course, is self-expression. From its traditional association with narratives about the representative public and famous man unambiguously situated in history to the "memoir boom" of the last few decades, the impetus and logic of the genre has always been the possibility of expressing the self in one's own terms.[1] Defined by influential French theorist Philippe Lejeune as a "retrospective prose narrative written by a real person concerning his own existence, where the focus is his individual life, in particular the story of his personality" (*On Autobiography* 4), literary autobiography functions as a way for writers to take control of representation and serve up a version of the self that is deemed fit—idealized or otherwise—for public consumption. But where classic examples of autobiographical writing worked from an assumption of a coherent and integrated self that could unproblematically be expressed in narrative, modern developments in the understanding of the subject cast doubt on such straightforward representation. Citing Freudian psychoanalysis, Marxism, and Saussurean linguistics, Sidonie Smith and Julia Watson note that these "radical challenges to the notion of a unified selfhood in the early decades of the twentieth century eroded certainty in both a coherent 'self' and the 'truth' of self-narrating" (200). Along with the later critical interventions associated with poststructuralism, which decisively ungrounded the idea of a single and static self, these challenges have led to a view of the subject as fractured, multiple, and always in process. Consequently, the postmodern decentering of the self has enabled critics such as Elizabeth Bruss, Paul John Eakin, and Smith to theorize the autobiographical subject as a performative construct that is instantiated in narrative and through the autobiographical act itself.[2] As Smith, following Judith Butler, has argued, "there is no essential, original, coherent autobiographical self before the moment of self-narrating," and therefore "the interiority or self that is said to be prior to the autobiographical expression or reflection is an *effect* of autobiographical storytelling" (17, 18; emphasis in the original), a perspective that unambiguously links the production of autobiographical texts to the formation of identity and subjectivity.

In combination with the recent critical re-evaluation of autobiography, which has both opened the genre to a plurality of new perspectives and emphasized other forms of life writing as equally valid, the notion that self-narration can be constitutive of selfhood means that the genre has obvious political potential for people on the cultural margins. Silenced or excluded by hegemonic master narratives privileging a perspective that is white, male, heterosexual, and able-bodied, people with marginalized identities might employ autobiography to insist on individual agency and in that way transform themselves from being objects in the narratives of others to the subjects of their own stories. Taking this view, Françoise Lionnet has argued that such writing can be seen as "an enabling force in the creation of a plural self, one that thrives on ambiguity and multiplicity, on affirmation of differences, not on polarized and polarizing notions of identity, culture, race, or gender" (16). In its ability to tell alternative stories and in the reconceptualization of the subject as discursively constructed to transform life writing, as Kate Douglas and Anna Poletti have summarized, the genre has moved "from being a cultural form associated with the lives of 'great men' to being a dynamic and influential means for people and communities to write themselves into culture and history" (8). Going further, Gillian Whitlock notes the centrality of the genre to contemporary debates about inclusivity and social justice, arguing that "autobiography is fundamental to the struggle for recognition among individuals and groups, to the constant creation of what it means to be human and the rights that fall from that, and to the ongoing negotiation of imaginary boundaries between ourselves and others" (10). Affording its practitioners both a speaking position and the ability to assert the self through personal voice, autobiography therefore contains the capacity to renegotiate individual relationships between the self and its surrounding cultural spaces.

Although autobiography offers a way for politically marginalized people to insert themselves into the culture, the decentering of the subject can be viewed both as an opportunity and an obstacle in terms of what it offers to the project of self-representation. On one hand, as Lionnet suggests, a plural and ambiguous sense of self might support notions of difference and a multiplicity of histories in the face of imposed monolithic identities. Edward Said, in his memoir *Out of Place*, takes this perspective: "I occasionally experience myself as a cluster of flowing currents. I prefer this to the idea of a solid self, the identity to which so many attach so much significance" (295). As a description of the potential benefits to conceiving of the self as unfixed and in flux, Said's passage is in step with both dominant cultural notions of the subject and current theories of autobiography. On the other hand, there might be something politically troubling about doing away with the idea of a cohesive self, especially for people who have been marginalized by various processes of social power. As Nancy Hartsock has asked, "Why is it that just at the moment when so many of us who have been silenced begin to name ourselves, to act as subjects rather than objects of history, that just then the concept of subjecthood becomes problematic?" (163). Considering this predicament from a feminist perspective, Leigh Gilmore notes that "many women autobiographers tend to attribute to speech, presence, political enfranchisement, and cultural authority the same tonic effects contemporary critics associate with the (more or less) free play of signifiers" (*Autobiographics* 75). In light of these objections to postmodernism's radical reconfiguration of subjectivity, the dilemma of how to insist on representing a marginalized self in a culture valorizing the dissolution of a coherent position from where to speak is evident.

In literary autobiography this dilemma is accentuated somewhat by the abstraction of the speaking subject—what in autobiography criticism is referred to as the "narrated I" (Smith and Watson 73)—into language. Appearing on the page both regularly and with consistency of expression, the "I" of literary autobiography serves as an obscuring formal convention that can both suppress the individuality of the speaking subject through an assumption of universality and act as a leveling effect that allows writers to mask themselves in its abstraction. In sharp contrast, autobiography in the visual-verbal comics form lacks the ability to abstract subjectivity into a universal signifier—as Michael A. Chaney has pointed out, comics "make abstractions of identity visible" (*Reading Lessons* 15)—and must instead insist on visualizing the self on the drawn page, where it is afforded a concretized reality through performative and repeated iterations. By being able to simultaneously dissolve the self into multiplicity and insist visually on presence and a specificity of representation, autobiographical comics might be said to split the difference between postmodern notions of subjectivity and more cautious approaches that resist the effacement of a coherent self in the face of marginalizing discourses. At the same time that life writing in comics form might in this way get beyond some of the impasses of literary autobiography, however, such visual embodiment also risks falling victim to the same cultural scripts that work to efface the subjectivity of certain groups.

Embodied Selves

As a necessary fiction of the genre, the narrated autobiographical "I" has often been considered in isolation, irrespective of its embodiment. The privileging of a universal subject that effaces bodily specificity and difference is a perspective that can be traced to Western culture's classic dualism between the material body on the one hand and the spirit or soul on the other. As José Alaniz points out, this opposition has traditionally been unequally balanced, and there exists "a long-standing hierarchy of Platonic-Cartesian metaphysics in which ethereal minds direct and mechanical bodies obey" (*Death* 15). Alaniz goes on to note the last few decades' critical interventions in studies of the body as both nature and social construct, which together highlight the exclusionary processes that have made certain bodies worth less than others. Bodies, it is clear, are inherently political, a perspective that has been taken up in both autobiography and the attendant criticism since the 1990s. Shirley Geok-lin Lim argues that "to recognize a material self is to begin to write politically" (449), and autobiographical engagements with what it means to inhabit certain bodies have become a prominent strand in the genre as authors work through the relationship between identity and representation through a focus on embodiment. In the introduction to a 2017 special issue of the journal *a/b: Auto/Biography Studies* about the future directions of the genre, editors Emily Hipchen and Ricia Anne Chansky cite the recent "material turn" in autobiography criticism, in which "making visible the invisible, the forgotten ones who want to be seen" (143) has appeared as a dominant current. But where the material and visible self is in literary autobiography abstracted into language, autobiographical comics put the body front and center for the reader to look at, evaluate, and engage with. In comics, the unmarked, universalized, and invisible body becomes an impossibility, and the inclusion of images, therefore, is significant to the political potential of self-representation, as readers (and viewers) are all but forced to visually confront an embodied subjectivity on the page.

In literary life writing, supplementing the text with images has often been a favorite strategy of autobiographers. Snapshots or portraits of the author at various ages and in diverse contexts appeal to the perceived status of photographs as documents of historical truth, but even nonmechanical images perform the dual acts of visualizing the written self and affirming authorship upon a "real person" situated in a recognizable cultural space.

Because images serve to make the invisible visible, they have the potential to recalibrate the relationship between reader and autobiographer. Bart Moore-Gilbert takes this perspective in his reading of former slave Olaudah Equiano's autobiography *The Interesting Narrative* from 1789: "Equiano's engraved portrait in the frontispiece of his text *embodies* his equality with the reader, notably by virtue of its direct (even challenging) gaze. This is aimed at precisely those readers who are traditionally privileged in scopic terms" (48; emphasis in the original). The perspective of the gaze as it pertains to autobiographical comics is a topic that will in various ways be taken up in the chapters to follow, especially with regard to possible ways of resisting it, but what is also implied in Moore-Gilbert's reading is the idea that images rarely communicate directly or unproblematically. Taking this view, Tobin Siebers has argued about the ability of certain images to resist imposed meanings that "images too complex to be read refuse this control, and they challenge the authority of reading as a privileged activity because they demonstrate a surplus of meaning untranslatable into linguistic terms" (*Disability Aesthetics* 122). The inclusion of intricately coded images in autobiography in this way allows for a more complex form of embodiment than what language alone is capable of, at the same time that it further compounds the genre's ability to insist on selfhood and agency. These observations naturally have important implications for how we view and encounter drawn subjects in autobiographical comics.

Putting the political body on display, autobiographical comics engage with representation in a way that can both directly address the reader and potentially reshuffle received notions of identity. As Kylie Cardell has argued, "comics *literally* enable new ways of seeing, new ways of being seen, and new ways of representing the self" (121; emphasis in the original). Elsewhere in the scholarship on autobiographical comics, this perspective has been taken up by Chute, who notes "the enabling role of the visual in self-articulation" (*Graphic Women* 7), as well as by Charles Hatfield, who points out that "visualization can play a vital role in the understanding and affirmation of individual identity" (115). But while the political *potential* of visual self-representation is a well-established critical paradigm, such representations, this study will show, rarely signify in uncomplicated ways and need to be understood as part of a wider context of visual culture that might include—or in some cases even rely on—unwelcome codes and traditions. As Sarah Brophy and Janice Hladki note about the dialectic quality of visually representing the self, "visual autobiography is both resistant to and conditioned by the imperatives associated with new and old forms of 'optical scrutiny'" (12). The particular properties of the visual—namely, those that involve seeing and being seen—mean that its enabling power is always balanced by an implied element of danger, as self-representational agency might slip into stereotypical capture with almost imperceptible ease. In a form that relies on a simplified visual language derived in part from the history of stereotype and caricature for its effects, this issue requires a delicate balancing act on the part of artists making autobiographical comics. While these considerations in different ways inform all of the chapters to come, they are especially pertinent to my discussion of El Rassi's *Arab in America* in chapter 5, in which I also examine the relationship between the comics form and the history of ethnoracial stereotypes in detail.

While in traditional prose autobiography the author can both hide behind and be hidden by the "I," comics simultaneously visualize the self and put it on public display. For the artists discussed in this book, therefore, the challenge becomes how to accurately portray a sense of the self as individual agent without becoming subject to such marginalizing representational traditions as those, for example, that turn women into visual spectacle and the disabled into freak shows. The comics form, I argue, allows these authors to meet and engage with this challenge by deploying its specific formal features in adventurous and often playful ways.

Drawn Selves

Formalist scholarship on comics has long been concerned with the form's ability to present the reader with a complex network of visual and verbal codes, including also the possibility of creating productive tensions among the many gaps and spaces between individual elements. In this view, the comics page is an unstable construct that offers a multiplicity of interpretative options and therefore relies on a high level of readerly engagement in order to create meaning. Most famously, practitioner and theorist Scott McCloud has introduced the concepts of "closure" and the "gutter" to explain how readers interpret this profusion of semiotic codes (63, 66). The gutter is the space between individual comics panels, and closure is the act performed as the reader moves between panels, imaginatively bridging the gaps and creating a narrative from a mixture of text, images, and the usually white (though sometimes black or otherwise colored) empty spaces of the gutter. McCloud's central ideas have been enormously influential, and much current comics scholarship focuses on the instability of meaning in the hybrid form as compared to traditional prose. In this vein, Hatfield has called comics "an art of tensions," and focuses his analysis on the interplay between the form's verbal and visual elements in order to argue that "the fractured surface of the comics page, with its patchwork of different images, shapes, and symbols, presents the reader with a surfeit of interpretive options, creating an experience that is always decentered, unstable, and unfixable" (32, xiii–xiv). Similarly, Frank L. Cioffi has argued that a key characteristic of comics is the ability to open up a "field of play" through "image-word disjunctions" (98, 113) that can interrupt fluid interpretation and disturb or otherwise unsettle the reader. More comprehensively, Thierry Groensteen has argued for a system of "arthrology" (*System* 6), by which meaning is created not only through connections between individual elements on the same page but also through the reader's ability to discern connections throughout the text as a whole. In Groensteen's analysis, drawings at opposite ends of a comics narrative might speak as easily to each other as those on either side of a gutter, an approach that gives rise to a view of the form as a vast network of visual and verbal codes that always have the potential to forge new interpretative connections.

Although most formalist comics scholarship focuses on the relationship between the visual and verbal elements, a more expansive consideration might enable us to understand the form's incorporation of several additional codes as a fuller expression of multimodality. As theorized by the New London Group of literacy scholars, the concept of multimodality was developed to account for cultural forms "in which written-linguistic modes of meaning are part and parcel of visual, audio, and spatial patterns of meaning" and therefore require a more expansive set of tools—what the group calls "multiliteracies" (Cope and Kalantzis 5)—to properly decode. Taking the broadest perspective possible, group member Gunther Kress has claimed that "all texts are multimodal" (184), by which he means to draw attention to the fact that even a traditional literary text, for example, will by necessity also include at least a visual or audio element, depending on whether it exists as a print or audio book. As further theorized by Bill Cope and Mary Kalantzis in the introduction to the group's first collection of essays, "there are six design elements in the meaning-making process: those of Linguistic Meaning, Visual Meaning, Audio Meaning, Gestural Meaning, Spatial Meaning, and the Multimodal patterns of meaning that relate the first five modes of meaning to each other" (7). Somewhat surprisingly, perhaps, the group has only intermittently made brief reference to the comics form, which would appear to be an obvious candidate for an extended analysis of multimodality.

Filling this critical space, Dale Jacobs has applied the group's framework to comics and has convincingly argued that the form creates meaning not only in the linguistic and visual realms but across all six of the outlined design elements.[3] Arguing that "reading comics involves a complex, multimodal literacy" (*Graphic Encounters* 3), Jacobs has shown through detailed close reading how the comics form takes advantage of the full arsenal of other meaning makers. These include not only the spatial mode (as also theorized by McCloud, Hatfield, and Groensteen), which "can be conceived of as the layout of panels on the page and the relation between these panels through use of gutter space," but also the "motion lines, sweat beads, posture, etc." of the gestural mode, and even "voice inflections, tone, cadence, and emotional tenor—that is, the audio element—[which] are indicated by way of lettering, punctuation, and the shape of the word balloons" ("Multimodal Constructions" 67, 66). As an argument for the complexity of the form and the equally sophisticated set of skills required to decode it, the concept of multimodality opens the discussion to a more inclusive perspective that allows for attention to how autobiographical comics might employ a variety of design elements in their sustained preoccupation with representing the self on the page. These include, for example, the gestural mode, which is of special importance to my discussion of how Doucet and Davison stage visual encounters between their drawn characters and the reader in chapters 1 and 5, as well as the spatial mode, which is fundamental to chapter 2's analysis of the way Gloeckner uses the form to narrate her experience of childhood sexual trauma.

In addition to the volatility produced by the form's multimodal mixing of different design elements, a central aspect of the form—and one that is of special significance to autobiography—is its use of sequential imagery to produce narrative. Prominent comics artist and early theorist of the form Will Eisner has famously called comics a "sequential art" (*Comics* 5), a perspective that is also central to McCloud's influential definition of the form as "juxtaposed pictorial and other images in deliberate sequence" (9). Following McCloud, it has become something of a critical consensus to observe that in comics, time equals space, and in autobiographical comics, therefore, the presentation of the drawn self happens in a temporally unfixed and theoretically endless proliferation of subjective incarnations of visual identity. Contrary to visual representation in film, for example, where the individual frames replace each other to create a fluid motion, the sequential panels of comics remain visible on the page, their materiality always present in the peripheral vision of the reader. Speaking generally about self-representation in visual media by women, Watson and Smith have argued that sequentiality "enables women artists to propose subjectivity as processual rather than static and to insist that identity is performative, not essentialized. No single pose or frame of the sequence is the 'definitive' or 'truthful' self-portrait" (34). Bringing the same point to bear specifically on comics, Ann Miller argues that "the sense of continuing identity is precarious for any *bande dessinée* character, given that it is drawn anew in each panel. This very instability makes the medium peculiarly apt for the portrayal of the autobiographical self" (250). In combination with the multimodal tensions outlined above, then, the autobiographical performance of the plural and unfixed self across space and time throughout a comic—similar to what Ramzi Fawaz, speaking of superhero comics, has called the form's ability to engage in "bodily fluxing" (18)—means that notions of a single, monolithic identity are always in danger of giving way to a potential redefinition that may unsettle established ways of seeing.

The proliferation of drawn selves throughout a comic is often accentuated by the form's traditional reliance on seriality. In addition to the serial aspects suggested by the sequential nature of the form, comics have often been published serially and in short installments. While the current vogue for one-volume graphic novels to some degree obscures this history—and is in contrast to our culture's increasing valorization of seriality in, for example, prestige television—the serial publication format has not only been a successful way for large publishers to produce habitual readers and consumers but also a way for creators and independent publishers to decrease the financial risk of publishing alternative work while generating a steady stream of income. Although these considerations have been important to the publication history of such authors as Doucet, the production of serial life narratives also has implications for the presentation of the self in autobiographical comics. As Nicole Stamant has observed in her book-length study of serial memoir, the practice "makes the process of self-production transparent" at the same time that it presents "a discursive mode that embraces multiplicity, relationality, and historicity" that in turn allows for "expansive, relational, and culturally contextualized self-representational positions, which dismantle grand autobiographical and historical narratives" (4, 5). As a further undermining of a singular, coherent identity that is liable to having its individual subjectivity subsumed by integrative and marginalizing cultural practices, the serial publishing format joins the sequentiality of the comics form itself as a tool to be employed by autobiographers wishing to write and draw their own multiple selves. With the exception of El Rassi, whose *Arab in America* was published in one volume and in a single unchanged edition, all of the authors whose work I discuss here have published their work serially: Doucet in the classic format of a serialized comic book, Gloeckner in successive iterations of the same basic story, Schrag in a series of accumulative memoirs, and Davison in differently organized and increasingly lengthy editions of the same book. Schrag, especially, in progressively longer and more complex narratives, investigates the development of the queer teenage self through an engagement with the form's serial properties, as I discuss in chapter 4. Multimodal, sequential, and serial, these and other autobiographical comics can thereby be read as rejecting unifying and difference-obscuring conceptualizations of selfhood in favor of a fragmented speaking position, the flip side of which is the heightened rhetorical power suggested by the visual embodiment of the self on the page.

In autobiographical comics, this embodiment is further informed by the fact that we as readers infer a certain relationship between the drawn page (including, of course, its central character) and the real-world author responsible for its creation. This relationship has often been theorized in terms that consider visual style as expressed in drawings as an articulation of the artist's subjectivity. As Kai Mikkonen notes, "traditionally, graphic style has been seen as a kind of signature of the story's creation, the image bearing the sign of its making," and therefore "the cartoonist's subjectivity can be detected in the use and combination of stylistic conventions such as the graphic line, lettering, or the spatial organization of the page" (101). Consequently, critical attention has focused on the individual artist's stylistic signature, as expressed through what Miller has called "a subjective vision, traced on the paper by the artist's hand" (245). Because the drawings on the page contain a recognizable and highly individual "trace" of the author, therefore, the mark of the "graphiateur" (Baetens 147, borrowing from Philippe Marion) is seen as providing the reader with the impression that "the hand and the body—as well as the whole personality of an artist—is visible in the way he or she gives a visual representation of a certain object, character, setting or event" (Baetens and Frey 137). As a final addition to the present consideration of how creators might represent themselves visually in autobiographical comics, the twin concepts of graphiation and the trace suggest not only that subjectivity of expression is embodied in graphic style itself but also that the material real-life author is embodied in the drawings on the page—including, of course, in self-representational characters. This interpretation views the form as especially intimate and therefore highly capable of engendering empathy for (or identification with) autobiographical characters. Reading an autobiographical comic may therefore at times feel like reading a private missive from its author, whose labor and body is present before one's eyes.

As unpredictable but highly personal constructs that are by default engaged with the various processes concerning seeing and being seen, autobiographical comics show us how their creators want to be perceived, and can establish new relationships between authors, characters, and the visual realm. Chaney, noting the "inherently pedagogical comics form" (*Reading Lessons* 7), has argued convincingly and at length that comics teach us how to read them, a perspective that might in this view therefore be extended to say that autobiographical comics can teach us how to see the world in new and different ways.

Unruly Selves

While the drawn character emerges in some autobiographical comics as what French artist Christophe Menu has called "a hieroglyphic shorthand" that "enables the narrative to progress without making an issue of representation" (qtd. in Groensteen, *Comics and Narration* 98), the authors discussed in this study are not primarily interested in such unproblematized forward momentum. Instead they employ the unique aesthetics of comics autobiography for the purposes of structuring personal identity and externalizing subjectivity, in a direct visual engagement with the various cultural processes that marginalize them. As the internal vision of the autobiographer translates into the external form of the comics page, the artists studied here aim precisely to make an issue of representation.

Chapter 1 begins the discussion of the comics form's potential for visualizing subjective notions of the self by focusing on its opportunities for depicting alternative versions of femininity. The chapter discusses the work of artist Julie Doucet in the context of traditional representations of women in comics. I interpret Doucet's loosely autobiographical comics, which are inflected by both dream logic and the fantastic, in light of Mikhail Bakhtin's concept of the carnivalesque and its aesthetic expression as grotesque realism. Through subject matter and a visual style grounded in the grotesque, Doucet's comics challenge normative notions of the female body through a process of resignification based in parody and unruly embodiment. The chapter thereby argues that Doucet's comics perform a feminist critique by redeploying masculinist tropes belonging to "high" culture as grotesque images in the "low" form of comics, and shows how Doucet's combination of subject matter and a nontraditional visual style unsettles the visual pleasure commonly associated with looking at women in comics.

Chapter 2 examines comics autobiography as a system for depicting the lived experience of marginalized and traumatized subjectivity. By focusing on the relationship between visuality and childhood sexual trauma in the work of Phoebe Gloeckner, I show how the visual and fragmented form can be employed as a means to assert agency for a victim of trauma. The comics form, I argue, can function as a kind of visual scriptotherapy, which allows the author to displace the traumatic memory onto the page and create a narrative from a series of disjointed memories. In readings of Gloeckner's two books *A Child's Life* and *The Diary of a Teenage Girl*, I illustrate how her use of the comics form takes advantage of its inherent ability to present traumatic memory and construct a literal eyewitness in the reader. Finally, the chapter argues that the form's ability to establish narrative from fragmented, repetitious, and disjointed images allows Gloeckner to organize painful memories into a coherent sense of self, and in this way work through her trauma.

Chapter 3 examines how the serial comics form can be used to visually examine and archive changing and in-process selves. While the form traditionally introduces a split between the present tense of the images and the past tense of the autobiographical narration, the comics of queer artist Ariel Schrag—several of which she drew and published while still a high school student—lack a self-conscious separation between author and character and are infused with a sense of visual becoming that lends urgency to her depiction of such adolescent experiences as first love, heartbreak, and coming out as gay. In addition, Schrag's personal maturation is mirrored by her gradually increasing skills as a comics artist, and her work therefore constitutes a kind of self-imposed apprenticeship in the art of making comics. In this context I read Schrag's approach to style as an expression of queerness and argue that the form's serial nature, multimodality, and association with zine culture provide Schrag with the tools to experiment with visual and verbal codes in order to delineate and assert a sense of the in-process lesbian teenage self.

Chapter 4 continues the book's exploration of authorial agency in autobiographical comics by examining how the form can help the author elude the objectifying gaze commonly associated with looking at disability. As such, the chapter examines Al Davison's *The Spiral Cage*—a memoir about living with spina bifida—in light of its engagement with his highly visible impairment in order to show how the comics form allows for the autobiographical character to meet the stare of the implied observer. Theorized by Rosemarie Garland-Thomson as the primary mode of looking at disability, the stare differs from the objectifying gaze because it is a dynamic interaction that produces an interpersonal relationship with the potential for an unexpected outcome. The multimodal comics form, I argue, allows for the construction of what I call a counterstare, and Davison shows us how this exchange of looks can be staged by frequently drawing himself to meet the reader's stare in self-portraits that are at once vulnerable and defiant, but always on his own terms.

Chapter 5 examines the relationships among racist stereotypes, visuality, and comics through a reading of Toufic El Rassi's *Arab in America*. In the book, El Rassi consistently portrays himself as an Arab stereotype, and includes numerous scenes in which he explores what it means to always be associated—in life, as well as in comics—with the long history of such derogatory imagery. Where the present volume's other chapters argue that the multimodality of comics allows the artists discussed to perform their autobiographical selves in ways that are multiple, serial, and against cultural expectations, I therefore conclude by suggesting that the particular and extensive history of racist stereotypes in the form complicates such an approach for artists of color, whose self-portraits are always in danger of slipping into images that marginalize or exclude. The chapter thereby expands the book's central argument by arguing that El Rassi's repetitive and self-conscious appropriation of the Arab stereotype serves both to undermine its power and to act as a rhetorical strategy that allows him to assert subjectivity through an insistence upon those very ethnoracial markers that set him apart and make him an easy target for anti-Arab sentiment in post-9/11 America.

Together these artists provide five different perspectives on—and engagements with—what it means for people with marginalized identities to represent themselves in autobiographical comics. Putting the form to decidedly more adventurous uses than a simple parade of nondescript talking heads in evenly sized panels, the artists I write about are all interested in investigating the very nature of visuality itself: with looking, showing, and being seen, and with drawing self-representational characters that in various ways meet, challenge, and resist the reader's would-be objectifying gaze. In short, these comics are unruly comics—comics that refuse to be polite, to keep silent, to conform to generic boundaries, and to keep their eyes to themselves.

1

Female Grotesques

● ● ● ● ● ● ● ● ● ● ● ● ●

The Unruly Comics of Julie Doucet

Until recently, comics have largely been a man's world. This is true in terms of their creators, who have historically been overwhelmingly male; their subject matter, which has generally been portrayed from the point of view of men and male characters; and their readership, which is often stereotyped as consisting of mostly boys and middle-aged men on the model of Comic Book Guy from *The Simpsons*.[1] Although this view is currently being conclusively upended by the large number of women making and reading comics today, as well as by the increasingly visible participation of women in the fan culture surrounding the comics world, it is nevertheless the case that to a degree unfamiliar in most other art forms, comics have historically and inescapably been gendered male. Such a view of the form is not least evident in terms of its customary way of representing women, who—in both mainstream comics and in work by underground or alternative cartoonists such as Robert Crumb—are often reduced to sexualized objects and erotic spectacle for the implied male reader. In comics, the female body is typically put on display for the reader to enjoy, in drawings that routinely but unrealistically exaggerate certain physical features or postures. This representational model is accentuated by the slick drawing style of most mainstream comics, which provides the reader with glossy fantasies that heighten the sexually inflected pleasure commonly associated with—and sometimes almost expected of—the act of looking at women in comics. As a vehicle for the depiction of male sexual fantasy, the comics form offers both creators and readers the opportunity to untether from a realistic approach to depicting female characters and instead produce and enjoy images of women that fall within a narrow range of acceptable femininity characterized by bodies that may be voluptuously sexual but are nevertheless always contained and neatly appealing to the male eye. Although this could, perhaps, to some degree equally be said about male superheroes (whose bodies tend to bulge with impossible but perfectly sculpted muscles), the specific way comics have tended to portray women as objects of visual pleasure is bound up with the broader patriarchal structures that regulate how female bodies appear and are represented in the culture. Because the comics form has in this way traded in images of women as erotic spectacle since its inception, the challenge for women creators of especially autobiographical comics becomes how to draw the female body and its cultural space without succumbing to established sexist and objectifying visual paradigms. How, in other words, might female comics autobiographers resist what Kaja Silverman has called "imaginary capture" (206) by the culture's dominant ways of seeing and representing women? In one answer to that question, this chapter examines the comics of French Canadian artist Julie Doucet, who in a series of autobiographical comics and book collections from the 1980s and 1990s mounts a striking challenge to patriarchal ideologies that discipline and limit the female body and its representations.

Although Doucet's comics are particularly unwavering in their insistence upon portraying alternative versions of femininity, her work is part of a tradition of comics by women that began with the underground comix movement based in San Francisco in the 1970s. As noted in the introduction, the cartoonists associated with the underground approached the anodyne cultural form of comics with intentions of subverting it through taboo-breaking and often offensive personal content. For several of the movement's leading figures, this project sometimes involved depicting their sexual fantasies, often in unsavory or plainly sexist fashion. Crumb, for example, made a habit of drawing women with large legs and backsides, which he then subjected to various sexually explicit and humiliating scenarios. In addition to the frequently misogynistic content, the fact that the underground consisted mostly of male cartoonists did not aid in providing a more inclusive perspective or artistic environment. As pioneering female cartoonist Trina Robbins remembers, "The big problem, if you were one of the few cartoonists of the female persuasion, was that 98% of the cartoonists were male, and that they all seemed to belong to a boy's club that didn't accept women" (vii). Responding to this situation, Robbins and a group of other female cartoonists published the comic book *It Aint Me Babe* in 1970, subtitled *Women's Liberation* and featuring drawings of such classic characters as Wonder Woman and Olive Oyl on the cover, marching and with their fists raised in a presumed protest against the patriarchy. After a single issue, *It Aint Me Babe* soon morphed into the regularly published series *Wimmen's Comix*, which lasted for seventeen issues under a democratically rotating editorship before ending its run in 1992.

Almost single-handedly, *Wimmen's Comix* opened a cultural space for women to draw and publish comics, and it is nearly impossible to overstate its lasting influence on the comics world. In addition to Robbins, its many contributors over the twenty-year run included such celebrated and widely read cartoonists as Lynda Barry, Alison Bechdel, Mary Fleener, Melinda Gebbie, Roberta Gregory, Aline Kominsky Crumb, Diane Noomin, Sharon Rudahl, and Dori Seda, as well as Phoebe Gloeckner and Doucet (who appeared together in issue 15 from 1989, which Gloeckner also coedited), among many others. The list of contributors is noteworthy for being an almost complete lineage of female alternative American comics creators during the period, most of whom used the new forum to engage directly with issues concerning gender and its associated injustices. But where artists such as Robbins, for example, often drew politically earnest critiques of contemporary society or stories of female goddesses set in the mythical past, and did so in a relatively slick visual style, other cartoonists were particularly inspired by the form's potential for self-representation. For her contribution to the first issue, for example, Kominsky Crumb drew an autobiographical story that depicted her having sex, throwing up, and masturbating with assorted vegetables while overcome with guilt. As Hillary Chute has argued about Kominsky Crumb's work in general, her "political project is to visualize how sexuality, even when disruptive, does not have to be turned over to the gaze of the other" (*Graphic Women* 30). For Kominsky Crumb, this goal is accomplished through a combination of an intimate focus on lived female experience and her highly unusual style, which at first sight appears unschooled and primitive, but which Chute shows to be a conscious political choice and a "deliberately erotic mode of production that inscribes her own messy body in her work" (*Graphic Women* 59). By positioning both Kominsky Crumb's style and subject matter as direct challenges to the dominant male perspective and its accompanying gaze, Chute highlights the form's potential for challenging established ways of depicting—as well as looking at—women in comics. Although this potential was often in evidence throughout the run of *Wimmen's Comix*, few artists more directly followed Kominsky Crumb's example of drawing autobiographical comics with a confrontational and explicitly feminist slant than Doucet, whose first comics began to appear as self-published zines in the late 1980s. But where Kominsky Crumb's autobiographical stories are generally focused on depicting everyday events as filtered through a neurotic and often crippling self-doubt, and are drawn in a style that accentuates a corporeal and resolutely nonidealized female body, Doucet's approach to autobiography is preoccupied with depicting an emotional life consisting of dreams, desires, and sexual fantasies, as well as with unconventional representations of the undisciplined female body and its capacity for a joyfully transgressive sexual agency.

Born in Montreal in 1965 and holding degrees in fine arts and printing, Doucet began self-publishing (that is, photocopying and distributing to local bookstores and through the postal service) her mini-comic *Dirty Plotte* in 1988. The original series—advertised, on its covers, as a "fanzine"—lasted fourteen issues and fluently switched between French slang and imperfect English. Eventually, upstart Montreal publisher Drawn & Quarterly picked up the comic in 1991, and the series continued in (mostly) English with another twelve full-size issues and a number of book collections throughout the 1990s.[2] During the Drawn & Quarterly run of *Dirty Plotte*, Doucet lived in Montreal, New York, Seattle, and Berlin, and her work was widely published in English and French, while also being translated into other languages. Appearing around the same time as several other autobiographical titles, Doucet's comics are often grouped with the other cartoonists published by Drawn & Quarterly in its early years, such as Chester Brown, Joe Matt, and Seth. Aside from sharing a publisher and an inclination for self-representation, however, *Dirty Plotte* has little in common with, for example, Matt's series *Peepshow*, which includes detailed stories about the author's many arguments with an on-again, off-again girlfriend, as well as his increasingly pathological cheapness and the failure to rid himself of an unflattering obsession with pornography. Closer in spirit to especially the early issues of Brown's *Yummy Fur*, which did not yet include autobiographical material but instead serialized the explicitly surrealistic narrative later collected as *Ed the Happy Clown*, the early issues of *Dirty Plotte* (both as mini-comics and in their Drawn & Quarterly incarnation) contained a freewheeling and impressionistic mix of short strips and collage work. The covers, especially, are examples of grunge-era collages mixed with almost Dada-esque absurdities, such as random shout-outs like "Hey you," "Read her sexy," and "Disco frog" yelling at the reader from wherever space permits. Although Doucet would eventually turn to a longer narrative in a story line originally serialized in the final three issues of *Dirty Plotte* and later collected as *My New York Diary*, the majority of the early strips feature few connective threads and instead rely on one-offs, most of which gradually come to concern the adventures of a clearly self-representational character named Julie. Although without a doubt autobiographical in spirit, Doucet's comics never simply depict the quotidian details of her everyday life, and the stories tell the reader little to nothing about her childhood, her various jobs, or her romantic partners. While incarnations of the latter appear regularly throughout her stories, they are often interchangeable and—with the exception of the boyfriend in *My New York Diary*, which is partly the story of the decline of the relationship—seem to come and go undramatically. Instead Doucet approaches her autobiographical character with an irreverent attitude that emphasizes fantasy, in stories that embrace her desires and excessive appetites for sex, alcohol, and sometimes even violence. A direct kick in the groin to both propriety and idealized versions of femininity, Doucet's comics are both a politically astute critique of patriarchal attempts to regulate and restrict the female body and a curiously innocent celebration of sex, death, and everything in between.

Doucet's position as a woman challenging a dominant male point of view made her both something of a feminist icon and a relative outsider in a world of alternative comics dominated by men. Despite such incursions into broader feminist culture as having her comics reprinted in quintessential 1990s alternative teen girl culture magazine *Sassy* and being name-checked along with such figures as Joan Jett and Gertrude Stein (in a list of feminist heroes that also include fellow cartoonist Ariel Schrag, the subject of chapter 3) in the song "Hot Topic" by riot grrrl descendants Le Tigre, however, Doucet nevertheless often expressed reservations about being ascribed a feminist agenda. As she told me in a 2013 interview, "In the late '80s and beginning of [the] '90s it was not really sexy to call yourself a feminist. I got influenced by that. Today I would say *of course* I'm a feminist!" ("Words into Pictures"; emphasis in the original). Doucet's initial ambivalence is typical of 1990s third-wave feminism and its popular incarnations as riot grrrl or girl power—the icons of which, as Rebecca Munford has pointed out, have "perceptibly distanced themselves from the political agendas of second wave feminism" (143). Representing "young women whose experiences and desires are marginalised by the ontological and epistemological assumptions of a feminism that speaks for them under the universalising category of 'woman'" (Munford 145), the third-wave riot grrrl ethos encompasses both Doucet's embrace of zine culture and her rejection of working within a specific feminist tradition associated with the policing of cultural practices in the name of a serious and potentially dulling political correctness.

Working within a punk and riot grrrl–inflected feminist framework, Doucet's comics consistently engage with concerns about women's bodies, and do so in ways that make them impossible to describe as dully serious. In the course of Doucet's many stories, characters unzip their skin, snakes perform oral sex, cats get tangled in their owner's snot, noses are picked, penises are severed, cookies are used for masturbation, tampons are inserted into penises, razor blades are used for self-inflicted cuts, and guts are spilled and eaten by stray dogs. Exemplifying Doucet's thematic preoccupation with the body, its functions, and the boundary-obscuring links between its inside and outside, these often troubling events are generally depicted as occasions for joy or even, in some cases, transgressive sexual excitement. Mixing imagery of the unruly and uncontained body with a joyful attitude anchored in parody, Doucet's comics use the misogynistic concept of grotesque female materiality as a generative principle from which she articulates a critique in both form and content of normative and restricting representations of the female body.

The subversive joy that Doucet associates with bodily transgression can be understood through Mikhail Bakhtin's concepts of carnival and its intrinsic connection with the grotesque. As articulated in *Rabelais and His World*, medieval and renaissance carnivals were liminal moments of play associated with such spectacles as feasts, pageants, and various iterations of festivals and markets. They were pure manifestations of folk or popular culture that functioned to release the transgressive energies of society. Employing inversion, mockery, and travesty in order to break taboos, carnival "celebrated temporary liberation from the prevailing truth and from the established order; it marked the suspension of all hierarchical rank, privileges, norms and prohibitions" (10). Concerned with change, becoming, and renewal, the carnivalesque worked within the cultural forms and protocols of the dominant class but also mocked high culture through a strategy of leveling and debasement that had the potential— temporarily, at least—to unsettle and disrupt authority.

The aesthetic expression most closely associated with the carnivalesque, according to Bakhtin, is the concept of grotesque realism and its concretization as a bodily principle. "The lowering of all that is high, spiritual, abstract," grotesque realism is "a transfer to the material level, to the sphere of earth and body" (19) and its corporeal incarnation is therefore concerned with "the lower stratum of the body, the life of the belly and the reproductive organs" (21). While the classical, bourgeois body is closely identified, as Kathleen Rowe notes, with the "'upper stratum' (the head, the eyes, the faculties of reason)" (33) and its spiritual and abstract associations, as well as with notions of individuality and containment, the grotesque body is concrete, material, and constantly overflowing its boundaries. The emphasis here is on the orifices, bulges, and protrusions of the human form, and on what Rowe calls "the drama of 'becoming,'" such as "intercourse, giving birth, and dying" (33). In this conceptualization, as Rowe makes clear, the grotesque body almost by default becomes the female body, which through its regenerative capabilities and its capacity for "menstruation, pregnancy, childbirth, and lactation" (33) transgresses its own limits and enacts a carnival of unbounded process. Aligning the masculine with the abstract and "high" and the feminine with the material and "low" is, of course, part of a misogynistic philosophical tradition privileging the former, as explorations of the female body as subject to various cultural inscriptions have demonstrated. Central to feminist challenges to these aspects of carnival and the grotesque is the insight that the body itself is a site of political struggle that functions, according to Elizabeth Grosz, as both "the means by which power is disseminated and a potential object of resistance to power" (12). Transgressive corporeal expression can therefore have potentially destabilizing effects on ideological codifications of the female body, much like the release of subversive energies associated with historical carnival could produce certain disruptive effects.

But in a sexist and somatophobic framework that defines the female body as low and grotesque, what constitutes a transgressive body from a feminist point of view? In part of her discussion concerning the subversive potential of unruly womanhood, Kathleen Rowe Karlyn draws on Bakhtin and argues that "the term grotesque is not negative but rather ambivalent, deriving its representational and social power through its embrace of conflicting poles of meaning. By this definition, unruliness is implicitly feminist because it destabilizes patriarchal norms" (11). In Bakhtinian carnival, the subversive power of this ambivalence stems from a combination of a liminal sense of play and the leveling effects of debasement. Drawing on the work of social anthropologist Mary Douglas, Judith Butler notes that "all social systems are vulnerable at their margins, and that all margins are accordingly considered dangerous" (*Gender Trouble* 180). Connecting this insight to Julia Kristeva's work on abjection, which can be understood as an expulsion of a debased "other" across the boundary of the self, Butler argues that "the construction of the 'not-me' as the abject establishes the boundaries of the body which are also the first contours of the subject" (*Gender Trouble* 181). Abjection, in this formulation, is integral to the formation of the self, and is a process through which the subject can achieve a sense of identity and agency. The abject itself, much like the Bakhtinian grotesque, is usually associated with bodily functions such as sex, defecation, and death, which are physical aspects of life that, as M. Keith Booker points out in his work on literary transgression, "are common to us all, male or female, white or black, capitalist or worker, king or peasant. As a result, they reveal the basic commonality of human experience and the fundamental factitiousness of all systems of rationalization for the exclusion or oppression of particular marginal groups" (13). Following Butler and Booker, the carnivalesque expression of the female body through the leveling effects of the grotesque and the abject may in this way undercut dominant social systems of repression at the same time that it may give rise to a sense of individual agency and identity.

For Doucet, aligning herself with a tradition of material and grotesque embodiment is precisely what allows her to capitalize on its subversive potential and take advantage of the transgressive energies inherent in the mimetic yet excessive approach to carnivalesque imagery. Challenging patriarchal logic, Doucet appropriates the point of view of the male comics world and rearticulates its interpellation of her from a point of view of debasement in order to expose its intrinsic misogyny. Consider, for example, the opening page of the first issue of the standardized run of *Dirty Plotte* (see fig. 1.1).[3] *Plotte* is Quebecois slang for vagina, or cunt, but in the mostly

FIG. 1.1. Julie explains the meaning of "plotte," from *Lève ta jambe mon poisson est mort!*

anglophone context of the comic, this needs to be explained to potentially unaware readers. Doucet therefore opens with a map of "French Canada," which geographically identifies the "plot" of land from where the word originated. Flanking the map are two figures labeled "A" and "B," which correspond to differing masculine interpellations of a woman as a "plotte": "A" is a traditionally sexy incarnation wearing only underwear and with her tongue suggestively touching her upper lip, and "B" is disheveled, dirty, and smelly; her makeup is running and her vagina is barely contained by her underwear—she is the grotesque plotte. The first proper panel shows Julie in front of a medical chart of a vagina, identifying it matter-of-factly: "So this is a plotte." Julie continues the tour in the following two panels, where first a conventionally beautiful woman is subjected to both the male gaze and the interpellation as a plotte, and then Julie herself, hair on end, is hailed as a plotte by two men on the street. The final panel shows plotte "B" intimating to the reader that "You know, plotte is a very dirty word," and the implication is that of the two possible significations, Doucet opts for identification with the grotesque version while reminding the reader of the harmful potential of such language. Speaking from the point of view of the grotesque, Doucet resists the regulatory effects associated with depictions of women in comics through a joyful and unapologetic graphic embodiment that concretizes all of the possible meanings of the term *plotte* as drawings on the page, reclaiming the word for herself in the process. The title of Doucet's comic is therefore also a feminist rebuttal through appropriation—and not coincidentally did some of the issues of the original mini-comic run of *Dirty Plotte* warn on the cover: "Fanzine feministe de mauvais gout" (Feminist fanzine of bad taste).[4]

While Doucet's employment of the grotesque female body opposes the sexism inherent in Bakhtin's model through cheerful and generative embodiment, such transgressions, critics have noted, may be ephemeral in nature. According to Terry Eagleton, for example, medieval carnival was "a licensed affair in every sense, a permissible rupture of hegemony, a contained popular blow-off" (148), and consequently not capable of lasting effects. This "paradox of legalized though unofficial subversion," as Linda Hutcheon (99) notes, is in modern times a function of democratic social structures and legislation protecting freedom of expression, and in the contemporary world, art commonly exists within the limits permitted by official culture, into which avant-garde or revolutionary artistic expression is eventually assimilated and made harmless. Similarly, Rowe points out that the inversions of carnival "are invariably righted and its temporary suspensions of boundaries appear only to reinforce existing social forces" (44). The combination of assimilation into the mainstream and the inevitable correction of revolutionary impulses seems an inescapable bind for transgressive art, but as Rowe has argued about women attempting to subvert established gender roles and common notions of bodily propriety, it is "important not to discount the impact of the symbolic, the lingering and empowering effect of the sign of the woman on top outside and beyond privileged moments of social play" (44). Similarly, Eagleton admits that the carnivalesque functions as a sort of utopian fiction, "a temporary retextualizing of the social formation that exposes its 'fictive' foundations" (149), and Peter Stallybrass and Allon White, in a passage about the transgressive potential of the grotesque that is not about comics but nevertheless seems to speak directly to the form's mixing of different verbal and visual codes, note that "hybridization . . . produces new combinations and strange instabilities in a given semiotic system. It therefore generates the possibility of shifting *the very terms of the system itself,* by erasing and interrogating the relationships which constitute it" (58; emphasis in the original). While the transgression may therefore always be licensed and temporary, the image itself—and perhaps especially through its destabilizing combination with words in the comics form— remains of value as both a possible inspiration to others and a revealing moment of affirmative transcendence.

Considering the political implications of carnival, Mary Russo has noted that it is its heterogeneous nature that "sets carnival apart from the merely oppositional and reactive; carnival and the carnivalesque suggest a redeployment or counterproduction of culture, knowledge and pleasure" (218). By appropriating cultural forms and standards and redeploying them as grotesque images, the carnivalesque can therefore become subversive through regeneration. In a similar way Butler, writing famously about the performative aspect of gender, claims that the subversion of embodied norms is possible (though always restricted) through the agency of performing differently: "perpetual displacement constitutes a fluidity of identities that suggests an openness to resignification and recontextualization; parodic proliferation deprives hegemonic culture and its critics of the claim to naturalized and essentialist gender identities" (*Gender Trouble* 188). As a form of imitation characterized by what Hutcheon has called "ironic inversion" (87) and performed with critical distance, parodic repetition has important transgressive implications. Crucial to the political project of resignification, however, especially when it comes to gendered representations, is a production of excess. In a critique of Cindy Sherman's *Untitled Film Stills*, Maura Reilly warns about the dangers of this particular kind of reproductive mimesis: "if mimicry fails to produce its difference, via excess or a gesture of defiance, for instance, then it runs the risk of reproducing, and thereby affirming, the very tropes it has set out to dismantle" (119). Conversely, Reilly suggests, successful subversive mimicry "must uncomfortably inhabit the paternal language itself; which is to say that it must be unruly, defiant and aggressive" (129). Reilly concludes that Sherman, in many cases, fails to reproduce this difference. While certain analyses might in this way view the eerie and uncanny work of Sherman as insufficiently unruly to subvert the source material, such a perspective is unlikely to be upheld by anyone taking even a brief look at Doucet's drawn engagements with femininity. In Doucet's comics, the conscious appropriation of the unruly grotesque is the excess that gives rise to defiance and agency and allows for the symbolic dismantling of male authority over her body. Doucet's carnivalesque performance of her own body, in other words, does away with what Hélène Cixous has called the "divine composure" of the "well-adjusted normal woman" (876) and challenges the prevailing cultural constructions of femininity through a parodic and troubling repetition of tropes belonging to patriarchal discourse.

In the story "Heavy Flow," for example, a giant, menstruating Julie wreaks havoc on downtown Montreal.[5] After waking up one morning to discover that she has started her period, Julie rushes to the bathroom only to realize that she is out of Tampax, a circumstance that causes first a panic attack and then a Hulk-like fit of uncontrollable rage. Unable to avert the crisis, Julie kicks down the door to her apartment and rushes into the street, where she terrorizes the downtown area by throwing cars around while people cower at her feet. The grotesque vision of unruly femininity reaches its peak in a page-size panel showing Julie as a growling King Kong–like version of herself rampaging among the skyscrapers, menstrual fluids cascading from her loins and with her clothing unable to contain her breasts (see fig. 1.2). Excessive and corporeally undisciplined in every way, including also her unshaved legs, unwashed hair, and unpedicured feet, Julie is the male nightmare of loss of control over the female body. Holding a man in each hand—appearing to be a businessman and a punk, affirming the inclusiveness of the critique—Julie is an unstoppable

FIG. 1.2. A giant Julie goes on a rampage, from *Lève ta jambe mon poisson est mort!*

force of pure feminine rage. The tongue-in-cheek absurdity of the situation is further accentuated by the exclamation of a bird perched on a nearby skyscraper that the city "smells like fish!" As a parody of male concern over "that time of the month," Doucet's story jokingly appropriates and exaggerates the stereotype of the unclean and emotionally unstable menstruating woman in order to reconfigure it as a grotesque image of female empowerment.

The final image of the story shows a smiling Julie who, after securing a package of Tampax by smashing a hole in the roof of a pharmacy, has returned to normal size and is now surrounded by the patriarchal figures of the police and fire departments. Covering her naked body with blankets and affirming their male authority by the display of such accessories as trucks, helmets, and hand weapons, they are the safeguards of male dominance over unrestrained female embodiment. Crucially, it is the mere presence of a package of Tampax, and not its application, that secures Julie's docility, a detail that affirms the product's symbolic power over a woman's reproductive cycle. Because Julie is finally, but ironically, brought back within the safe confines of femininity maintained by a combination of Tampax and the fire department, the story exemplifies the temporary nature of carnivalesque transgression. But by its production of parodic excess in its representation of a giant menstruating woman—exemplified formally by the large and memorable centerpiece dwarfing all other panels—Doucet creates a powerful image of the feminine grotesque that may have lingering effects.

A similar attempt at controlling female appearance takes place in the story "Dirty Plotte vs. Super Clean Plotte," which specifically references the world of comic book superheroes.[6] Here, "Mary White, reporter at 'Neat Housekeeping' Magazine" reveals her secret identity as Dirty Plotte's antagonist Super Clean Plotte upon hearing—superhumanly—Julie picking her nose. Changing into a skintight outfit in a nearby phone booth, Super Clean Plotte rushes to Julie's apartment, which is filled with empty bottles, dirty clothes, and assorted comic books. After smashing through the window and calling the apartment a "pig-sty," Super Clean Plotte attempts to use her "super bleach gun" to clean it up. Representing mainstream femininity's efforts to domesticate the filthy and nose-picking Julie, Super Clean Plotte eventually goes too far when she targets Julie's comics, an event that sets off a violent confrontation between the two. No match for Julie's unchecked rage, however, Super Clean Plotte is eventually rendered unconscious by a cartoon-style kick. "Me dirty?" a victorious Julie asks, before stuffing Super Clean Plotte into her unwashed sheets and farting in her face: "Yeeeeah! . . . And proud of it!" The story concludes with Julie proclaiming, over the expired body of her propriety-obsessed antagonist and with a crazed look on her face, "Never! Never! They will never get me!!!" The display of an unclean female body and its messy environment is a challenge to the acceptable expressions of womanhood advocated by the emissary from a magazine devoted to maintaining the social status quo. But where "Heavy Flow" ironically ends with the victory of the alliance between patriarchy and Tampax, "Dirty Plotte vs. Super Clean Plotte" presents a scenario in which Julie resists and eventually defeats the domesticating impulses and is allowed to express her authentic feminine self through an appropriation and reversal of the superhero battles of mainstream comics. In the world of *Dirty Plotte*, the bad girl wins the right to pick her nose by literally farting in the face of authority.

The theme of resistance to normalizing impulses is further explored in "My Conscience Is Bugging Me," which tells the story of Julie's struggle with a highly unusual "conscience."[7] Visually reminiscent of the "dirty" version of the interpellated plottes from *Dirty Plotte* no. 1, Julie's conscience is in fact an embodiment of her unruly and grotesque side, the incarnation of which follows her on the street as a double. Sloppily dressed, dirty, and with needle marks on her arms, the conscience farts in public, spits on the heads of children, climbs around on parked cars, and is sexually aggressive toward men (see fig. 1.3). The conscience is a constant embarrassment to Julie, who finally leaves her on the street and complains that "I don't know where I'm at anymore . . . My brains are scrambled." The story ends back in Julie's apartment, where the returned conscience kisses her on the forehead before the two are rejoined in a tender embrace. The final acceptance of Julie's transgressive side is telling, as is the identification of it as her "conscience." The implication is that Julie's less decorous double is in fact a more genuine version of herself, which she has had to discipline and subdue in order to appear in the outside world. In response to this repression of Julie's natural impulses, her conscience is defiantly aggressive and openly flouts patriarchal ideas of how a woman should act and look. The final embrace thereby becomes a rebellious act of noncompliance and an affirmation of a nonstandard feminine side that is in direct opposition to gendered bodily and behavioral norms.

Apart from being an exploration of repressive masculinist ideology, "My Conscience Is Bugging Me" also indicates how Doucet frequently deploys various psychoanalytic concepts in unexpected ways—such as, in this case, through the portrayal of an embodied conscience separate from herself. According to Bakhtin, much of the subversive potential of the carnivalesque derives from the incorporation and inversion of "high" culture into "low" forms associated with folk culture, where it is recycled, debased, and

FIG. 1.3. Julie's conscience is bugging her, from *Lève ta jambe mon poisson est mort!*

ridiculed. As Russo compellingly phrases the argument, "The masks and voices of carnival resist, exaggerate, and destabilize the distinctions and boundaries that mark and maintain high culture and organized society. It is as if the carnivalesque body politic had ingested the entire corpus of high culture and, in its bloated and irrepressible state, released it in fits and starts in all manner of recombination, inversion, mockery, and degradation" (218). In carnival, the artificial boundary between high and low culture is a favorite target of parody, and one that Doucet examines with her usual playful enthusiasm in the low cultural form of comics. In her approach to psychoanalysis, a trope of high culture associated with metaphorical abstraction, Doucet's strategy is one of mischievous literalization as she explores such concepts as dream interpretation, castration anxiety, and penis envy through a series of stories from *Dirty Plotte* collected in a volume jokingly—but also teasingly—entitled *My Most Secret Desire*.

In "A Night," the collection's opening one-page story, Doucet cleverly plays with the common dream of losing one's teeth, a dream image that has been subject to much and varied interpretation since Freud, who links it to "masturbation, or rather the punishment for it—castration" (*Introductory Lectures* 203). Similarly, Freud elsewhere notes "the frequency with which sexual repression makes use of transpositions from a lower to an upper part of the body" (*Interpretation* 398). According to contemporary psychoanalyst Salman Akhtar, moreover, "the dream of teeth falling" is "in the direction of turning us into toothless babies, innocent, harmless, and ready to be nourished by the maternal breast . . . in women it implies a wish to be pregnant" (301). Doucet's original spin on this common dream image is simple yet disturbing: Julie is not dreaming, but wakes up from sleep to discover her bed covered in blood and her teeth falling out (see fig. 1.4). The story begins and ends with a black square symbolizing the oblivion of sleep, and the nightmarish events that take place between them are therefore presented as real. This is especially noteworthy in the context of the collection as a whole, where several other stories end with Julie waking up from an odd dream. In a misguided attempt at calming her down, Julie's boyfriend comes to the bathroom while she is "barfing" out her teeth, and tells her to "Come back in bed it's late" before tapping her gently on her behind and turning out the lights with "Go back to sleep my baby." His complete failure to comprehend Julie's bodily chaos is a parody of ineffectual male attempts at reassurance when faced with the reality of a nonidealized (and, in this example, malfunctioning) female body. The reversal of dream and reality in this introductory story, additionally, sets the thematic frame for the rest of the collection, in which Doucet portrays her dreams as consisting of exactly the kind of primary psychological material that is supposed to be converted into less overt images by the Freudian dream-work.

FIG. 1.4. Julie barfs out her teeth, from *My Most Secret Desire*.

Instead of dreaming of her teeth falling out as a consequence of repressed masturbation urges or a pregnancy wish, Doucet's upside-down world relegates the traditional dream images to "reality" and conversely presents her dreams as literalizations of her subconscious desires. Over the course of the collection's other dream stories, Julie masturbates using a cookie (given to her by her mother for this very purpose, which eliminates the practice's association with shame and the repression of urges), accepts as a gift a cut-off penis (which she proceeds to gleefully eat as if it were a hot dog), gives birth to an untold number of cats (in a convoluted sequence of dreams and dreams within dreams that prompts Doucet to ask the reader "What does it all mean?"), makes love with her masculine reflection in a mirror (a development that follows from Julie proclaiming that "I say in this dream I'm a man!"), and, in a series of stories, is excited to have gained a working penis. As a playful engagement with the idea of penis envy, these last stories are especially suggestive for the way they combine a joking and deflating appropriation of psychoanalytic concepts with a feminist critique anchored in the carnivalesque.

In "Regret: A Dream," for example, Julie wakes from surgery to discover herself the subject of a double mastectomy and a total phalloplasty, a situation that after a brief moment of bewilderment fills her with joy when she discovers that "It . . . works!" With fresh confidence, a masculine swagger, and a new leather jacket, Julie discovers that her new situation makes her sexually desirable to both a female friend and—randomly, but very happily—Micky Dolenz of the Monkees, who tells her that "Two men together, it's possible, you know!" The story—the latter part of which takes place in what appears to be an actual traveling carnival, complete with a knife-throwing booth and a sideshow—ends with Julie experiencing a quiet moment of contemplation that leads to the titular regret: "But . . . What if I don't like it with this? Ooh what if . . . I . . . I miss my vagina?" In this dream story, penis envy literally turns Julie into a carnivalesque and sexually flexible man, but the imagined pleasures of masculinity, such as the ability to aggressively approach potential sexual partners, turn out to be both fleeting and hollow in comparison with the lost comforts of femininity represented by her missing vagina. A playful engagement with gender roles and their ambiguous connection to biological sex, "Regret: A Dream" thereby portrays the trying on—or performance—of masculinity as initially alluring, but nevertheless as having lasting and potentially undesirable consequences.

In a pair of stories, both entitled "If I Was a Man," Doucet further explores what it would be like to have a penis, an experiment that has two widely differing outcomes. In one story, she completes the title's statement with "I would have a useful penis." In the peculiar dream-logic world of Doucet's comics, this means that the head can be detached and the shaft used as a container for pornographic magazines or as a vase for flowers.

Naming her "funny penis" Mustang, Doucet draws her masculine self with a fully erect but also comically large penis, to the point where it must literally be harnessed. The story has a playful feel as Julie explores various possibilities of putting the penis to increasingly ridiculous uses, all of which serve to undermine it as a symbol of power. The lighthearted innocence of this story, however, is undercut by its namesake episode, in which a male Julie proclaims that "if I was a man, I would have a girlfriend with big tits . . . because I gotta huge penis." This new identity leads Julie to sexually assault a woman on the street, drooling on her and rubbing the penis between her breasts before ejaculating on her panicked face (see fig. 1.5). Here the penis is a source of sexual violence and degradation in a scene that represents masculinity at its worst. Significantly, the comic is portrayed from the point of view of a sexually confident but masculine version of Julie, who after the assault exclaims: "Haa the great mysteries of nature!" This particular mystery, it is implied, concerns why masculinity should be so toxic as to immediately lead to sexual assault, a question that is left unanswered. Here and elsewhere, Doucet investigates the central role played by the penis in the culture, as both bodily reality and symbolic seat of power and violence. As literal interpretations of the concept of penis envy, Doucet's stories critique both traditional masculinity and the assumption that having a penis is worth aspiring to, in a freewheeling and stream-of-consciousness appropriation of an often mocked psychoanalytic trope. But psychoanalytic accuracy is not on Doucet's agenda; instead she jokingly regurgitates components from official high culture in the low form of the carnivalesque comic book in order to undercut their descriptive authority through various strategies of literal or figurative debasement.

While these examples of Doucet's comics are characterized equally by narrative representations of undisciplined femininity and satirical engagements with masculinity, her thematic preoccupations are accentuated by her adventurous and sometimes unorthodox approach to form. In addition to the impact created by her depictions of undisciplined femininity, such features as her sometimes jarring combinations of words and images, her offbeat use of language, her rough but instantly recognizable drawing style, and her occasional posing of the autobiographical character as looking directly at the reader all contribute to the project of authentic self-representation that seeks to escape the repressive patriarchal codes inherent in both traditional comics visuals and the culture at large. As such, Doucet's comics can be strange to look at and difficult to read, and they often require more decoding

FIG. 1.5. Julie plays at being a man, from *My Most Secret Desire*.

work by the reader than traditionally drawn and narrated work in the form. Michael A. Chaney argues that Doucet "combines the aesthetics of punk rock with the anxious sensibilities of a hoarder" (*Reading Lessons* 131), an apt description of the confrontational and disquieting effect of her work at the level of formal expression, in words as well as pictures.

A significant part of Doucet's comics' appeal is her use of language in an idiosyncratic way that is potentially upsetting but more often deflating. As an example of the former, Doucet often allows text and images to ironically play off each other in unsettling ways. In a story entitled "Dogs Are Really Man's Best Friend," for example, Doucet depicts the gruesome knife murder of a young girl at the hands of an older man, after which his dog eats the body and thereby eliminates the evidence.[8] The unusual illustration of an innocuous proverb as misogynistic crime suggests that threats of violence against women are hidden, and perhaps implied, throughout language as well as culture. Moreover, the tension between the storybook-like title and the horrific images drawn in a rough and expressionistic style exemplifies Doucet's penchant for combining the verbal and visual modes in the service of disrupting predictable thematics and linear narrative. In addition to this strategy, Doucet often playfully undercuts the authority of language by peppering her text with half-formed sentences, profanity, and various unusual outbursts. In "Heavy Flow," for example, Julie's response to waking up and discovering her period leaking onto the sheets is "Ho no fuck," and she later exclaims "Glub glub glub glub" before beginning her aforementioned transformation into a menstruating giant. This deflating aspect of Doucet's use of language is heightened by her habit, especially early in her career, of writing in a combination of French and English. As Doucet explains in the introduction to *Fantastic Plotte!*, a book collection reprinting the *Dirty Plotte* mini-comics in their original mixed-language form, bilingualism was always an important aspect of her comics. Although from a francophone background, Doucet first attempted publication by entering a comic strip competition in the anglophone alternative weekly the *Montreal Mirror*. Using, as she says, "whatever was left of my highschool english [sic] classes" to write and submit short parodic strips about *Star Trek*'s Kirk and Spock urinating on various planets in order to possess them, Doucet did not win the competition.[9] Finding, however, that "writing in another language could be a lot of fun," her imagination was set free and her comics continued to switch between French and English before her linguistic promiscuity was roped in by the demands of unilingual publishing.[10] As a consequence of this approach to language, the English words in the earlier comics often seem slightly awkward, as when Julie professes to chew gum "to help my mouth stir better" or tampons are described as having reached "max of blood capacity."[11] In the context of the tense Quebecois language politics of the late 1980s and early 1990s—a period that saw the aftermath of, as well as the buildup to, unsuccessful independence referendums in 1980 and 1995—this slightly inverted use of English constitutes a further challenge to authoritative models through the playful redeployment of the dominant Canadian language. By uneasily inhabiting the "paternal language" of English, Doucet thereby contests "correct" ways of speaking and writing English while affirming her artistic and personal identity in opposition to standardizing and prescriptive norms.

In addition to her experiments with language, either alone or in combination with images, one of the most instantly noticeable aspects of Doucet's comics is her highly unusual and idiosyncratic visual style. In direct opposition to the codes of mainstream comics, especially as regards their polished and frequently sexualized representations of female characters, Doucet's drawing style is characterized by a messy and imprecise looseness—one might call it grotesque—that rewards attention but disinvites sexualized visual scrutiny. Comparing it to the classic *ligne claire* style of the Franco-Belgian tradition most often exemplified by Hergé's *Tintin*, Ann Miller and Murray Pratt refer to Doucet's style as "ligne crade" (n.p.), and Charles Hatfield, noting the underground movement's influence upon her work, calls it "comix brut" (61). Hatfield further argues about Doucet and a number of comparable artists that their style "subverts the cultural and ideological reassurances proffered by the Clear Line" (61), and in a North American context a similar claim could be made about her stylistic opposition to the slick world of mainstream comics. Examining the visually simple Donald Duck comics by Carl Barks, for example, Donald Ault has argued that "Barks's clean lines insist on an absolutely clear distinction between inside and outside: a world in which the desire to hold things in their place is secure" (132–133). As an argument for the political implications of style, Ault's analysis suggests the necessity of repressing certain excessive urges—one must draw on model and within the lines, so to speak—in order to avoid upsetting the status quo. Discussing the comics of Lynda Barry, which are similar to Doucet's in their frequent use of collage and lack of features marking them as technically sophisticated in the eyes of a mainstream comics reader, Özge Samanci writes about the "clear-cut, uniform" style of mainstream North American comics and notes that because it is based on "the idea of progress—fluent perception and the idea of hierarchy . . . the professional aesthetic implies the masculine way of thinking" (185). In contrast, Samanci cites the "clumsy and childish" (182) drawing style of Barry, which offers a disorderly feminine perspective that disrupts clear boundaries and forward momentum, thereby upending the conventions of the male-dominated world of comics. Similarly, Chute characterizes Kominsky Crumb's style as deliberately "ugly" in the sense that it constitutes a "specifically feminist aesthetic response to an idealized and culturally male methodology of style" (*Graphic Women* 59, 60)—a methodology, that is, that has dominated the comics world and thrived on the representation of women as sexual objects. Style, in this analysis, is inherently political, and Doucet's shaky lines and untraditional representational strategies function as a feminist corrective to the objectifying impulses built into most iterations of the form.

Along with their freeing disregard for conventional notions of beauty in comics art, Doucet's panels are overstuffed and obsessively detailed. As such, interior spaces are rendered with attention to the wallpaper and invariably littered with the assorted debris of bohemian life such as bottles, books, and dirty laundry, and street scenes are crammed with passersby and—in a peculiar eccentricity of Doucet's—anthropomorphic garbage. Over the course of the twelve full-size issues of *Dirty Plotte*, Doucet's tendency to fill in every available space with background detail intensified, reaching its peak in the serialized story later collected as *My New York Diary*. Drawn with heavy black cross-hatching and filled with an almost claustrophobic amount of clutter, Doucet's panels in *My New York Diary* constantly threaten to overwhelm the eye and disturb narrative momentum, as readerly attention is directed away from the main characters and toward a cockroach or a dirty tissue on the floor. This effect is intensified in the book collection, which shrinks the original comic's pages noticeably and thereby diminishes the white spaces between the black inks. In addition to functioning, perhaps, as a visual expression of Doucet's struggle with epilepsy—a condition that looms in the background of *My New York Diary*, which is otherwise the story of her move to New York and her life there with a slacker boyfriend—this remarkable attention to detail also has political implications. In an examination of comics by Doucet, Debbie Drechsler, and Phoebe Gloeckner, Alisia Chase reads the prominence of visual clutter in the drawn backgrounds as "symbolic shorthand for the emotional confusion that accompanied the lived experiences of the protagonists as well as their subsequent artistic narration by the creators" (221). While Chase highlights the feminist potential of visual style in comics art, in which artists can symbolically externalize fraught interior states as drawings on the page, Doucet's particular approach seems less inspired by emotional confusion than compelled by an obsessive need to fill every available space in a deliberate insistence upon the material circumstances of her life that obscures clear boundaries and disturbs visual hierarchies of seeing.

Traditionally, much comics art has been characterized by a certain realistic verisimilitude and the expert deployment of such features as perspective and well-defined borders between various elements. In contrast hereto,

Doucet's drawings avoid regular use of depth and three-dimensionality almost completely, as lines often do not converge at a unified vanishing point. As a result, furniture looks ready to slide off the floor in her interior scenes, and characters inhabit their spaces awkwardly. Combined with the detailed backgrounds and a lack of color, the flatness of many panels creates a monotonous effect that makes characters blend in with their surroundings instead of being clearly defined within them. Additionally, Doucet's uneven lines, drawn with an attention to the creases, folds, and dents of the used and the everyday, give each object a materiality that further democratizes the visual field. The result is a decentered reading experience that avoids accentuating certain elements over others. Even in scenes where Doucet depicts her own body naked and in sexual situations, the busy flatness of the visuals invites the eye to roam freely among the many possible focal points. Therefore, in the significantly more traditional narrative that makes up *My New York Diary*, which relies less on fantastic and carnivalesque subversions than on straightforward storytelling, the grotesque excess that can disrupt established ways of seeing is instead expressed in Doucet's unusual approach to visual style, which de-emphasizes the visual objectification of the female body familiar from mainstream comics.

These stylistic challenges to objectification are further advanced through Doucet's deployment of her autobiographical character as exhibiting an active sexuality and a sometimes antagonistic stance in relation to the reader. Although Julie is most commonly drawn as a relatively plain young woman, the materiality of Doucet's unsteady line resists the smooth surfaces associated with traditional representations of women in comics art. Despite the pervading nudity, moreover, Julie is never sexualized in a way that panders to a male readership, and any thematic sexualization is always resolutely from the point of view of Julie/Doucet herself. In a one-panel drawing entitled "Self-Portrait in a Possible Situation," for example, a cut-up and bloodied Julie holds a razor blade between her teeth, uses her left arm to hold up her hair, and looks straight at the reader with a dazed look that, despite the circumstances, is highly sexually charged (see fig. 1.6). In *Lève ta jambe mon poisson est mort!* the image appears alongside two similar drawings of a naked Julie cutting herself with a razor blade, and the series concludes with an image of Julie looking at the reader, knife in hand and with a collection of sharp objects laid out before her, saying, "Hey listen men I need a model for some little drawings! Heh heh heh." Explicitly

FIG. 1.6. Doucet's "Self-Portrait in a Possible Situation," from *Lève ta jambe mon poisson est mort!*

"END"

FIG. 1.7. Julie castrates Steve the reader, from *Lève ta jambe mon poisson est mort!*

linking the act of drawing with sexual pleasure and bodily injury, these images directly confront a male readership looking for scopophilic pleasure in Doucet's comics.

The implicit threat of castration is carried to its conclusion in a story entitled "Le striptease du lecteur," in which Julie introduces Steve, a male reader who has responded to her previous request and sent her an unsolicited naked photograph of himself with the note that "My body belongs to you." Taking the offering quite literally, Julie kills, cuts, and castrates Steve with what seems like ritualistic sexual pleasure, a procedure that culminates in the dismembering of his penis, the bloody end of which she uses to write "Fin" on the wall at the story's end (see fig. 1.7). The sexuality on evidence in these drawings is not one of invitation, proposition, or inhabitation of various norms for what it means to be "sexy," but one of violent defiance. Doucet, making no concessions to a traditional male readership or the images of women expected in a comic book, instead stages sexually charged but confrontational encounters between herself and the reader that insist on individualized female sexuality and agency.

Doucet thereby combines often unorthodox subject matter with the multimodal features of the comics page—including what the New London Group would call the gestural mode as expressed through the autobiographical character's facial expressions, posture, and general stance—which work together to disturb the scopophilic pleasures associated with the male gaze. According to Laura Mulvey's influential work on visual pleasure in cinema, "the presence of woman is an indispensable element of spectacle in normal narrative film" (841), and the male gaze familiar from feminist film theory is one that fixates the feminine object in a position of passive entrapment as spectacle. Rowe, however, suggests that transgressive texts that "show women using in disruptive, challenging ways the spectacle already invested in them as objects of a masculine gaze . . . might suggest an alternative view of female subjectivity" (5). The word "spectacle" is reminiscent of the terminology of Bakhtin, and the connection is made explicit by Booker in his discussion of Angela Carter's *Night at the Circus*: "By appropriating the male stereotype of the woman as object of the gaze and driving it to its extreme in spectacle, Fevvers [a half-human, half-swan circus performer] is able to undercut the original stereotype by carnivalizing it" (226). Similarly, Doucet's carnivalesque performance of femininity as spectacle can constitute such a disruption of the male gaze at the same time that it can stare back in ways unavailable to traditional prose. In an emblematic image summing up many of the concerns noted here, for example, Doucet depicts herself as a naked Medusa, the prototypical unruly woman, complete with six arms, snakes for hair, her tongue sticking out, and her vagina and breasts bared (see fig. 1.8). Surrounding her are the tools of her trade, ink and brush, but also items associated with excess, intoxication, and womanhood, such as coffee, alcohol, and a tampon. Her blank eyes make her impossible to pin down, and as unruly femininity meets the reader's gaze, Doucet assertively insists on her own subjective vision of what it means to be a woman in comics, both on and off the page.

After almost fifteen years of working in the form, Doucet stopped making comics in the late 1990s. Her last publication in the form is *The Madame Paul Affair*, a humorous but by her standards rather tame story about her unusual landlady, which was originally serialized in French (a first for Doucet) in the Montreal weekly *Ici* in 1999. Doucet has explained in a number of contexts her decision to abandon comics for other avenues of visual art as a combination of being overworked and feeling like an outsider in the boy's club of alternative comics.[12] Despite her voluntary retirement from the comics world, however, Doucet's work has remained influential and continues to inspire new generations of cartoonists. The influence of her irreverent approach to both form and subject matter, for example, can be seen in work by such contemporary female artists as Kate Beaton, Lisa Hanawalt,

FIG. 1.8. Julie as Medusa, from *Lève ta jambe mon poisson est mort!*

and Julia Wertz. But while Doucet's more recent work in screen printing, collage, mini-zines, and short abstract animation projects does not fit within a form recognizable as comics, it is nevertheless thematically consistent with her earlier work and similarly concerns both autobiographical constructions of the self and a resistance to dominant representational paradigms. In many ways, her most traditional postcomics work is *365 Days*, a handwritten diary of a year in her life that incorporates various drawings, collages, and abstract designs. In *J comme je*, more radically, which is her prose autobiography up to the age of sixteen, Doucet writes exclusively with words cut out from old French-language magazines, ransom note–style. Meanwhile, art books such as *Elle-Humour*, *Lady Pep*, *Long Time Relationship*, and *Carpet Sweeper Tales* (the latter, according to the book's flap, "Meant to be read aloud") juxtapose drawings, cut-out words, and images reprinted from what among

FIG. 1.9. Example of Doucet's collage work, from *Elle-Humour.*

other things appear to be decades-old lingerie ads and Italian photo comics in ways that continue her exploratory interrogation of gender in general and femininity in particular (see fig. 1.9).

A recent work that constitutes a near return to the kind of image making associated with comics is Doucet's collaboration with French filmmaker Michel Gondry, published as *My New New York Diary* in 2010. An experimental comics/video hybrid, both the book and short film version of *My*

New New York Diary detail Doucet's visit to New York City in order to shoot the footage used in the production of the video. A whimsical project typical of Gondry's artistic sensibilities, the central conceit of the video is to replace the book's drawn image of Doucet with live-action video of the author herself, as she interacts with the drawn backgrounds and characters. The result, according to Gondry's foreword, is an investigation of the "special status" (n.p.) of the author in autobiographical comics, and the intrusion of the video image of Doucet into her drawn universe offers a novel way of reconsidering the position of the artist in her work. By removing the autobiographical character from the frame and replacing it with a live-action video recording of the author, the short video highlights the artificiality of the drawn self and denaturalizes the surroundings in order to bring attention to the visual style that is a direct expression of its author. The result is a simultaneous omnipresence and obliteration of authorial visibility as the gap between author and character is thoroughly exposed. The collaboration thereby illustrates the construction of the self on the comics page as just that—a construction—but also allows the viewer to find traces of the author elsewhere. For Doucet, that authorial presence is undergoing constant creative change, in a continually renewing performance of herself that constitutes a persistent challenge in form and content to dominant ways of looking at women, in both the comics world and beyond.

2

Working It Through

● ● ● ● ● ● ● ● ● ● ● ●

Trauma and Visuality in
the Comics of Phoebe
Gloeckner

In an article about self-representation in graphic memoirs of illness created
by women, Theresa M. Tensuan describes the routine function of women
in comics as "the tabula rasa onto which male authorial desires are projected"
(182). The context for Tensuan's comment is a discussion of the "ideological
underpinnings of supposedly objective illustrations" (182) in scientific (and
therefore implicitly male) medical discourse, and her argument suggests that
representations of the female body in comics are tied up with a history of
medical illustration portraying women as idealized objects of male authority and desire. Tensuan's example is American cartoonist and medical illustrator Phoebe Gloeckner's drawing "The Breast," which consists of a series
of images depicting a variety of naturally shaped female breasts paired with
their post–augmentation surgery counterparts, which appear uniform and
in line with the "'ideal' breast," where the "angle of inframammary fold to
nipple is 20–35 degrees" (Gloeckner, *Child's Life* 142). A parody of attempts

to quantify a body ideal through its reduction to a mathematical angle, Gloeckner's illustration further illuminates how, Tensuan argues, different "systems of representation ranging from comics to medical illustration simultaneously reveal and reinscribe the metaphorical and material violence enacted on women's bodies" (182). By setting her focus equally on both the reveal and reinscription of bodily norms and the ideals implicit in their visualization, Tensuan understands that depictions of the female body always run "the risk of representation," to borrow a phrase used by Hillary Chute in her discussion of graphic life narrative by women (*Graphic Women* 3). In the largely male-dominated world of comics, the possibilities offered by the form for the representation of women's lives thus carry within them the risk of succumbing to normative and sexist models supporting a privileged male point of view. In the comics of Julie Doucet, the solution to this bind is the defiant appropriation of the dominant tropes from masculinist ideology in order to turn them on their head through exaggeration, inversion, parody, and grotesque carnivalization in both form and content. The result, as I have argued, is a disruption of the visual pleasure associated with looking at women in comics and a shattering of expectations concerning representations of traditional femininity.

But where Doucet turns the gender hierarchies embedded in the visible world upside down in the service of parody, Gloeckner's feminist project as expressed in her finely drawn comics is an altogether different challenge to patriarchal norms. In both the all-comics collection *A Child's Life* and her innovative text/illustration/comics hybrid *The Diary of a Teenage Girl*, Gloeckner mines the autobiographical material of her sexually traumatic childhood and early teens, and does so with a visual honesty that insists on making the invisible visible through depictions of sexual abuse and other scenes of childhood and teenage trauma involving the covert and illicit behavior of male authority figures. For both artists, it is the use of the form itself that becomes a radical act of self-articulation: Doucet as grotesque medusa challenging normative patriarchal gender roles, and Gloeckner as composed artist in charge of her own life narrative who incorporates traumatic events from early life into adult experience. But where Doucet's approach is informed by a playful jouissance, Gloeckner's comics are for the most part serious in tone, and her work is imbued with a sense of the emotional investment needed to live through these experiences and the immense creative necessity of documenting them. Strikingly and even confrontationally visual in their insistence upon showing as well as telling, and preoccupied with questions of truth and representation, Gloeckner's two books offer an opportunity to explore the relationships among autobiography, trauma, and comics. Chute, examining Gloeckner's work, argues that her images consist of an ambivalent combination of pleasure and degradation made evident through her "ethical and troubling visual aesthetics," and although she rightly points out that Gloeckner's images are "consistently informed by trauma" (*Graphic Women* 91, 61), her reading stops short of fully exploring the resonance between comics form and theoretical work on the representation and working through of trauma. Extending Chute's influential discussion, this chapter examines the close relationship between Gloeckner's aesthetic strategies and the visual nature of traumatic memories in order to argue that the formal properties of autobiographical comics offer unique opportunities for the representation of the largely visual memories associated with trauma, and that the narrativizing potential of the form can be productively mobilized both for therapeutic purposes and as a means to assert agency for the victim of trauma.

Despite having drawn comics since childhood, Gloeckner has not been very prolific as a comics artist, instead often working as a commercial and medical illustrator. Born in Philadelphia in 1960, she spent most of her later childhood and teenage years in San Francisco, where she moved with her mother and younger sister in the early 1970s. Gloeckner attended a series of different Bay Area schools, several of which she was expelled from for truancy and poor academic performance, and spent a period experimenting with drugs as a teenage runaway among the hustlers and drug dealers of San Francisco's Polk Street. Gloeckner later studied art and biology at San Francisco State University and earned a master's degree in biomedical communications from the University of Texas Southwestern Medical Center at Dallas. She is currently a tenured professor in the School of Art and Design at the University of Michigan. Gloeckner's relatively small body of comics work has been sporadically published in such anthology projects as *Twisted Sisters*, *Weirdo*, and *Wimmen's Comix*, the latter of which she also edited issue 15 of in 1989. Influenced by the confessional autobiographical work of the underground comix movement in general, and the form's potential for feminist work in particular, Gloeckner's comics join Doucet's in taking inspiration from the previous generation of female cartoonists. *Twisted Sisters*—Aline Kominsky Crumb and Diane Noomin's response to what they considered *Wimmen's Comix*'s too-strict interpretation of what proper feminism ought to look like—was especially influential for Gloeckner, who in an interview with Andrea Juno mentions discovering her mother's copy of its first issue when she was around fifteen years old (150). One particularly notable addition to Gloeckner's comics work is her illustrations for a special 1990 edition of J. G. Ballard's *The Atrocity Exhibition*, which consist of semiclinical drawings of sex, injury, and internal anatomy, including prominent images depicting genitalia and cross-sections of fellatio. Preoccupied with the human body and its workings, many of Gloeckner's comics similarly portray sexual situations in a direct way, and her work has therefore often been the object of controversy and outright censorship, such as being removed from several public libraries.[1] Gloeckner's comics work was collected for the relatively slim volume *A Child's Life* in 1998, which also includes a large sample of her illustrations, sketches, and other artwork. A second edition, including two additional pieces and a new cover image, was published in 2000.

Many of Gloeckner's most celebrated comics stories feature her alter ego Minnie Goetze as a child and teenager in 1970s San Francisco. Her second book, the text/illustration/comics hybrid *The Diary of a Teenage Girl*, is explicitly based on Gloeckner's diary from when she was fifteen, with approximately half of it reproduced verbatim from the original.[2] Perhaps surprisingly, Gloeckner has often expressed reservations about her work being labeled as autobiographical. Whereas the work of artists such as Alison Bechdel, Marjane Satrapi, and Art Spiegelman has achieved an unprecedented level of critical acclaim partly because it engages with the authors' real world of nonsuperheroes, Gloeckner has repeatedly insisted on the essential fictionality of her work. In the *Diary*, she pointedly includes in the front matter the disclaimer that "This account is entirely fictional and if you think you recognize any of the characters as an actual person, living or dead, you are mistaken" (*Diary* iv). In an interview with Whitney Joiner from the time of the publication of the *Diary*, Gloeckner further explains: "By reading that book, you're not experiencing what I experienced. You're perhaps experiencing my *interpretation* of it, but you're bringing yourself to it. In that way, I always hesitate to say this is a true story. I'm not attempting in any way to make documentary. You can never represent everything. It's always a selective process" (n.p.; emphasis in the original). Despite this, later in the interview Gloeckner interchangeably refers to herself and her character Minnie, who is drawn to look like her and is the protagonist of both books, and the cover of the *Diary* itself features a photograph of a teenage Gloeckner, identified in the list of illustrations as "the real Minnie Goetze" (*Diary* xiii). In addition to indicating Gloeckner's unease with designating an artistic representation as being "true," even if the event described really happened, her ambivalence also aligns her with theories of life writing contesting the truth/fiction binary of autobiographical expression.

While Gloeckner acknowledges the use of her own life as the raw material for the book, she also stresses the need to imaginatively reshape events in order to make them cohere as a narrative and arrive at a different kind of truth: "sometimes you have to distort 'reality' in order to express what you feel is the true feeling. A recounting of facts can carry little meaning. An artist imposes a certain order on perception" (Groth 92). Elsewhere, Gloeckner has insisted that "this is not history or documentary or a confession, and memories will be altered or sacrificed, for factual truth has little significance in the pursuit of emotional truth" ("Autobiography" 179). Gloeckner thereby points both to the fundamentally creative nature of all life writing and the impossibility of adhering to arbitrary standards of truth. In her study of contemporary autobiographies informed by trauma, Leigh Gilmore similarly notes that "conventions about truth telling, salutary as they are, can be inimical to the ways in which some writers bring trauma stories into language," and therefore "the autobiographical project may swerve from the form of autobiography even as it embraces the project of self-representation" (*Limits* 3). Elsewhere Gilmore argues more generally that in the face of expectations concerning autobiographical writing that often privilege a male perspective, "women may choose forms other than straightforward, contractually verifiable autobiography for self-representation" (*Autobiographics* 96). As Gilmore suggests, women and other life writers marginalized by the culture might in this way seek out alternative genres or forms, which may offer a more congenial environment for the project of self-representation than the demands made by traditional monolithic autobiography.

As a multimodal and inherently discontinuous form, comics offers one such alternative way of representing the lived truth of marginalized lives. As Jared Gardner argues about the form's inherent inability to comply with the supposed responsibility of autobiography to adhere to a version of the truth:

> The comics form necessarily and inevitably calls attention through its formal properties to its limitations as juridical evidence—to the compressions and

gaps of its narrative (represented graphically by the gutterspace between the panels) and to the iconic distillations of its art. The kinds of truth claims that are fought over in the courts of law and public opinion with text-based autobiography are never exactly at issue in graphic autobiography. The losses and glosses of memory and subjectivity are foregrounded in graphic memoir in a way they never can be in traditional autobiography. ("Autography's Biography" 6)

Both the unreliability of memory and the highly subjective nature of all life writing are thereby emphasized in autobiographical comics, which self-reflectively announce their status as products of a subjective consciousness through their formal expression. Through its abstracted images and multi-modal tensions, in other words, the comics page draws attention to itself as self-evidently different from that which it represents, and the form there-fore becomes resistant to truth claims in a way that can free artists to struc-ture the narrative according to larger emotional truths. Combined with the ability to externalize subjectivity on the page in a way that is constitutive of selfhood while remaining true to notions of the self as fragmented or mul-tiple, the form itself, as this book argues throughout, can therefore be enabling for marginalized authors because it offers opportunities for self-creation that may be unavailable elsewhere. That this view has implications for fem-inist authors of autobiography such as Doucet and Gloeckner should be clear from the discussion thus far; that the form is also well suited for the representation and working through of trauma follows from many of the same observations.

The concept of post-traumatic stress disorder first appeared in the third edition of the American Psychiatric Association's *Diagnostic and Statisti-cal Manual of Mental Disorders* in 1980 and was originally a result of increas-ing attention to the psychological stress experienced by returning soldiers during and after the Vietnam War. The types of events able to cause trauma have undergone significant revision in the decades since, and now commonly include social as well as sexual traumas, in addition to exceptional and large-scale incidents such as war and natural disaster. According to an influential view exemplified by Ruth Leys, trauma is characterized by psychic fragmen-tation and the splitting of the subject: "The idea is that, owing to the emo-tions of terror and surprise caused by certain events, the mind is split or dissociated: it is unable to register the wound to the psyche because the ordi-nary mechanisms of awareness and cognition are destroyed. As a result, the victim is unable to recollect and integrate the hurtful experience in normal consciousness; instead she is haunted or possessed by intrusive traumatic memories" (2). The perspective that victims are unable to recollect traumatic memories has been challenged by psychologist Richard J. McNally, who in an authoritative overview of current clinical studies argues that "people remember horrific experiences all too well" and that "victims are seldom incapable of remembering their trauma" (2). Nevertheless, common to most conceptualizations of trauma is the idea that certain memories are dissociated from everyday experience and manifest themselves in normal consciousness in intrusive and hurtful ways. The working through of traumatic events, therefore, requires the transformation or rescripting of these traumatic memories into an organizing narrative in a way that allows for the subject to assimilate the event itself into lived experience and eventually put it in the past. To this effect, clinicians Bessel A. van der Kolk and Onno van der Hart have observed that "traumatic memories are the unassimilated scraps of overwhelming experiences, which need to be integrated with existing mental schemes, and be transformed into narrative language" (176), and psychiatrist Judith Lewis Herman argues that the "work of reconstruction actually transforms the traumatic memory, so that it can be integrated into the survivor's life story" (175). Crucially, as McNally observes, "autobiographical recollection is a reconstructive, not a reproductive, process" that "is not like replaying a videotape of one's life in working memory" (35), a phrasing that highlights the necessarily creative aspect of incorporating certain memories into a cohesive narrative of the self.

In addition to the integrative potential of trauma narrative, great emphasis is regularly placed on its externalization. "In the telling, the trauma story becomes a testimony" (181), Herman notes, and her point is echoed by Shoshana Felman, who, according to Suzette A. Henke, asserts that "a surrogate transferential process can take place through the scene of writing that allows its author to envisage a sympathetic audience and to imagine a public validation of his or her life testimony" (xii). Similarly, psychiatrist Dori Laub has ascribed significant importance to the role of the witness in the process of working through traumatic memories, either at "the level of being a witness to oneself within the experience [or at] the level of being a witness to the testimonies of others" (61). The idea of the displacement and narrativization of trauma through externalizing testimony is as old as Freud's "talking cure." In *Studies on Hysteria* from 1893, Freud and Josef Breuer argue that "the injured person's reaction to the trauma only exercises a completely 'cathartic' effect if it is an adequate reaction—as, for instance, revenge. But language serves as a substitute for action; by its help, an effect can be 'abreacted' almost as effectively" (Breuer and Freud 8). Language has therefore also occupied a central role in much theory concerning the literature of trauma, which commonly relies on a version of what Henke has called scriptotherapy as the paradigm through which such texts work.[3] Defining the term as "the process of writing out and writing through traumatic experience in the mode of therapeutic reenactment" (xii), Henke, drawing on Herman, argues that "the object of psychoanalysis—and of autobiography as scriptotherapy—is to 'reassemble an organized, detailed, verbal account, oriented in time and historical context' out of 'fragmented components of frozen imagery and sensation'" (xviii). While language in the form of narrative is in this way often theorized as crucial to the processing of trauma, whether in a therapeutic or literary context, Henke's comments also suggest the potential contradiction of attempting to represent in words that which is often described as being inherently visual or sensory.

The notion that traumatic memories are predominantly visual in nature is supported by both clinical studies and the vocabulary of visuality that is commonly employed when describing trauma. According to van der Kolk and van der Hart, "cognitive psychologists have identified three modes of information encoding in the CNS [central nervous system]: inactive, iconic and symbolic/linguistic" (172). Because traumatic events are by definition unbearable in their horror and intensity, they argue, people exposed to them "experience 'speechless terror'" that "cannot be organized on a linguistic level, and this failure to arrange the memory in words and symbols leaves it to be organized on a somatosensory or iconic level" (172). Similarly, McNally notes that clinicians studying post-traumatic stress disorder have shown that "sometimes intrusive recollections are so vivid that it seems as if the trauma is actually happening again. In these *flashbacks*, the person may see, hear, smell, or feel the original sensations while remembering the trauma" (106; emphasis in the original). Traumatic flashbacks, McNally elaborates, "involve intense visual imagery" and "like autobiographical memories in general . . . inevitably entail reconstruction and distortion" (114, 117). In addition to these clinical accounts, literary theorists also commonly describe the nature of traumatic memories in visual terms. To that effect, E. Ann Kaplan mentions "trauma's peculiar visuality as a psychic disorder" (13), Leigh Gilmore argues that traumatic memory "expresses itself in flashbacks and fragments" (*Limits* 29), and Suzette A. Henke, again following Herman, describes its "stereotyped, repetitious" quality and explains how its "iconic and visual" images "intrude on the consciousness as 'a series of snapshots or a silent movie'" (xvii–xviii). Consisting of intrusive images in the form of flashbacks or snapshots, traumatic memories are thereby overwhelmingly considered to be visual, a circumstance that both contributes to their disruptive potential and posits a theoretical dilemma for literary theorists working with literature of trauma.

The recognition that traumatic memories consist of predominantly visual material that is unsuccessfully integrated into lived experience has meant that literary theorists have sometimes asserted the essential unrepresentability of trauma, at least in terms of traditional written forms. As Gilmore notes, referring to Cathy Caruth's influential view of trauma as "unclaimed experience," such perspectives contend that "language fails to adequately convey trauma and thus those who survive it stand outside an experience they cannot fully claim" ("Witnessing" 158). Language thereby occupies a peculiar double role in the theorization of trauma, where it is positioned as the tool for creating an organizing narrative—through the model of, for example, scriptotherapy—at the same time that it is considered somehow inadequate to the task of representing the particular nature of traumatic memories. This conceptual paradox is at the heart of literary trauma studies, and theorists working with trauma have therefore been at pains to develop a framework in which the written word can be equal to the representational task at hand. Caruth, for example, insists that trauma must "be spoken in a language that is always somehow literary: a language that defies, even as it claims, our understanding" (*Unclaimed Experience* 5), and Anne Whitehead argues that "the impact of trauma can only adequately be represented by mimicking its forms and symptoms, so that temporality and chronology collapse, and narratives are characterized by repetition and indirection" (3). The notion that trauma must be represented in fragmented or experimental forms has been so influential as to be named, by Alan Gibbs, "the trauma paradigm," which posits that "trauma texts should aim to transmit or convey trauma rather than represent it, and if they are to represent it, then it should be done according to the most indirect and experimental aesthetic forms possible" (1, 26). Gibbs goes on to examine several texts that, in his view, portray trauma in ways that escape this paradigm, but the question of whether trauma might best be represented through experimental or more traditional representational strategies is made significantly less urgent by the comics form, the inbuilt features of which—mimetic visual representation and narrative fragmentation—can do both simultaneously.

Allowing for multimodal representation that can be at once realistic and estranging, sensitive to the specific nature of traumatic memories while remaining true to their disruptive nature, comics appears to be a particularly apt form for narratives of trauma. As Chute has written about Lynda Barry's trauma-inflected autobiographical comic *One Hundred Demons*, Barry "does not need to 'translate' the nonverbal, affect-laden, sensory images into verbal narrative to approach her past; rather, she *includes* them" (*Graphic Women* 134; emphasis in the original). In addition to representing that which is visual and fragmented to begin with, however, the formal characteristics of the comics form may also be helpful for the gradual assimilation and working through of the traumatic experience. As a result of representing traumatic events as drawings on the page, comics narratives of trauma may thereby help the victim come a step closer to "claiming"—to use Caruth's terminology—the original experience, which can be both externalized and put into visual narrative by the autobiographer.

Alongside the aforementioned models theorizing the linguistic testimony of trauma as scriptotherapy, the visual arts are commonly acknowledged to possess therapeutic potential. Regarding the specific limits of the verbal as compared to the visual, Herman has noted about the therapeutic process that "as the narrative closes in on the most unbearable moments, the patient finds it more and more difficult to use words. At times the patient may spontaneously switch to nonverbal modes of communication, such as drawing or painting. Given the 'iconic,' visual nature of traumatic memories, creating pictures may represent the most effective initial approach to these 'indelible images' (177). According to psychotherapists Barry M. Cohen and Anne Mills, further, the concept of isomorphism, which refers to "the similarity in structure between a person's internal state and its outward expression . . . allows clients to externalize deeply personal experiences or sensations through the strategies and styles in their art, conveyed by lines, shapes and colors" (203). Therefore, they note, visual art is "the medium of choice . . . for externalizing [the patients'] perceptions and concerns and accessing material that has been visually encoded" (218). The therapeutic practice of art, in this perspective, can be used to dissociate traumatic experiences, and since traumatic memories are predominantly visual, yet are theorized as depending on the establishment of verbal narrative for their integration into a victim's life story, the visual-verbal form of comics may therefore be able to both represent and help work through the trauma in ways that are impossible in either mode alone.

Through its multimodal combination of fragmented verbal and visual codes that together create narrative, the comics form is particularly germane to the therapeutic representation of traumatic memories. In the context of trauma narrative, further, the split of the subject in autobiographical comics (between the narrating I and the narrated I, or between autobiographer and the drawn autobiographical character) can also function as a way to externalize and represent the dissociated and traumatized memories that cannot be integrated into the psyche. On the page, these representations can be arranged into narrative, and much in the same way that scriptotherapy works to disclose the trauma "in a format that promotes sequential organization of thoughts and narrative formation" (Smyth and Greenberg 139), so does the "sequential art" (Eisner, *Comics* 5) of comics produce narrative from still images through the process of what Scott McCloud—borrowing from gestalt psychology and using a term that has unmistakable implications for the working through of trauma—calls the "closure" (63) within and between panels. Thierry Groensteen, similarly, in a more rigorously theoretical explication of essentially the same process, uses the term "arthrology" to describe the relationship between discrete panels and the production of narrative that results from their juxtaposition. Groensteen distinguishes between "restrained arthrology" (the relationship between panels in sequence) and "general arthrology" (the relationship between panels in the comics network in its entirety), but common to both types is the construction of narrative from individual units of largely visual information (*System* 103, 144). The frameworks of McCloud and Groensteen are meant to describe the process from the perspective of the reader, but the split subject of comics creates a similar position for the autobiographer, who, as Gardner has argued, can be "both victim of the trauma and detached observer" ("Autography's Biography" 12). By externalizing visually encoded material as sequential drawings, the comics form is therefore not only able to represent traumatic memories but can also help construct a coherent narrative of the autobiographical self that may help the painful events be assimilated into lived experience through the creative arrangement of images on the page.

The comics form's ability to establish narrative from the "unassimilated scraps" of visual memory can be a creative act that enables what Dominick LaCapra has called the "articulatory practice" (22) of working through trauma. As Gloeckner herself has acknowledged, "my motivation is, 'This all happened to me. I feel really totally fucked-up. I don't understand any of this. Let's look at it. Let's not look at it sideways or make it look prettier, but let's just look at it for what it is'" (qtd. in Joiner, n.p.). Gloeckner's use of the word "look" is telling, as is her implication that her autobiographical project constitutes an attempt to make meaning out of confusing and painful memories by putting them into comics form. McNally notes that in clinical trials of verbal testimony "decreases in fragmentation over the course of therapy predicted improvement in PTSD symptoms" (135), and comics thereby can be seen as offering the autobiographer the ability to approach healing through the construction of a coherent narrative from the fragmented memories of painful past experience. Speaking of the importance of imagination to trauma texts in general, Gilmore argues that "part of what we must call healing lies in the assertion of creativity" (*Limits* 24), and as Gloeckner depicts traumatic childhood memories of sexual abuse on the comics page, their simultaneous representation and narrativization constitute a powerful act of creative recovery in the face of the cultural effacement of her subjectivity as both a woman and a victim of trauma.

Gloeckner's collection *A Child's Life* (2000) consists of stories and illustrations created over a period of more than twenty years. The earliest included work is a three-page autobiographical comic she drew in 1976 at age sixteen, and the most recent is a sequence of seven stories collectively entitled "A Child's Life" from 1998. The book's other comics are organized into sections called "Other Childish Stories," "Teen Stories," and "Grown-Up Stories," indicating Gloeckner's impulse to organize and compartmentalize what is in most cases highly autobiographical work. Indeed, most of the book's stories include a character bearing an unmistakable visual resemblance to Gloeckner, even if her name rarely appears on the page. Instead, Gloeckner's most frequently used pseudonym is that of Minnie Goetze, who acts as an alter ego in several of the stories and also returns as the first-person protagonist in *The Diary of a Teenage Girl*. In "It's Mary the Minor" from 1976, however, Gloeckner's autobiographical stand-in is named Mary, but the short narrative includes many of the same events and lines of dialogue that would later feature prominently in both *A Child's Life* and the *Diary*. The story "The Girl from a Different World," likewise, includes a Gloeckner look-alike named Penny, who confides similar events to an unsympathetic boyfriend, from whose point of view the story is told. This multiplicity of self-representational characters is illustrative of Gloeckner's approach to autobiography, which returns continually to the same events but from different perspectives and with a variety of narrative conceits.

The seven stories making up the title sequence of *A Child's Life* depict Minnie as a child of about eight, living with her younger sister, mother, and stepfather in an unnamed American city. The stepfather, Pascal, is significantly older than Minnie's mother, who is portrayed as easily dominated and looks not much older than a teenager herself. From the beginning, it is clear that Pascal has an excessive temper that often turns violent, and it later appears that he has a sexual interest in Minnie. Although Pascal never directly acts on this desire, he is drawn as an angry, leering, and slightly creepy-looking man, with curled lips and narrow, hard eyes. Minnie, in turn, is drawn as an intense-looking child with large, dark eyes, and Gloeckner's detailed drawing style adds realism to both the characters and their environments. The stories cover such material as Pascal losing his temper and hitting Minnie and her sister while driving, his attempts to talk the mother into an open marriage, and his inappropriate interest in whether Minnie's friends have begun to develop breasts.

In the course of the title story sequence, one image in particular stands out in relation to both the overall narrative and as an illustration of Gloeckner's use of the form to represent the specific nature of certain traumatic memories. McNally, summarizing clinical studies of "flashbulb memories," notes that "during a traumatic event, people often experience the illusion of time slowing down," that "attention is riveted to the most important aspect of the scene," and that such memories "seem unforgettably engraved on the mind and resistant to decay" (51, 52, 54). All of these qualities are represented visually in Gloeckner's art. Taking up the entire second page of a three-page vignette entitled "Hommage [*sic*] à Duchamp," the image depicts Minnie and her sister discovering Pascal masturbating in the bathroom (see fig. 2.1).[4] A pane of glass has been knocked out of the door, and the girls peer in through a frame that is bordered by the broken glass. What they see is their naked stepfather with his penis in his hand and clearly close to orgasm, his head turned slightly toward them but the direction of his gaze indeterminable. The image is constructed in three layers: the girls, the broken window, and Pascal occupy three different planes, creating the identifying effect of standing behind the girls and looking into the bathroom with them. The sizes of Pascal's head and penis have been exaggerated greatly, suggesting their importance to the visual memory of the scene. In addition, the penis occupies the focus of attention by virtue of

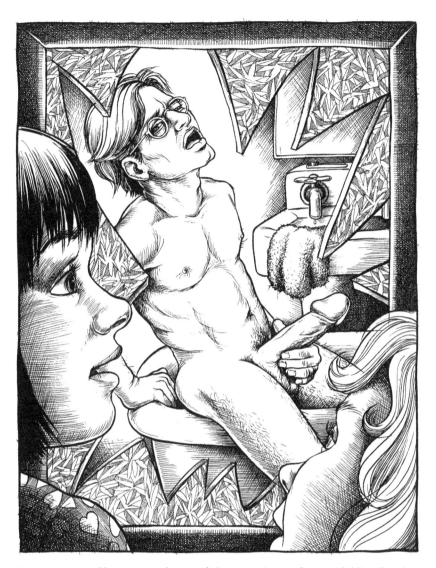

FIG. 2.1. Minnie and her sister see their stepfather masturbating, from *A Child's Life and Other Stories*.

both the composition of the image and the direction of Minnie's gaze, which is fixed upon it in a way that extends time and suggests a lingering moment despite the swift and surprised feel of the scene. From the vantage point of the reader, only Minnie's right eye is visible, but it is wide open in a way that suggests both curiosity and the burning into visual memory of the scene. The size of the panel, moreover—taking up a full page—creates an effect of shock, permanence, and disruption of the narrative. When compared to its surrounding images, the panel has no visual indicators of time passing, such as motion lines or speech balloons, and the stillness adds to the effect of a moment frozen in time. The splintered glass, finally, creates a jagged edge that both frames the image and adds a symbolic layer suggesting the splintering of childhood and the sharp edges of adult consciousness. As Chute has perceptively pointed out about the image, "Minnie and her sister are both attracted and repulsed" (*Graphic Women* 72), and this ambivalence is clearly at the thematic center of the story, which concludes with the girls running away and trying to understand what they just witnessed. Serving as the story's centerpiece, the image stands out and even interrupts the sequence in a number of interrelated formal and thematic ways that together suggest trauma. Caruth has argued that "to be traumatized is precisely to be possessed by an image or event" ("Introduction" 4–5), and while the memory is perhaps not necessarily or overtly traumatic for Gloeckner, the drawing's design, size, and narrative placement nevertheless indicate the ability of the comics form to represent the kind of disruptive visuality commonly associated with traumatic memory.

Gloeckner's perhaps best-known story, included in the "Teen Stories" segment of *A Child's Life* and titled "Minnie's 3rd Love, or, 'Nightmare on Polk Street,'" is from 1994, and is a longer and more sophisticated narrative that employs several of the strategies made possible by the comics form to depict scenes that are explicitly traumatic. The story takes place in 1976, after the family has moved to San Francisco, and Minnie is now a teenager living with her alcoholic mother and younger sister. In addition to the lack of domestic stability resulting from alcoholism, Minnie is also involved in a secret sexual relationship with her mother's boyfriend, who is approximately twenty years older than she is. Escaping an often tense home situation, Minnie spends most of her time on Polk Street, where she hangs out with various hustlers and junkies in the hope of finding drugs. She soon becomes infatuated with a young junkie named Tabatha whose mother was a heroin addict and "put Tabatha in porno films when she was a small child," a circumstance from which she "did not emerge intact" (*Child's Life* 72). Tabatha, however, intends only to use Minnie as a trade to her dealers in exchange for drugs, and soon uses her power over Minnie to trick her into taking too many Quaaludes, after which Minnie's drugged-up and unconscious body is serially raped in a "week-long nightmare of sex + drug taking" (*Child's Life* 75). The story culminates with a violent fight between Minnie

FIG. 2.2. Minnie and her mother's boyfriend, from *A Child's Life and Other Stories*.

and Tabatha, before a coda in which the two meet randomly on the street eighteen years later, exchanging a few awkward words. The relatively short comics narrative thereby contains several instances of sexual abuse and violence, which Gloeckner portrays in ways that are both unflinchingly visual and take full advantage of the specific formal properties of comics.

Minnie's sexual relationship with her mother's boyfriend is visually depicted in a large panel taking up almost a full page early in the story (see fig. 2.2). Set in a dark laundry room, the scene depicts the boyfriend hunched ominously over a kneeling Minnie, with his pants at his ankles and his hand on her head. The boyfriend is drawn as a large man who is barely contained by the panel borders—a strategy that both accentuates his size compared to Minnie and symbolizes the way his memory looms large in her consciousness. In stark contrast hereto, Minnie looks younger in this image than in the rest of the story, is sitting on her Hello Kitty diary, and—in a rare moment of wry humor that suggests the narrative presence of the adult autobiographer—is clutching a bottle labeled "The kind of good cheap California wine that makes girls cry and give blowjobs to jerks" (*Child's Life* 73). The center of the frame is occupied by the boyfriend's erect penis pointing directly at Minnie's crying face, and the image thereby condenses a great deal of visual information in a single panel. Communicating at once the illicit nature of the scene, the alarming age difference, and the abusive nature of the relationship despite the absence of overt force, the composition of the image is also in important ways similar to ones that both precede and succeed it, and together they inform and echo each other across the narrative.

The first of these is the panel immediately preceding the laundry room scene, which depicts Tabatha performing oral sex on a gay man in women's clothing in exchange for drugs (see fig. 2.3). The second depicts the unconscious Minnie sprawled on a bed and the victim of the aforementioned rape by Tabatha's drug dealers (see fig. 2.4). All three images depict an erect penis (or two penises, erect or otherwise, in the image with Tabatha) pointing left and in the direction of a vulnerable young woman, suggesting both the sexualized nature of patriarchal power and the pervasiveness of such abuse. The inclusion of Tabatha performing oral sex further generalizes the trauma beyond the strictly autobiographical while simultaneously suggesting a commonality of experience despite the two women's widely different circumstances. Together the images portray various scenes of female victimization at the hands of men, and the laundry room image is especially haunting because of its striking visualization of the often silenced sexual abuse by male authority figures in domestic situations. The effect of *showing* an adult man pointing his erect penis at a crying girl constitutes a radical political act of visualization that would not be possible in traditional literary autobiography. The comics form, further, allows for the establishment of narrative between the different traumatic events, both through the linking of the scenes in question via intermediary panels and because the visual resemblance serves to arthrologically form its own thematic narrative within the story. Depicting increasingly severe cases of sexual abuse and linking them all with the consumption of drugs and alcohol, the images together suggest a certain causality between the scenes, in a potentially endless chain of victimization and abuse. The repeated depiction of erections, moreover—a

FIG. 2.3. Tabatha exchanges sex for drugs, from *A Child's Life and Other Stories*.

FIG. 2.4. Minnie is raped by Tabatha's drug dealers, from *A Child's Life and Other Stories*.

striking taboo in Western culture—is an empowering act that refuses both their habitual veiling and the associated power of absence through disturbingly matter-of-fact representation.

By visualizing and narrativizing the traumatic events, Gloeckner bears witness to the experiences of her younger self in a confrontational and direct form that allows for the representation and externalization of haunting images. In the case of the image depicting the rape, the drawing is also a visualization of an event that is not accessible to the memory of the author because she was unconscious while it happened. While the story, which is told in the third person, gives no indication of how exactly Minnie learns of the rape, the same event occurs in the first-person *Diary*, where it is represented by a narrative absence—a blackout of experience by the unconscious Minnie. Tabatha later informs her in great detail how "I let them fuck you" (*Diary* 264) for a bottle of Quaaludes. In the short story, therefore, the scene constitutes Gloeckner's creative "recovery" of a horrifying event, the extent of which she can only imagine. The image is in this way a reconstruction that allows her to make witnesses of both herself and the reader so that the scene can be simultaneously integrated into her life story and externalized as visual testimony on the comics page. Because of the uncompromising nature of the narrative and its visuals, "Minnie's 3rd Love" is often singled out when Gloeckner's work has been subject to censorship. As Elizabeth Marshall and Gilmore have argued, however, Gloeckner's work "is not explicit and graphic in relation to the prevalence of sexualized and violent imagery but, rather, in relation to the norms of not representing rape and incest from the girl's perspective" (108). Unreasonably likened to child porn and in one case even deemed "a how-to-book for pedophiles" (qtd. in Chute, *Graphic Women* 77), Gloeckner's work in this and other stories functions as both an important visual reminder of the regularity of such abuse, as well as a potentially therapeutic tool for its author as she organizes and bears witness to the traumatic events.

Another story from *A Child's Life* that arranges lived experience using the visual logic of the comics form, and does so in a way that suggests trauma in both form and content, is the explicitly autobiographical "Fun Things to Do with Little Girls" (see figs. 2.5–2.7). Placed in a section of the book simply entitled "Other Childish Stories," which includes a number of short comics unrelated to the central narrative about Minnie, the three-page story is credited to "Phoebe 'Never gets over anything' Gloeckner" and is told in the first person without the mention of any names. The characters are

FIG. 2.5. Page 1 of "Fun Things to Do with Little Girls," from *A Child's Life and Other Stories.*

unmistakably the same as in the Minnie stories, however, both in appearance and characterization, but the switch from using autobiographical pseudonyms indicates a more direct engagement with self-representation, and as a result the story has a more intimate feel than the ones featuring Minnie. The comic depicts how the Pascal character, now simply referred to as "my stepfather," tries to convince the two girls to try a glass of red wine.

FIG. 2.6. Page 2 of "Fun Things to Do with Little Girls," from *A Child's Life and Other Stories*.

The Phoebe character, "anxious to please and wanting to appear sophisticated" (*Child's Life* 66), drinks a little, while her younger sister, only six years old, refuses. The main story now continues on the left-hand side of the relatively classic six-panels-per-page layout, and culminates as the stepfather fills

FIG. 2.7. Page 3 of "Fun Things to Do with Little Girls," from *A Child's Life and Other Stories*.

his mouth with wine, holds the sister to the floor, and spits the wine into her mouth when she opens it to scream. The panel in which Pascal holds the sister, wine dripping from his mouth, is placed on the right-hand side of the page, and is similar in pose to other memories that are interpolated into the narrative. The first of these is an image showing the Phoebe character having sex with her mother's boyfriend years later, the boyfriend hunched over her and dripping with sweat while she looks indifferently toward the reader. This panel also contains the narration: "Years later, the first time I had sex was with my mother's boyfriend. I was eager to be sophisticated and wanted nothing more than to please" (*Child's Life* 67). Making the connection between being encouraged to drink wine and having sex with a man more than twice her age, the two images in their similarity suggest the impression that both events made on her, while the words underscore the immaturity of Phoebe's point of view. The next inserted memory is more general, and shows Phoebe fighting with her sister and pinning her to the floor in a pose reminiscent of both aforementioned images. Admitting that "I was no angel. I used to beat up my sister mercilessly" (*Child's Life* 67), Gloeckner uses these similarities to link her own aggressive behavior with both the violence of her stepfather and the sexual exploitation by her mother's boyfriend, while also suggesting the potential for a causal relationship between the various manifestations of power.

The resemblance of these images illustrates Groensteen's notion of general arthrology, which describes how the visual resonances across the network of a comics page can create correspondences of meaning. Adding to and complicating the meaning of each individual panel, what Groensteen refers to as the "braiding" (*System* 146) of the different images throughout the spatial field exemplifies how additional layers of narrative can appear outside of strict chronological progression in comics. In Gloeckner's story the last two of these images are inserted into the narrative *before* the event that brings them to mind takes place, and the splintering of linear temporal progression into fragmented space and time is thereby resonant with the conceptualization of trauma as a visualization of repetitious frozen images brought to consciousness through flashbacks reminiscent of snapshots. Anne Whitehead has argued that "if trauma is at all susceptible to narrative formulation, then it requires a literary form which departs from conventional linear sequence" (6), and the jumbled chronology creates the effect of both a gradual revelation and a serial compounding of the trauma, as one memory functions to uncover others.[5] The effect of placing the similar images on the right-hand side of the page creates a fragmented yet sustained disruption of the narrative that suggests the split consciousness of trauma, wherein traumatic memories manifest themselves as intrusions into normal experience. The traumatic experience of seeing her sister violated in this way by her stepfather thus blurs into Gloeckner's visual memory of other events, to the point where she conceptualizes sexual violence and sibling infighting as similar, but of course fundamentally different, manifestations of transgression.

In a sort of arthrological framing device, the two images that appear on the right side before and after the three panels depicting abuse both have to do with alcohol. In the first of these, Gloeckner notes that the girls' biological father was responsible for a car crash that "killed his best girl" when he "was drunk and 16" (*Child's Life* 67). In the second, which is also the final image of the story proper, the mother is depicted alone in the kitchen, where she would usually just "drink + cry during such episodes," without responding to a cry for "Mommy!!" (*Child's Life* 68). The motif of alcohol further links these two events with the main narrative, and suggests that the wine acted as a catalyst for their remembrance. Finally, another layer of framing depicts a story that seems to have triggered the whole traumatic series of memories. In addition to the intense stare of Gloeckner's adult face, the title panel depicts a woman in a supermarket putting a bottle of whiskey into her purse while her daughter asks for a package of cereal. After the reader is informed that "this bonus story concludes on p. 3 frame 5," the woman is shown in the penultimate panel as being arrested for shoplifting. In the last panel of the comic, the woman's daughter is depicted in an otherwise blank panel, looking scared and—in an arthrological echo of Phoebe and her sister's cry for their own mother in the panel directly above—crying out "Momma!" (*Child's Life* 68). This last scene takes place after Gloeckner has announced "the conclusion of bonus story" (*Child's Life* 68) in the previous panel, and the scared little girl can thereby be simultaneously read as the girl left behind in the supermarket and a generalized representation of the consequences of irresponsible parenting. McNally notes about the context for recollecting traumatic and other memories that "we are more likely to recall something when the context of remembering resembles the context of encoding" (40), and as the frame story links both alcohol and its relationship with parental neglect to the main narrative, the comic suggests that the traumatic memories were brought to the surface of the adult Gloeckner's consciousness when she observed this scene in a supermarket.

The final words of the story are written underneath the image of the scared little girl, and read "That's all there is there ain't no more" (*Child's Life* 68), a reference to the last line in the many film and television adaptations of Ludwig Bemelmans's Madeline series of children's books. Ending the story with a line from children's entertainment underscores the childhood perspective on the events portrayed at the same time that it emphasizes the theatricality of the reconstructed narrative. While Gloeckner humorously bills herself as unable to get over anything, the mere creation of the story and its extensive linking of traumatic memories from various points in her life similarly indicate a certain distance from them, to the extent that she is able to observe her life and work through the trauma by visually depicting it on the page. The disorienting and splintered visual chronology typical of traumatic memories, moreover, is alleviated somewhat by the textual narration running through the story, which posits an organizing authorial subject who is both distinct from the visually represented events and in control of the narrative. The combination of text and image native to the comics form, therefore, allows for the construction of an integrative visual-verbal narrative that is true to the nature of traumatic memories while retaining the therapeutic potential of the narrativizing act. Through its various layers of recursive remembrance and its use of the specific narrative opportunities offered by the comics form, the story can therefore be viewed as an instance of drawn scriptotherapy. Indeed, Gloeckner continued to dramatize and work through many of the same events in *The Diary of a Teenage Girl*, published in 2002.

In contrast to the several different autobiographical characters appearing in the stories collected in *A Child's Life*, the *Diary* is presented as the unified diary of fifteen-year-old Minnie Goetze, written over the course of a year when she was living with her mother and sister in San Francisco in the mid-1970s. The book consists of a mix of typed diary entries, illustrations, and narrative comics. As mentioned previously, the book is based on Gloeckner's actual diary from this time, but it was adapted and streamlined into a coherent story. As with most of her work, Gloeckner refuses the term *autobiography* for the book, but the expanded and less uniform category of *life writing* would easily accommodate it. The central story is repeated from "Minnie's 3rd Love" and concerns Minnie's yearlong sexual relationship with her mother's boyfriend, now called Monroe, as well as her increasing drug use and subsequent semiromantic involvement with Tabatha. Spanning nearly three hundred pages, the book covers significantly more ground than its twelve-page comics predecessor, and where the fragmented comics narrative mostly depicts Minnie as a drug-using runaway on Polk Street, the *Diary* expands to include many of the events leading up to and following directly after this time in her life. For example, the book also contains the story of how, after discovering and reading Minnie's diary—the one later made available to the reader—her mother drunkenly attempts to pressure a sheepish Monroe into marrying Minnie. Rightfully sickened by this proposition, Minnie leaves home and stays with various acquaintances from the city's hard drug scene. After several months of instability, during which she runs away and returns home more than once, the *Diary* closes first with Minnie promising herself never to use drugs again, and then with an epilogue describing a chance meeting with Monroe that gives her the opportunity to shake his hand, look him in the eye, and think to herself: "I'm better than you, you son-of-a-bitch" (*Diary* 293). In the illustration accompanying this scene Minnie is smiling, with her face prominently framed by her black hair, while Monroe is seen only from behind, his face obscured and his hair blending into the clouds, suggesting that both he and his memory are on their way to becoming immaterial (see fig. 2.8). Ending on a considerably more positive note than the comics version, and with Minnie asserting agency and control of her own situation, the *Diary* also elaborates on certain events and characters necessarily compressed in the comic, portraying them from a number of different perspectives through the multimodal interplay of various textual and visual forms.

According to Whitehead, trauma narratives tend to include certain key stylistic features, including "intertextuality, repetition and a dispersed or fragmented narrative voice" (84), all of which are present in the complex construct that is the *Diary*. In addition to the text entries, the book includes a large number of illustrations of objects, characters, and scenes from the narrative, as well as several sections told in comics of different length. The illustrations are of varied origin and include a large number of drawings made by Gloeckner as both a teenager and adult, a cartoon made by Gloeckner's father, who was a commercial artist, drawings by Aline Kominsky Crumb and Robert Crumb, with whom Gloeckner's mother socialized, and images taken from comics by Justin Green and Diane Noomin, among others. The comics fall into two categories: those drawn by Minnie/Gloeckner at the time of the diary's composition, and a much larger number created by the adult Gloeckner at the time of writing the book. The text itself is also multimodal, and includes letters from Pascal, who is at this point divorced from Minnie's mother, as well as written dialogues representing conversations between Minnie and others, transcriptions of self-help tapes, lists, poems, and song lyrics, in addition to the diary entries themselves. Changes in register are represented through differing font sizes, indentation, and italics, all adding to the amount of information communicated visually on the page. The plurality of perspectives, including the use of Gloeckner's own diary as the raw material from which the narrative is created, makes for an intricate structure containing several different

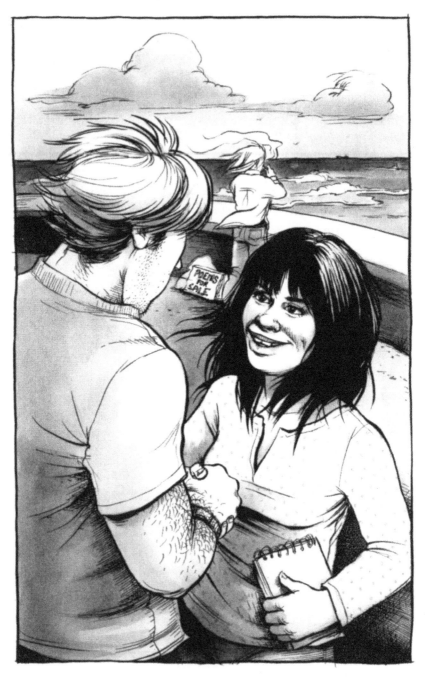

"I'm better than you, you son-of-a-bitch."

FIG. 2.8. Minnie says goodbye to Monroe, from *The Diary of a Teenage Girl*.

perspectives on the same events, and the multimodal nature of the book's many different strategies of representation suggests the complexity and fragmentation of the autobiographical subject.

In the published book, the text is a mix of actual diaries written by the fifteen-year-old Gloeckner and additions and edits made by her adult self twenty-five years later. Meanwhile, the comics created contemporaneously with the original diary do not advance the story but serve as allegorical interludes, and the comics made by the adult Gloeckner portray events omitted in the diary from her adult perspective. The illustrations, likewise, are adult glosses on events described by a teenager (whether from the original diary or made by Gloeckner as an adult). The grown-up perspective provided by the new comics and their realistic, almost documentary-like drawing style, along with most of the illustrations, thereby function as an adult commentary in which Gloeckner makes the long-ago teenage protagonist visible in an act of autobiographical remembrance and creation that embodies her marginalized teenage self on the page. Interspersed throughout the narrative, moreover, the comics and illustrations give the impression that some memories are more visual than others and can best be presented as such. The hybrid form containing multiple perspectives on her life also represents Minnie's ambivalence as she knowingly enters into the sexual relationship. Significantly, she is as active in pursuing Monroe as he is in seducing her, and she exhibits a substantial sexual appetite throughout the narrative—confiding to her diary, for example, that "I really like getting fucked" (*Diary* 26). While the sexually experienced and often mature-sounding voice of the written diary can sometimes obscure Minnie's youth, however, the images depicting a fifteen-year-old girl in bed with a much older man serve to remind the reader that the unequal relationship is also a clear case of sexual abuse (see fig. 2.9). The narrative's multimodal mixing of verbal and visual forms in this way accentuates the gulf between Minnie's feelings of sexual maturity and the fact that she is only a few years out of childhood. The diary entries themselves, by virtue of being from the point of view of a teenager somewhat excitedly caught up in events, lack the perspective brought to the book by the drawings made by the adult Gloeckner. Aware of the trauma, and of the effect it has had on her life since, Gloeckner offers the illustrations as a corrective to the first-person narrative's relative innocence, while remaining true to the authentic experience of her teenage self.[6] Although it contains no images as overtly disturbing as the laundry room scene in *A Child's Life*, the *Diary* employs its visual elements to subtly show what the text itself is

FIG. 2.9. Minnie in bed with Monroe, from *The Diary of a Teenage Girl*.

unable to tell, suggesting the full extent of the traumatic events only through implication and multimodal juxtaposition.

The images in *The Diary of a Teenage Girl* bear witness to a case of sexual abuse in a way that the words alone do not. According to Kaplan, victims of traumatic events "put their experiences in writing . . . for several reasons: to organize pain into a narrative that gives it shape for the purposes of self-understanding (working their trauma through), or with the aim of being heard, that is, constructing a witness where there was none before" (20). With the *Diary*, Gloeckner has created a narrative from scraps of text made by her younger self, which she has sifted through, organized, and made to cohere according to her adult subjectivity. In the process, the trauma is externalized onto the page through the visual representation of the younger self, and the comics and illustrations thereby construct both author and reader as literal eyewitnesses to the trauma. While *A Child's Life* and *The Diary of a Teenage Girl* use images in somewhat different ways, both works employ visuality in order to make the private public and restore a sense of agency to the traumatized self in the process. By visualizing examples of hidden but all-too-common sexual abuse, Gloeckner reminds us that patriarchal structures of sexual dominance and abuse govern women's private and interior lives, and that abuse is often silenced and denied by both victim and aggressor. The visual grammar of comics, moreover, offers a way of creating closure between the fragmented drawings representing traumatic memories, and the establishment of narrative from frozen images holds the potential to both work through the events and contain them within the compartmentalized panels of the comics page.

In the political act of showing hidden sexual abuse, as well as the use of comics to depict and work through scenes of personal trauma, Gloeckner's two books not only make a case for the potential of the form to serve a therapeutic purpose but also illustrate the problem of adequately representing an autobiographical self that is both fragmented and under duress. Where traditional autobiography aims to present the reader with a stable representation of a coherent subject, for Gloeckner the autobiographical project is an ongoing task bound up with the recursive portrayal of key events from different perspectives and in a variety of formats. Drawing on Caruth, Bina Toledo Freiwald argues about the tendency to produce multiple autobiographical volumes that "as a practice that allows a plural present self to grapple with its past(s), serial autobiography is both a symptom of and an antidote to the rupture that is trauma's aftermath—that 'breach in the mind's experience of time, self, and the world'" (234). Caruth herself notes that the "wound of the mind" created by trauma "is experienced too soon, too unexpectedly, to be fully known" (*Unclaimed Experience* 3). As Gloeckner continues to rewrite her life through an increasing number of panels, stories, and books, it is evident that in her use of the comics form she is highly indebted to the experience and rhetoric of trauma and that the form's specific features provide her with a set of tools with which to attempt the ongoing and always incomplete task of representing a traumatized subjectivity as it exists in the breach between the known and the unknown.

3

Queer as Style

● ● ● ● ● ● ● ● ● ● ● ● ●

Ariel Schrag's *High School
Comic Chronicles*

One particularity of the comics form is that the combination of text and images often introduces a split into a given narrative, between the present tense of the drawings and the past tense of the narration. In this view, the immediacy of the images causes them to present themselves to us as the diegetic present tense, even if the events portrayed are technically being recounted or remembered from a vantage point in the relative future. When looking at a single comics image, in other words, we tend to enter its temporality and experience it as if it were happening at the moment of reading. This ability to situate the reader in the past while maintaining a retrospective point of view in the text-based narration creates a productive tension between the past and the present that is especially valuable to autobiographical comics. By combining the power of the present-tense images to draw in the reader and make us live in the vivid past with an acute awareness of the reflecting author-narrator who is recounting the story and has constructed the images, autobiographical comics usually exist in the uneasy space between the visually represented lived experience of the past and the present-day narration, while giving prominence to neither.

In most autobiographical comics, then, two versions of the author are continually and simultaneously present in the narrative, and the tension created between them is a fundamental reason for the particular impact of, for example, Phoebe Gloeckner's stories of sexual trauma. Relying on the ability of images to depict the immediacy of the present, Gloeckner provides a perspective that is both contemporary with the events portrayed and, because of the organizing adult consciousness and its incarnation as a narrative voice, unmistakably the work of a reflective adult author using the form to make sense of past experience. By using her teenage diary as the raw material for an extended and multivolume meditation on certain key traumatic events from her adolescence, Gloeckner's series of self-portraits are in this way also about the author's relationship with the past, which the comics form enables her to sift through visually and present to the reader with the immediacy of images and from the relatively safe distance of adulthood. The combination of adult authorial distance and the labor-intensive method of creating comics as polished as hers, moreover, including the many artful elisions, compressions, and arthrological allusions needed to shape a narrative visually, allows Gloeckner to provide a perspective on her own life that is well considered, measured, and—in spite of the traumatic events— stylistically restrained in its visual representation. Her narratives and her characters, including her recurring semiautobiographical avatar Minnie, thus arrive for the reader fully formed, conceptualized from the comics' inception and drawn with the care and precision of a trained and mature artist.

Compared to that of Gloeckner, the serialized autobiographical work of queer American comics artist Ariel Schrag is thematically and stylistically untidy and is imbued with an urgency and sense of the self as being in-process that reflects the fact that Schrag drew and published several of her comics about her high school experience while still a high school student. At least initially lacking almost entirely in both a sense of retrospection and in the self-conscious separation between author and character that is commonplace in autobiography, Schrag's four comics—in sequence they are *Awkward*, *Definition*, *Potential*, and *Likewise*—each details one of her years in high school in Berkeley, California in the mid-1990s. In addition to the unusually young age of their creator, the four books have a rather convoluted publication history that is of interest because it speaks to Schrag's quick development as a professional artist and to such issues as authorial control, seriality, and her obsession with depicting the truth of her experience in spite of subject matter that might be controversial to the friends and family represented in the comics.

The first three of Schrag's high school comics were written during the summer after the year they chronicle, while *Likewise* took a full year to write. *Awkward* and *Definition* were inked and consequently self-published (photocopied and stapled) in the years immediately following the events they depict—1995 and 1996, respectively—and were distributed to friends and classmates, as well as sold at comics conventions such as San Jose's Alternative Press Expo by Schrag herself. Alternative comics publisher Slave Labor Graphics, based also in San Jose, picked up and published *Definition* in 1997 and serialized *Potential*, which took two years to ink, in six issues from 1998 to 1999.[1] This was followed by the delayed publication of *Awkward* in 1999 and the collected edition of *Potential* in 2000. Parts of *Likewise*, a lengthy and ambitious comic that took Schrag eight years to ink, were initially serialized in three issues in 2003–2004, but the book only saw full publication with Simon and Schuster's 2008–2009 reissue of the works in three volumes as *The High School Comic Chronicles of Ariel Schrag*, the first of which combines the much shorter *Awkward* and *Definition*.[2]

Schrag's comics differ from most other autobiography, in comics form or otherwise, by largely having been drawn and published shortly after the events they portray. In traditional autobiographies of childhood or young adulthood, the expected implication is that the narrating I (the self who tells) can be understood as a later incarnation of the narrated I (the self told about). In such narratives, Kylie Cardell and Kate Douglas have argued, "the child, along with his or her experiences, functions to explain the adult self that the subject becomes, and the adult controls the way that representation is told" (1). In Schrag's work, conversely, the distance in perspective is not that of an adult author looking back at her teenage years and reflecting upon their meaning and impact for her present-day self. Rather, the distance is between the individual events themselves and their being put on paper a few months later, while the adolescent author was still in the throes of such experiences as first love, heartbreak, and coming out as a lesbian. Where Gloeckner used her teenage diary as the raw material for the elaborate adult authorial construct that is *The Diary of a Teenage Girl*, Schrag's *High School Comic Chronicles*, while also based on her written diaries, are almost completely lacking a self-conscious separation between adult author and teenage character, for the simple reason that no adult has been involved in their creation.[3] Because of the circumstances of the comics' production and publication, therefore, they are less a reflective autobiographical account in the vein of Gloeckner's work—or Alison Bechdel's *Fun Home* or Marjane Satrapi's *Persepolis*, for that matter—than a concurrent and on-the-scene eyewitness report of what it was like to be a teenager in a very specific place and time.

Together, Schrag's four volumes of high school comics constitute a narrative of becoming, one that is both the story of her personal and artistic maturation and an account of her move away from what Adrienne Rich has famously called "compulsory heterosexuality" (130) and toward a firmly acknowledged lesbian identity, with a stop at bisexuality along the way. The comics form, crucially, is important to Schrag's project because it allows her to serially depict her changing sense of self through stylistic and narrative experimentation. Simultaneously a coming-out and a coming-into narrative, Schrag's comics chronicle begins rather innocently in *Awkward* by detailing her fleeting crushes and musical obsessions, but as the author matures, the material in the following books grows steadily darker and more structurally complicated. Similarly, the artwork progresses from a simple cartoony style to a more refined approach that relies increasingly on shading and perspective and also experiments with realistic watercolors and untraditional page layouts in key sequences. Focusing on the artistic and personal development on display throughout the four installments, this chapter provides a consideration of Schrag's work that argues that the books' origin in zine culture combined with the comics form's serial nature and visual instability provide Schrag with both a vehicle for self-expression and the tools to experiment with visual and verbal codes in order to delineate and assert the queer and in-progress teenage self as experimental artist. In doing so, Schrag's four books gradually begin to employ the full arsenal of the comics form in order to stylistically express the difference and excess associated with queerness that realistic depictions of bodies and faces often fail to produce without resorting to stereotype or caricature.

As Schrag's narrative becomes increasingly sophisticated in both storytelling and imagery with each new installment, it is evident that the multiple narrative and visual possibilities of the comics form are essential to her personal and artistic development and their implications for her depiction of a constantly changing, growing, and maturing self. For a young, queer, and female artist, this radical—in scope, as well as content—act of depicting both her exterior and interior realities constitutes a counterdiscourse initially made possible by the accessibility of the comics form and its concrete expression as part of handmade and self-published 1990s zine culture. Regarding the ability of the young to speak for themselves, Henry A. Giroux has argued that "Youth as a complex, shifting, and contradictory category is rarely narrated in the dominant public sphere through the diverse voices of the young. Prohibited from speaking as moral and political agents, youth become an empty category inhabited by the desires, fantasies, and interests of the adult world" (24). In this view, firsthand accounts of adolescence are subject to censorship in both form and content by an adult world controlling access to an audience and typically concerned with marketability. This cultural and commercial marginalization is further compounded for queer youth, who, social work theorist Jama Shelton notes, are routinely "denied public language with which to articulate their experiences, to name themselves, and to frame their needs." Noting the importance of self-articulation to personal development, Shelton further argues that "it is imperative that queer young people are provided the tools with which they can explore and express themselves in a manner that is consistent with their subjective and collective desires and are also offered safe spaces in which to do so" (70). While Shelton's sentiments are commendable, they nevertheless rely on an adult and predominantly heterosexual world to allocate—and therefore regulate—such spaces.

Zines, however, as identified primarily with 1980s and 1990s alternative or underground culture, can provide precisely such a self-claimed and unregulated space for personal expression. This is especially true in the genre known as the perzine, or personal zine, which is characterized, according to Anna Poletti, "by the authors taking their life and identity as the main focus" (35). As zines are given, sold, traded, or otherwise circulated through such avenues as local small press expos or the mail, they have the potential to exist as truly alternative culture unmonitored by adultist, heteronormative, and patriarchal society.[4] Mary Celeste Kearney, in an exploration of various girl-made media, has argued about the potential of the form as a whole that "as the young females who create zines are often adolescents transitioning from girlhood to womanhood, such texts provide a space for their creators' initial exploration of nontraditional identities, especially those that may be deemed inappropriate for individuals of their sex and age and thus are rarely permitted public expression" (146). While not all zines take comics form, of course, it is perhaps not coincidental that some of the

most lasting contributions to this corner of youth culture have been produced—or, rather, handmade—by adolescent girls and young women associated with such alternative expressions of femininity as the riot grrrl
movement.[5] But where Julie Doucet's early work from the late 1980s takes
advantage of the comics zine's marginal status to explore an interior life
dominated by unspoken desires or sexual fantasies, Schrag employs the form
to create an extended and exhaustively documented comics narrative that is
equal parts real-time meta-*Künstlerroman* and the intimate story of her personal and sexual maturation.[6] While the zine format enabled Schrag to
begin her public journey of self-discovery as both artist and lesbian, her collected comics are also a document of her quick professionalization from
making photocopied and self-distributed comics to emerging as the full-
fledged author of the ambitiously conceived and professionally published
magnum opus *Likewise*. Moreover, this journey from the diary-inflected
Awkward to the experimental autobiography of *Likewise* also follows Schrag
through an increasingly complex and obsessive engagement with lived experience and its representation that nearly threatens to consume both her life
and the comic by series' end—at which point the straightforward storytelling of the early installments has given way to narratively and stylistically self-
reflective ruminations about the intersection of life and art in comics.

Although Schrag's comics are in these ways insistently autobiographical,
they can nevertheless be difficult to classify in terms of genre, and exist
somewhat uneasily in the space between diary, memoir, and autobiography.
Like Gloeckner's *The Diary of a Teenage Girl*, Schrag's comics are in large
part based on her actual written diary, but unlike Gloeckner's work the narrative does not conform to either general expectations of diary writing or
to Philippe Lejeune's definition of the form as "a series of dated traces" (*On
Diary* 179). Despite Lejeune's emphasis on seriality and his notion of trace,
which can include "an image, an object, or a relic" (*On Diary* 179), Schrag's
comics fall outside this general definition by being a continuous and undated
narrative sequence. Her diaries instead constitute what Lejeune, in a further meditation on the generic properties of various autobiographical forms,
has called the "avant-texte" (*On Diary* 226) of the final narrative, the raw
material from which it is shaped. Similarly, Claire Lynch, in an article about
children's autobiography, coins the term "ante-autobiography" to refer to the
texts that come before, or exist instead of, a full-length narrative—the material that "has the potential to become an autobiography" (105). Insofar as
the written diary itself exists at all in Schrag's work, it is as a diegetic element

that functions to indicate her compulsive desire to record her life by keeping regular journal entries and writing about events that just happened. In this vein, Schrag often portrays herself writing in her paper diary or on a computer. Throughout the comics, this perpetual collecting of ante-autobiographical material reflects Ariel's determination to present as complete a record of events as possible, to the point where she also keeps files on her friends and family and tape-records both herself and her conversations with others.[7]

This aspect aligns Schrag's work with one of Lejeune's functions of the diary—namely, to "build a memory out of paper, to create archives out of lived experience, to accumulate traces, prevent forgetting, to give life the continuity it lacks" ("How" 107)—at the same time that it sets it apart from the different category of autobiography. As Lejeune explains, "autobiography and the diary have opposite aims: autobiography lives under the spell of fiction; the diary is hooked on truth" (*On Diary* 201). This difference, Lejeune is quick to point out, does not imply anything as simple as "autobiographies are false and diaries are true" (*On Diary* 201), but rather speaks to the two forms' relationship with the past and future. While "the past puts up only minor resistance to the powers of the imagination," Lejeune notes, "the same cannot be said of the future. Diarists never have control over what comes next in their texts. They write with no way of knowing what will happen next in the plot, much less how it will end" (*On Diary* 202). While diaries are thus by necessity ignorant of the future, they cannot, of course, exist entirely in the present but must inevitably refer back to previous entries and experiences. As Paul Robinson points out, "even the most circumstantial diarist occasionally steps back from his quotidian account to reflect on the larger meaning of his life" (262). But where diaries exhibit a perspective limited in scope because the moment of the story's telling is close to the diegetic present, other and more retrospective forms of life writing have the entirety of the subject's lived experience at their disposal. This perspective provides a significantly expanded potential for reflection, which in turn is a quality that is often considered essential to the artistic success of autobiographical work. Accordingly, Jane Taylor McDonnell comments that "the reflective voice is so important to memoir writing because self-revelation without reflection or understanding is merely self-exposure. We want the author of a memoir to have *grown up*, to have learned from earlier mistakes or experiences, and to be the wiser for it" (136; emphasis in the original). McDonnell's emphasis points to one of the expectations associated with autobiography and memoir—namely, that their authors have outgrown an immature or childish perception of both the world and themselves, and that this is reflected in their self-presentation. If autobiography and memoir are in this way concerned with the formation and retrospective life story of a mature self, then Schrag's temporally limited and inescapably youthful narratives do not easily conform to these generic expectations. By relying on "documentary" evidence from her diaries and other recorded ante-autobiographical material, and by writing and publishing her work in installments chronicling a year at a time—a model that significantly limits the potential for retrospection and causes her to write about such topics as her parents' messy divorce and her own ongoing romantic relationships while they happen—Schrag's comics straddle the line between the diary's present-tense immediacy and the more reflective and narrativizing genres of memoir and autobiography.

While the overall perspective of Schrag's comics chronicle is marked by a certain generic indeterminacy, the four-year narrative also exhibits an evident progression from an early approach that favors the accumulative and direct self-portrait typical of diary to one that increasingly privileges integrated storytelling and the authorial reflection of mature autobiography. In combination with an increasing complexity of narrative vision that follows Schrag's personal maturation as a writer, the drawings are a central part of this progression. Over the course of the four installments, Schrag's visuals gradually develop from the somewhat naive but fluidly drawn sketches illustrating her diaristic narrative in the early installments to a more considered but also visually promiscuous style that works in concert with the narrative to produce a highly complex representation of both her exterior and interior life.

Stylistic change or development over time is a commonplace of comics art. Because of the labor-intensive and time-consuming nature of producing comics, an artist's visual style often changes and eventually solidifies over years-long projects. Because of the circumstances of their publication, this phenomenon is especially evident in long-running newspaper strips like Jim Davis's *Garfield*, Charles Schulz's *Peanuts*, and even Bechdel's *Dykes to Watch Out For*, where changes in character design are often gradually imperceptible but ultimately so significant that early renderings can be almost unrecognizable compared to more recent iterations. In other more temporally and narratively contained single-artist work produced over a span of several years, developments in style are equally common though often less dramatic in nature. In order to achieve a coherent visual expression—obeying what Gert Meesters has called "a fundamental law of comic art: unity of style" (qtd. in Groensteen *Comics* 113)—artists will sometimes return to and redraw earlier pages or installments once a desired, or simply final, style has solidified.[8] While the stylistic development of comics artists is sometimes only visible from a decades-long perspective, or is erased completely by later reworking, it is, by contrast, front and center in Schrag's work, where it is also thematically coherent with, and eventually inseparable from, the two central narratives of becoming and coming out.

Since Schrag's extended comics project is in many ways a story about artistic and sexual experimentation, it seems only fitting that it should exhibit a heterogeneity of visual style that is at odds with what Thierry Groensteen calls the "imperative of harmony, the classical ideal" (*Comics* 114). Over the course of the four volumes, Schrag's artistic development is obvious from both the observable changes to the drawing style itself and the narrative purposes its variation is increasingly employed for. Accordingly, as Schrag gradually becomes a more confident cartoonist her variations in style become something more than merely a reflection of personal skill as regards drawing ability. Eventually, they include such sophisticated techniques as expressionistic indications of heightened emotion and abrupt shifts in the visual register in order to denote the different modalities of experience and memory depicted on a given page. Groensteen, building in part on the work of French linguist Alain Rey, has pointed out that "a claim to truthfulness is not necessarily to be equated with the most realist possible graphic modalization" as long as characters are "endowed with 'a stable identity for the duration of the story'" (*Comics* 112). In contrast, Schrag's comics provide an example both of an artist exploring the narrative functions of the form itself and actively and resolutely working against its conventions by eschewing stability of visual representation in favor of a queer aesthetic of multiplicity and excess.

The first volume of the extended narrative, *Awkward*, was written, drawn, and inked during the summer of 1995, and concerns Schrag's 1994–1995 freshman year. The events portrayed consist largely of various friendship cycles, a number of teenage crushes on mostly boys (with accompanying light kissing in a few instances), smoking pot, and attending shows. Ariel's personal preoccupations are similarly adolescent—and, from a contemporary perspective, charmingly emblematic of being a teenager in the 1990s—and include her obsessions with the actress Juliette Lewis and the all-female grunge band L7. At forty-nine pages, *Awkward* is by far the shortest of the four volumes, as well as the most direct in terms of narrative structure and the representation of personal subjectivity. The story line is straightforwardly organized as a series of events and conversations about them, and depicts life as it happens to Ariel, without much nuance or a significant outside perspective. Similarly, the narrative voice descriptively recounts the various events, and traces of a self-reflective and organizing consciousness are limited to Schrag's ability—by virtue of looking back over the school year from the vantage point of the summer—to construct events as short story arcs and provide commentary about, for example, "the past few months" (*Awkward and Definition* 41). Despite this potential for slight retrospection, the viewpoint is largely limited to the present tense, and foreshadowing of events exists only to set up various scenes or to hint about whether a new acquaintance will eventually become a good friend.

The most narratively adventurous quality of this early installment is when Schrag draws Ariel directly addressing the reader, in a breach of the fourth wall. After a boyfriend breaks up with her over the phone, for example—because, as he says, "I don't really like how you're always buying me presents"—Ariel protests by confronting the reader in the next panel (which is borderless, signifying heightened emotion), exclaiming with evident anger and bloodshot eyes: "Time fucking out! I got him one fucking Doors patch—and I didn't even buy, I stole it" (*Awkward and Definition* 20) (see fig. 3.1). In such playful uses of comics narrative to immediately refute the perspective of another character through commentary aimed directly at the reader, Schrag asserts control of the narrative and reminds us of her subjective viewpoint. Similarly, Ariel addresses the reader several times to give her opinion of new friends. In one sequence, a girl from art class impresses a skeptical Ariel by owning a certain early album by L7, an event that prompts Ariel to turn and face the reader, giving her stamp of approval with a thumbs up and the surprised assurance that "She's cool!" Brief and seemingly trivial as these instances of direct address are, they serve to create a sense of intimacy with Ariel, who evaluates her immediate experiences and confides her thoughts to the reader.

In even her earliest comics, then, Schrag demonstrates an ability to work with the conventions of the form beyond utilitarian and straightforward storytelling techniques, and also reveals an awareness of a prospective audience. As Isaac Cates has pointed out, "an ordinary prose diary is imagined to be a private undertaking, written for the sake of the diarist alone" (216),

FIG. 3.1. Ariel addresses the reader, from *Awkward and Definition*.

and while the sometimes confessional nature of *Awkward* is often diaristic in its privately quotidian summation of mostly banal events, the implication of a reader reveals that Schrag conceives of herself as a public artist from the very beginning of her extended project. In addition to gesturing toward notions of agency and mediated representations of marginalized teenage subjectivity, this early flirtation with the expectation of an audience also introduces Schrag's deliberate blurring of the line that separates life from art—a feature of her comics that becomes increasingly prominent as the series progresses. As Anira Rowanchild has noted, "Knowing that you are going to write about an event or an idea encourages you to frame, construct and interpret it, in the same way that carrying a camera on holiday shapes your visual experience" (203), and while Schrag's lived experience is as of yet seemingly uninfluenced by its future as a comic (and since there is no previous drawn and circulated comic to play a part in her life at this point, a circumstance that would change with future installments), the authorial asides and Schrag's awareness of her role as autobiographical storyteller anticipate her later predilection for staging key events at least partly for the benefit of her comics narrative and its readers. These few instances of emerging formal complexity aside, the narrative voice of *Awkward* is dependably straightforward and consistent with the exploits of its drawn central character, describing events as they happen and in a voice that is remarkably contemporary with the action and largely free from retrospection despite being in the past tense.

The visuals contribute to this unity of voice through their simplicity, serving mostly to drive the narrative forward or show what is simultaneously being told. Stylistically, Schrag's drawings are minimalist, cartoony, and unpolished, lending the book a youthful exuberance that is central to its appeal as a firsthand account of teenage experience. Compared to the studied roughness of Julie Doucet's comics, however, Schrag's drawings are unmistakably the work of a young but talented artist who is not yet in full control of her creative powers and is still working toward a personal style. As such, characters are often interchangeably drawn and rarely amount to more than sketches, and faces are rendered with a cartoony sense of expressionist exaggeration, with enlargements of eyes and mouths doing most of the emotional characterization. In the rare instances where background objects such as cars appear, they are drawn without apparent concern for verisimilitude, and while Schrag's page layouts are for the most part fairly standard, they often play with formal restrictions by letting characters or speech balloons burst through panel borders in key sequences. While exhibiting a few inspired flourishes, the visuals mostly function as an uncomplicated vehicle for the narrative, securing forward momentum and an overall sense of Ariel's freshman year being relatively untroubled.

That impression is tempered somewhat early in the book, however, when Ariel learns that a boy she is crushing on (and who often wears an L7 shirt, hence the nickname "my L7") has been the victim of a vicious beating where "some guys jumped him in the locker room and called him a long-haired faggot" (*Awkward and Definition* 3). Introduced visually by drawing Ariel with "L" and "7" instead of pupils, this event, which occurs on page 3, helps to balance the upbeat and carefree tone of the narrative somewhat by providing an early reminder of the urgent realities and intense feelings that are also part of regular teenage life, especially for those with unconventional styles or sexualities. As such, the event's inclusion functions as a powerful but—since the authorial perspective is limited by the narrative having been created the following summer—unintended foreshadowing of some of the more mature and introspective themes to be explored in the subsequent volumes, especially as regards Ariel's slow realization that she is a lesbian.

This slight but gradual introduction of a more serious tone is illustrated by a comparison of the cover images for *Awkward* and *Definition* (see fig. 3.2). Where *Awkward*'s cover simply shows Ariel in full figure on a light background, looking slightly dazed—or, perhaps, given the centrality of

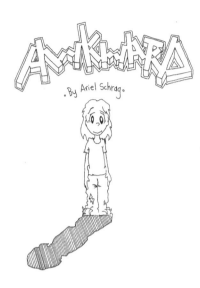

FIG. 3.2. The strikingly different cover images for *Awkward* and *Definition*.

marijuana to her ninth-grade experience, high—the cover of *Definition* depicts Ariel from the waist up, on a black background and with her arms and teeth anxiously clenched. The solid black background is accentuated by a white square behind Ariel, which is both a relatively sophisticated design element adding balance to the composition and a visual metaphor illustrating that the light and carefree days of ninth grade are behind her. In this vein, Schrag's narration introduces the book as follows: "Well, well, well it's been quite a year—awkward as usual, but as it turns out a whole lot more comes with being a sophomore. expectations, excitations, lacerations, aspirations, adorations, complications and everything and all of those—" (*Awkward and Definition* 1).[9] Introduced in this way by a retrospective comment foreshadowing the events to come, *Definition* was written and inked in the summer of 1996 and chronicles Schrag's 1995–1996 sophomore year. Slightly darker in tone and roughly twice as long as *Awkward*, this second installment continues the development of Schrag's increasingly self-aware and formally accomplished narrative.

The first panel of *Definition* is drawn from Ariel's point of view, as her friend Alicia points a finger in her direction and proclaims loudly: "You're a dyke!" (*Awkward and Definition* 1). Where discussions of sexuality in *Awkward* were limited to innocent and mostly unreciprocated crushes on boys, supplemented with friendship crushes on a number of girls, *Definition* foregrounds these issues from the very first page. According to Ariel, Alicia is "the definition of proud dyke" (*Awkward and Definition* 2), but her exuberant invitation of "Welcome to queer nation!" (*Awkward and Definition* 1) is met with only denial and affirmations of straightness by Ariel. While Alicia allows for the possibility that Ariel might in fact fall between 2 and 4 on the Kinsey scale (with herself being an unequivocal 6), Ariel's response is simply that this aspect of her sexuality is "not something I felt like dealing with" (*Awkward and Definition* 2). After admitting that she sometimes thinks about girls, however, Ariel is next seen drooling, cartoon-style, over a thought-bubble containing the sexy goth girl Rosary, who was briefly and insignificantly introduced in *Awkward* as simply a friend's older sister (see fig. 3.3). As the first visual object of desire in the comic, Rosary achieves a special prominence in the imagination of both Ariel and the reader, and her image functions to further provoke Ariel's increasing self-awareness. Admitting to herself that her interest in girls might in fact be sexual—she does, she admits, after all caress her Juliette Lewis poster every night before going to sleep—this dawning realization is represented as a giant (and humorously labeled) "boulder of truth" (*Awkward and Definition* 2) that hangs over Ariel and makes the weight of her backpack seem trivial in comparison.

Regrouping immediately to remind the reader that this situation "still doesn't deny my love for *boys*" and that "it's not over Michael till you're on the ground and *fucked*," Ariel's multivalent desire leaves her only with the option of pronouncing herself "bi" or, as she says, "one of the gang" of fashionable girls portrayed as remarkably eager to declare themselves bisexual (*Awkward and Definition* 2–3; emphasis in the original). While this seems like a convenient and, for her middle-class Berkeley environment, at least (the seemingly atypical attack on "my L7" in *Awkward* notwithstanding), socially acceptable position for Ariel to inhabit, she admits that she "was not too enthralled to take on the title" (*Awkward and Definition* 3). Declaring instead that "as far as I was concerned and the rest of the world would be concerned—*I'm straight*" (*Awkward and Definition* 3; emphasis in the original), Ariel's determination both goes directly against the evidence of her drooling response to the alluring Rosary on the previous page and is wittily undercut by a series of text boxes with sarcastically overeager affirmations exclaiming "Definition #1 straight = me" and "That's what I said!" (*Awkward and Definition* 3). In this short three-page opening

FIG. 3.3. Ariel fantasizes about Rosary, from *Awkward and Definition*.

sequence, Schrag introduces what will (unbeknownst to her at this point, of course) become a major recurrent theme of the rest of the series—namely, her gradual coming to terms with her own homosexual desire. In addition to its more reflective and introspective thematic content, however, the three pages also exhibit a variation in visual point of view, narrative perspective, expressionism, and an overall use of the comics form that is significantly more sophisticated than the rudimentarily constructed *Awkward*. Switching fluidly between various framings and experimenting with point-of-view drawings, illustrated metaphors, and spatiotemporal changes to other scenes or characters, all in the service of a narrative about her emerging sexuality, the opening of *Definition* represents both a significant step forward in Schrag's self-directed apprenticeship as a comics artist and a further queering of her style.

At a total of eighty-six pages, *Definition* also has a slightly more developed narrative than *Awkward*, with much of it devoted to Ariel's continued sexual experimentation. After a make-out session with a doting boy is disrupted because she fantasizes about Rosary, Ariel finally manages to kiss her object of desire. The kiss itself is drawn in an enlarged and focalizing circle that encroaches on the page's other panels as if to depict the subjective experience of time expanding during this euphoric moment. Moreover, the scene is subtitled "Definition perfection" (*Awkward and Definition* 13) and is drawn with considerably more detail and realism than the surrounding panels, signifying a moment of both heightened sensory input and lasting emotional importance to Ariel. As the rambling narrative voice explains in the subsequent panel, "It was as if suddenly everything about kissing made sense and all those other awful bland boring kisses I'd had vanished away with unimportance and insignificance all the doubts and wonders about kissing thrust aside with a laugh because now I knew" (*Awkward and Definition* 13). Along with this self-conscious use of language—unusual for the generally plainspoken narrative voice—the specific properties of the comics form are in this manner employed to visually depict the centrality of this kiss to Ariel's trajectory of sexual self-discovery. Although Rosary subsequently fails to return Ariel's interest, the kiss sets her on the course of further experimentation, leading first to more kissing and then to a comically clueless attempt at a lesbian threesome with two friends that includes such key dialogue as "So . . . what do we do?" and "Don't lezzie's [*sic*] finger each other?" (*Awkward and Definition* 16). Although her sexual development remains a thematic undercurrent throughout, the relative failure of this event seems to temporarily slow down the pace of Ariel's experimentation and allow other events to gradually take precedence in the narrative.

Accordingly, large sections of *Definition* depict such events as attending No Doubt shows and worshipping lead singer Gwen Stefani, but the narrative also includes Ariel's first visit to a comics convention in order to sell her self-published edition of *Awkward*. While the distribution and reception of

Awkward among her classmates is virtually absent from *Definition*'s narrative, Schrag's participation in San Jose's Alternative Press Expo features prominently and indicates her increasing professionalization and a growing awareness of an audience. Initially intimidated by the remarkably cool names of the other exhibitors listed in the program—such as Tina Piazza with Rock Snot Comics—Ariel nevertheless attracts the attention of "a large man in a business suit" (*Awkward and Definition* 61) who is rumored to have worked for hip publisher Image Comics and who expresses interest in adapting *Awkward* for an animated television show or feature film. Although nothing concrete happens as a result of this encounter, the event is important to an understanding of Schrag's extended project as at least partly a self-reflective narrative of artistic growth and professionalization, and is the first example of a previous year's comic having a direct influence on this year's life. Although Schrag draws herself as both tiny and overwhelmed by the fast-talking business-suited man, the scene establishes her as a teenage artist talented enough to be considered commercially viable and whose high school experiences are deserving of a readership beyond her immediate circle of friends and classmates. Additionally, the circular self-reflexivity of having one comic appear in another provides *Definition* with a complex autobiographical perspective as her life gradually intertwines with her developing art.

Both the visuals and narrative structure of *Definition* are, of course, intrinsic to this development. Where *Awkward*'s drawings are sketchy and airy and rarely deviate from a standard page layout of largely square panels in orderly rows, the second installment of Schrag's series is significantly more formally adventurous. Most notable, perhaps, is her increased use of heavy blacks and crosshatching for contrast, which combine to lend the visuals a more substantial and varied appearance. Schrag also experiments with drawings that are meant to indicate her subjective state, such as when Ariel gets drunk with friends or achieves the test results necessary to get into a particularly interesting chemistry class. Along with several other scenes, the latter of these events is presented as a flashback, for no other apparent reason than that Schrag seems to have been making up the narrative at least partly on the fly. But the technique also indicates a growing sophistication in her storytelling that serves to gradually untether her experiences temporally and spatially from episodic but strict causality. With the narrative freed from a diaristic and straightforwardly linear presentation of events, Schrag's comics chronicle edges closer to the domain of fully realized autobiography presented by an author in full control of her own story line. As Schrag gradually increases the narrative and visual complexity of her work, the comics form allows her to become the writer of her own experience in both text and image and provides her with an endlessly flexible tool for portraying a teenage self that is perpetually developing and sexually ambivalent. While Schrag varies her visual appearance somewhat from overtly feminine to slightly masculine depending on the context or the object of her desire in a given scene, these early experiments find fuller expression in *Potential*, the next installment in her extended narrative of incremental self-discovery.

Where the cover image of *Definition* hints directly at the sexual anxiety central to Schrag's sophomore year, the cover of *Potential* is a slightly more intricate rumination on similar themes—and one that is only fully decipherable in the context of the comic's narrative.[10] The main image, framed by a blue background, depicts Ariel partially hidden behind what appears to be trees in a dark forest, with an anxious look on her face and her eyes wide open (see fig. 3.4). Upon closer inspection, it is clear that the cover is modeled with perfectionist detail on Ariel's junior year biology textbook, a subject she has become particularly interested in because of its promising insights into the natural basis for homosexuality.[11] Functioning as an ambiguous visual metaphor for being lost in—or coming out of—the woods of her own biological homosexuality, the image encapsulates the book's major theme of Ariel continuing to explore and obsess about her sexual identity. Moreover, the subdued color scheme and intense darkness that surrounds Ariel sets the tone for a narrative that begins with first love and ends with heartbreak and emotional isolation.

Junior year begins on a note of optimism, however, as Ariel eats a chicken leg and proclaims that "Times have been fun, I know it, but from here on out we're talkin': A's to plow for, virginities to lose, proms to attend; we're talkin'—Potential so thick you can sink your teeth into it" (*Potential* 1). This sense of the increasing thematic weight of her material is mirrored in the book's ambitious visuals and its physical scope, which extends to 224 highly detailed pages that took two years to ink. Beginning much like *Definition*, the opening sequence of *Potential* finds Ariel with a boyfriend—"and a damn good one at that" (*Potential* 3)—but unable to suppress her desire for girls, to the point where she continually fantasizes about them appearing naked in the school hallway, bumping their breasts into her and suggestively telling her "I only like girls" (*Potential* 3). Literally casting aside a thought

FIG. 3.4. Cover of *Potential*, modeled on Ariel's biology textbook.

balloon containing her growing doubts and proclaiming that "This year was just not the time for frivolous sexual orientationing to take place" (*Potential* 3), Ariel instead decides to devote her time and energy to schoolwork. That same night, however, Ariel first realizes that she is constantly rejecting the advances of her boyfriend, and then dreams about kissing Stacy—Berkeley High School's "big dyke on campus" (*Potential* 5)—in a sequence that is

FIG. 3.5. Ariel dreams about kissing Stacy, from *Potential*.

drawn with a vivid realism that suggests its significance to Ariel (see fig. 3.5). The following day, after hugging an out lesbian girl and proclaiming it "one of the nicest things I've ever felt," Ariel finally acknowledges that "it's not like being bi was some prize to hold onto" and, with a visual joke that sees her stepping outside the panel border and determinedly flinging the bouquet of bisexuality to a group of eager girls, raises her fist to announce "Dykedom here I come!" (*Potential* 9) (see fig. 3.6). The final panel is contained by a significantly thicker border and placed by itself at the middle bottom of the page, signifying both the centrality of the act and the solidification of her sexual identity as a lesbian.

A remarkably untraumatic coming-out scene, the sequence also humorously indicates Schrag's realization that her newly acquired sexual identity is not visually self-evident. As Richard Dyer explains, "A major fact about being gay is that it doesn't show. There is nothing about gay people's physiognomy that declares them gay, no equivalents to the biological markers of sex and race. There are signs of gayness, a repertoire of gestures, expressions, stances, clothing, and even environments that bespeak gayness, but these

FIG. 3.6. Ariel embraces dykedom, from *Potential*.

are cultural forms designed to show what the person's person alone does not show: that he or she is gay" (19). In comics, the inclusion of gay characters has historically been subject to this same representational dilemma, which makes it difficult to visually indicate a character's homosexuality without resorting to exaggerated and often stereotyped signifiers. Compared to real life, further, comics work with a reduced number of modalities, a circumstance that significantly limits even the possibility for the representation of many of the most common (and offensive) stereotypes. Although gay and lesbian characters have appeared regularly in comics since the introduction of Papa Pyzon and Sanjak in Milton Caniff's long-running newspaper strip *Terry and the Pirates* in the 1930s, they also went mostly unnoticed by readers unaccustomed to decoding subtle signs of gayness. Indeed, the relative invisibility of queer sexualities when depicted in the comics form played a central role in both Fredric Wertham's *The Seduction of the Innocent* and the 1954 Comics Code largely inspired by its (highly contested) findings.[12] In the book, Wertham famously describes the relationship between Batman and Robin as "a wish dream of two homosexuals living together" (190), the implication being that although there was perhaps nothing in the comic books to overtly portray the characters as gay, a particularly disposed reader might interpret the situation as propaganda or—even worse, Wertham makes clear—identify with the pair. Although the Comics Code that in large part resulted from Wertham's book and the congressional hearings inspired by it does not explicitly forbid depictions of homosexuality, it includes a clause banning "sex perversion" (qtd. in Nyberg 168). As Hillary Chute points out, such language functioned as "a clear reference to homosexuality" (*Why Comics?* 350), even in the absence of explicitly gay characters or themes. Instead of such direct representation, Chute notes, "Comics used to be read paranoically as gay code" (*Why Comics?* 350), and the form's readers accordingly have a long history of reading between the lines for both censorious and affirmative purposes.

In more recent comics, the fact that gayness does not signify visually by itself has meant that long-established characters can suddenly acquire queer sexualities. The most notable example of this is perhaps the Marvel superhero Northstar, who was reconfigured as gay several years after first being introduced in 1979. Similarly, Edward H. Sewell Jr. notes about a regular *Doonesbury* character's sudden coming out that "there is nothing to visually distinguish Andy from any other character in the strip" (254). Indeed, Sewell argues, "queer characters in mainstream comic strips are well integrated into heterosexual society in that they look and act 'straight' before coming out as queer, and they look and act in a manner appropriate to the dominant heterosexual culture after coming out" (253). Gay characters in at least mainstream comics therefore often, as Sewell succinctly puts it, "come out and fade back in" (253), but even in such explicitly queer-themed work as Howard Cruse's *Wendel* strip for the *Advocate* or Bechdel's *Dykes to Watch Out For*, the queerness of characters is visually communicated by Dyer's "signs of gayness"—including, for example, certain hairstyles, clothes, or mannerisms—instead of through illustration of physical features as bearers of essentializing identity markers. In life as in comics, then, gayness must be performed in order to be visible, a circumstance that Schrag addresses explicitly in *Potential*'s coming-out scene and, more symbolically, in the gradual queering of her visual style throughout the extended high school narrative.

Following Ariel's proclamation of a lesbian identity, Schrag finalizes her coming-out sequence by portraying Ariel as acquiring the necessary visual signifiers. Through the assistance of two pairs of anonymous hands that reach into the panel in order to cut Ariel's hair short and dye it black, Schrag wittily plays on the fact that in the straightforward visual semiotics of high school, a little hair dye goes a long way toward indicating and affirming sexual orientation. Even more striking than this confident proclamation of a minority sexuality, however, is the way Schrag conflates sexual and artistic development with stylistic experimentation. As a portrayal of the final step in Ariel's journey of sexual self-discovery, *Potential*'s introductory chapter self-consciously combines extreme stylistic variation with such narrative techniques as dream sequence, fantasy, and visual metaphor. If, as John Nguyet Erni has argued, queerness "recognizes itself as a mode of articulation that is inherently excessive" and is characterized by a certain "textual promiscuity" (572, 577)—what Eve Kosofsky Sedgwick refers to as "the open mesh of possibilities, gaps, overlaps, dissonances and resonances, lapses and excesses of meaning" (7)—then Schrag's articulation of sexual orientation can be understood as part of her experimental and stylistically excessive use of the comics form throughout the four books. In this view, Schrag's queerness is expressed as increasing artistic mastery and the experimental breaking of stylistic conventions regarding narrative containment and visual uniformity. As a clear turning point in the narrative, moreover, the sequence's self-conscious engagement with form also indicates the more reflective nature of the material to come. From this point onward, Schrag largely abandons the portrayal of external events without commentary that characterizes both *Awkward* and *Definition* and instead moves toward an increasingly introspective and subjective form of narrative that is closer to the self-reflection of autobiography than to the immediacy associated with diary. As form and content merge and artistic self-consciousness is born, it becomes clear that coming out as a lesbian represents a momentous change in Schrag's understanding of the relationship between life and art, and that it sets her on an experimental course of self-discovery through visual life writing that continues throughout *Potential* and finds full creative expression in *Likewise*.

After this personally and artistically significant beginning, the remainder of *Potential*'s narrative largely concerns Ariel's romantic relationship with Sally, who is introduced as the older sister of a friend. The trajectory of the relationship moves quickly from courtship through official relationship to eventual rejection and heartbreak. At issue at all times is the suspicion—of Ariel, the reader, and Sally herself—that Sally is predominantly

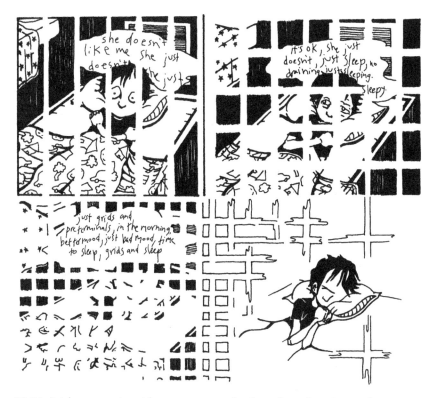

FIG. 3.7. Ariel uses a comics grid to compartmentalize her sadness, from *Potential*.

straight despite her involvement with Ariel. The particular dynamic of their relationship leads Ariel to become increasingly needy and emotionally demanding the more she is rejected, which in turn leads only to further rejection. After Ariel's sexual advances are continually declined, she begins to experience what she calls "this draining feeling" (*Potential* 127) whenever Sally turns away from her, and which Schrag represents visually as first the word "drain" written vertically on Ariel's chest and later by drawing her as shapelessly melting into the mattress in a moment of despair. In a key scene, the comics form itself becomes a way for Ariel to keep her emotions in check, as she imagines an orderly and increasingly narrow grid overlaid on her life, compartmentalizing her sadness into smaller and smaller units until she is calm enough to fall asleep (see fig. 3.7). Segueing from there into a realistically drawn nightmare dream sequence, the visual style of *Potential* is constantly attentive to the various registers of reality and states of emotion experienced by Ariel and becomes increasingly complex and subjective in accordance with her fraught mental state. As the narrative progresses, for example, drawings often become sketchier in key scenes, and characters—Sally, chief among them—gradually lose facial features such as mouths or noses, indicating Ariel's subjective memory and selective attention in moments dominated by intense feeling. In examples such as these, the unconventional use of the form itself becomes a key participant in the storytelling, providing a visual externalization of Ariel's interiority that blurs the line between life and art to the point where her repressed emotions find their fullest expression as drawings on the page.

Where *Awkward* and *Definition* were comparatively lighter in mood and theme—focusing as they did on the more innocent aspects of being a teenage girl—*Potential* represents a departure for Schrag, who by now depicts more emotionally difficult material such as her own growing insecurities and the intimate minutiae of rejection and heartbreak. Evidently driven by a desire to produce as "truthful" as possible an account of her experience, Schrag's third autobiographical comic lays bare her most private thoughts and actions, including a number of explicitly drawn sex acts, but is completely lacking in the exaggerated but playfully self-conscious depiction of personal disagreeableness in vogue with such contemporaries of hers (in publication history if not in age) as, for example, Joe Matt. Where Matt makes an entertaining spectacle of his own failings, however, Schrag's directness is both disarming and at times perhaps slightly disturbing, considering her age and the fact that her work is meant for public consumption. In his extensive study of the diary as a genre, Lejeune notes that "ever since we developed the vile habit of publishing diaries, many people put on a suit and tie to write about their private lives" (*On Diary* 175), and Schrag's work is therefore notable for its refusal to dress up a chaotic emotional life and messy sexual experiences for the reader. In this sense, Schrag's work is compulsively and even indiscriminately self-revealing, but where artists like Doucet and Gloeckner veil their autobiographical narratives with, respectively, a stylized layer of grotesque exaggeration and the implication that an accomplished adult consciousness is involved in the depiction of abusive childhood scenarios, Schrag's work can be somewhat jarring in its matter-of-fact depiction of events. Combined with the lack of adult authorial distance from the events described in the narrative and the externalization of subjectivity in the visuals, this unrestrained approach to life writing serves to produce the effect of immediacy as the reader experiences Ariel's life as it unfolds and without apparent self-censorship.

In this vein, Schrag's dedication to authenticity logically also extends to her friends and family, whose lives and experiences her serialized and extended self-portrait by necessity includes. Documenting the beginning and eventual disintegration of her romantic relationship over the course of the year, for example, involves a depiction of Sally that is sometimes unflattering in its account of her bad moods and insensitive rejection of Ariel's advances. In an early scene near the beginning of the relationship, Sally mentions that she has heard about Ariel's comics from a friend who appeared in one, and admits to having consequently asked herself whether "I really wanna be hanging around Ariel Schrag. I don't think I'd wanna be in the comic" (*Potential* 47). Because she ultimately becomes the narrative's most prominent character besides Ariel, Sally's initial reservations about having her intimate life put on display in a published comic indicates the risks Schrag is willing to take in the service of representing her subjective experience of life as truthfully as possible. Similarly, *Potential* documents the time of Ariel's parents' divorce, during which both parties are insensitive around the children and immature with each other—or, as Ariel simply says, "Both of my parents were completely insane" (*Potential* 143). In addition to the relationship with Sally, the divorce is a key event in Ariel's junior year, and its announcement during a family dinner is the occasion for a visually dense sequence. Here Schrag uses halftones, heavy blacks, and scraggly line work to claustrophobic effect in a portrayal of the anxiety surrounding the impending dissolution of the family. While Ariel's parents are never depicted as directly addressing Schrag's critical exposure of their personal failings during an emotional time, it is nevertheless striking that Schrag—at seventeen, no less—feels comfortable depicting such personal material in a book meant for publication.

While *Potential* perhaps surprisingly does not include scenes about Ariel's further professionalization—this was the year, after all, when she secured a publishing contract for *Definition*—her earlier work nonetheless also plays a prominent role in the narrative. As the most recent installment, *Definition* becomes an especially important metatext for both the current year's experiences and the comics project as a whole. In a key scene depicting Ariel and her friend Harriet chatting and getting high, Ariel pulls out a box of files she keeps for the comic, including several folders with the names of friends written on them and one enigmatically labeled "The Truth" (*Potential* 42) (see fig. 3.8). This prompts Harriet to exclaim: "Wow, this is giving me a really weird feeling like we're in the comic book, like everything I say

FIG. 3.8. Ariel and Harriet get high and read *Definition*, from *Potential*.

is a new panel!" (*Potential* 42). Ariel replies, "Yeah, I get that a lot," and as they proceed to read *Definition*, Harriet further notes that "it's like we're trapped in the comic book and we can't get out" (*Potential* 42). This marijuana-induced commentary about the intertwining of life and art is further developed by the visual appearance of the sequence's panels, which from the first depiction of Ariel's box of files are drawn to look like three-dimensional sheets of paper loosely arranged on the blank page. Presenting the panels as near tangible and implying that the archive represents the genesis of the comic—turning, as it does, in both this scene and in Ariel's "real life," everything it touches into panelized comics form—this sequence both illustrates Ariel's compulsion for telling the truth and significantly blurs the line between her life and art in order to suggest that the difference between the two is always subject to interrogation.

Near the end of the short sequence, Schrag includes an image that explicitly alludes to the complex relationship between her lived experience and its expression in comics form. Drawn from Ariel's point of view as she holds and looks at a page from *Definition* concerning her sixteenth birthday, the image also includes her realistically drawn and life-size thumb and part of her hand. In this complex and layered image, then, the reader is looking at a realistic drawing of Ariel's hand holding a cartoony image drawn by herself a year prior, all of which is presented in a panel advertising its own comics-ness through peeled-off corners. Reminiscent of a few celebrated images from Bechdel's *Fun Home* in which the adult narrator is shown to examine photographs from her father's past but, of course, predating them by almost a decade, Schrag's image functions as both a sudden encounter with a heightened sense of reality and a multilayered wormhole into the past.[13] Where Bechdel's drawings, according to Julia Watson, "call readers' attentions to our voyeuristic looking at her intimately personal acts of investigating her father's hidden history and her own identification with it" (33), Schrag's image, crucially, implicates the reader in her voyeuristic engagement with both *her own* actual life experience and its translation into comics form. Representing Ariel's contemplative encounter with the person and artist she simultaneously still is and has ceased to be, the image comments on both her artistic and personal maturation and suggests that her past life has become indistinguishable from its representation in the comics. Admitting elsewhere in the sequence that being trapped in the comic is "kind of scary" (*Potential* 42), Ariel thereby further anticipates the main theme of *Likewise*—namely, her increasing inability to separate her life from her art.

The culmination of Schrag's extended comics project, *Likewise* is both a significant step forward in terms of formal sophistication and an unapologetic dive into the rabbit hole of self-reflexive meta-autobiography. This shift is signaled by the book's cover, which does away with the series' convention

FIG. 3.9. Ariel at work drawing comics, on the cover of *Likewise*.

of featuring Ariel as a focalizing design element and instead shows her to the side and from the back, seated at her desk in her room and drawing (see fig. 3.9).[14] Moreover, where the previous covers were relatively undetailed and somewhat loosely drawn, the cover of *Likewise* is a hyperdetailed and ruler-precise depiction of her room and its contents—most of which represent the usual clutter of teenage life, including a guitar, Converse Chuck Taylor sneakers, a stolen "No Parking" sign, and a patched-up backpack. In addition to these objects, however, the drawing also shows several books scattered around the room, including Gustave Flaubert's *Madame Bovary*, Dean Hamer and Peter Copeland's *The Science of Desire*, James Joyce's *Ulysses*, Simon LeVay's *Queer Science* and *The Sexual Brain*, the aforementioned *Biology* textbook, and copies of Schrag's own *Awkward* and *Definition*. Because the cover depicts Ariel at work on inking *Potential*, of course, that book is not yet in existence. Along with the folder labeled "The Truth" and another one marked "Sally," these textual references serve as an introduction to Schrag's senior-year obsessions with the intersections of truth, desire, and queerness, all of which are themes in the formally ambitious and at times unwieldy final chapter of her high school narrative. Combined with the many allusions to other texts, the cover's decentering of Ariel also symbolizes Schrag's literal and figurative turn away from the reader and into the comics project itself, which comes to dominate both her senior year and its depiction in *Likewise*.

In both form and content, *Likewise* is a significantly denser and more challenging reading experience than Schrag's previous work, to the point of being a sometimes willfully difficult text. As such, the book has often posed a challenge to critics, who frequently seem unable to make sense of its constant shifts in tone, storytelling technique, and visual style and instead explain the inconsistencies away by speculating that perhaps Schrag grew tired of her final book midway through and simply finished sloppily and without a plan.[15] This is far from the case, however, and *Likewise* is an intricately constructed text that is all the more impressive for having been conceived by someone who just graduated from high school. At 359 numbered pages (in addition to a 20-page unpaginated sequence near the middle, after which the page numbering simply resumes where it left off) the book is also exactly the same length as all three previous installments combined. Moreover, the page length of each of *Likewise*'s three sections line up exactly—although in reverse order—with *Potential*'s 224 pages, *Definition*'s 86 pages, and *Awkward*'s 49 pages, indicating an intertextual relationship that goes beyond simply relying on previous and accumulative life experience in order to tell a new story.[16] Lacking an overarching and straightforward narrative arc such as the one provided to *Potential* by Ariel's relationship and eventual breakup with Sally, *Likewise* is more a collection of episodic scenes than a straightforward narrative. While events like

Sally's periodic visits home from college in Portland, Oregon, and Ariel's own college applications are important to the story, its main current is a sometimes impressionistic and always subjective depiction of Ariel's post-breakup mental state and its eventual expression in comics form.

The book opens with a one-page prologue set in the summer of 1998, between Schrag's junior and senior years, during which time she was drawing *Potential*.[17] Hanging out with Sally—who remains a friend at this point, despite the end to their romantic relationship—Ariel discusses her progress on the new book, which causes Sally to express relief that she will be away when it comes out. Realizing that Ariel will be busy inking the book over the course of her senior year, Sally then suggests to her that she "might as well call the next book 'writing potential'" (*Likewise* n.p.). The use of lowercase for the title is significant (in a mention of the book in just the previous panel, the title is both capitalized and underlined) and indicates a double meaning that hints at Ariel's growing obsession with writing and her development as an artist. In addition, the pun also highlights the fact that Schrag did in fact spend her senior year writing *Potential*, and was therefore in a sense living in a past dominated by the dissolution of her first real love affair. As such, part 1 of *Likewise*—running, as mentioned, the exact same page length as *Potential*—is predominantly concerned with Ariel's lingering feelings for Sally, as well as a continued fascination with the possible biological foundation for homosexuality.

With *Likewise* in this way mirroring *Potential* in both theme and structure, Schrag's highly referential framework continues in parts 2 and 3, which self-consciously engage with the legacies of *Definition* and *Awkward*. As such, part 2 finds Ariel reconnecting with some of the more innocent fun of *Definition* by going to rock shows and attending a comics convention, just as she had done in the earlier book. Similarly, the brief part 3 speeds things up toward the end with sixteen—again, just as in *Awkward*—episodic and very short chapters detailing such adventures as Ariel's visit to a strip club with a male friend and her long-awaited high school graduation. Presented as near simulacra of her own previous work, the three parts of *Likewise* thereby find Schrag seemingly trapped in a recursive feedback loop of re-engagement with the past and its recycling as a public comic book. Consequently, it is not until the book's last page that she can finally exclaim "It's over" and "I am now experiencing a private moment" (*Likewise* 359). As Ariel proceeds to pop a zit, the entire four-volume narrative comes to a carefully unceremonious end as she looks at herself in the mirror and thinks to herself that "This is the most important year of my life and this is what I do with my time" (*Likewise* 359). Having finally and metaphorically popped the zit of her life to release its contents for public inspection, Schrag's conclusion simultaneously refers backward to her extensive body of work and forward to a new and more private life.

As a final sentiment of release from the demands of the comics project, however, the end of the narrative must be understood in the context of *Likewise*'s intricate structure and constantly shape-shifting visual style, which are both deeply connected to Schrag's growing obsession with recording and depicting the many perspectives making up the truth of her experience. Commenting on what he perceives to be the increasingly common tendency for stylistic variation within single works by contemporary comics artists, Groensteen has argued that "there is an obvious parallel between these modulations of graphic style and the changes in tone, style, and writing technique practiced by James Joyce in the novel that is emblematic of modernity, *Ulysses*" (*Comics* 113). The *Ulysses* comparison is especially apt in the case of *Likewise* because of the prominence of that novel in the narrative and its influence upon the comic's conceptual organization. As Ariel continues to grieve over the dissolution of her relationship in part 1 of *Likewise*, obsessing over who Sally might be having sex with at college, and whether they are boys or girls, she remembers that Sally read *Ulysses* and that it "made her who she is" (*Likewise* 74). Impressed with Sally's precociousness in reading the famously difficult novel, Ariel wonders "Well—why can't I!" and decides "By Jove I'll read it! One day at a time and what will she have ahead of me then! Nothing!" (*Likewise* 75). The decision to read *Ulysses* therefore represents the beginning of Ariel coming to terms with the end of the relationship by helping her feel like Sally's intellectual equal. As Ariel continues to read the novel, however—renowned for its extensive use of stream-of-consciousness narration and a number of distinctive styles to represent different modes of experience—it also begins to act as something of an artistic talisman that ultimately influences the way Schrag approaches storytelling in both text and image. While Groensteen is referring mostly to artists whose experiments with an inconstant visual style reinforce the narrative thematically, Schrag's comic is a truly experimental construct that shifts between both storytelling techniques and a large number of drawing styles in order to represent the diverse registers of her life in different ways.

At the textual level, the influence of *Ulysses* upon *Likewise* is most obvious in Schrag's extensive use of stream-of-consciousness narration that is often unconnected with the images and their dialogue. In one of the book's most unconventional and challenging sequences, for example, Ariel takes the bus alone while her thoughts are represented as both narrative text boxes and inserted images, the latter of which appear like suddenly recollected visual memories inside the larger panels. As a representation of the life of her mind, this technique is both intimate and somewhat alienating in its excess of information, and at times makes for a narrative that can be diffi-cult to follow. Stream-of-consciousness narration is only one of several sto-rytelling techniques that Schrag employs in *Likewise*, though, and the book is also heavily reliant on dialogue, typed diary entries, and transcribed tape recordings. As a tapestry of different voices, *Likewise* thereby attempts to represent a comprehensive account of Ariel's experience of both her inte-rior and exterior worlds. The visuals are a crucial part of this strategy, and Schrag varies her drawing style according to the narrative technique and the category of experience being recounted in a given scene. As Italian visual artist and theorist Renato Calligaro argues, "just as a text can be, in turn, descriptive, allusive, moralistic, stream of consciousness, onomatopoeic, etc., so the image can become, successively, naturalistic, cubist, abstract, graphic or picturesque" (qtd. in Groensteen, *Comics* 114). Employing different draw-ing styles almost as if they were discrete textual categories used to represent various kinds of experience, *Likewise* shifts frequently and abruptly between visual idioms in ways that are never random but always adhere to the book's elaborate structure.

According to this scheme, Schrag represents the various modalities of her experience using seven different drawing styles (see fig. 3.10). Most com-monly, present-day scenes are always represented in a simple cartoony style embellished by crosshatching and narrated by stream of consciousness and dialogue. Whenever Sally enters the action, however, the panel borders dis-appear and the images flow together, as if to represent Ariel's heightened and emotionally fraught mental state. Flashbacks from the main action, moreover—even when, as in the already mentioned bus sequence, they occur *inside* the present-day panels—are presented in less substantial grayed-out halftones and without solid blacks, while the text relies on dialogue and Ari-el's written thoughts. Further, imaginary scenarios are represented by impressionistic stippling and usually contain little or no dialogue, as if to indicate brief flashes of Ariel's imagination. Finally, as the narrative pro-gresses and Schrag begins to rely increasingly on various types of ante-autobiographical material in order to construct her story, the three methods

FIG. 3.10. The different drawing styles used by Schrag to represent various modalities of experience in *Likewise*, from *Likewise*.

used for recording are each given their own distinct visual and textual expression. Ranked in vividness according to the technology used, sequences based on Ariel's audio recordings of events are drawn in high-contrast black and white and contain only transcribed dialogue, while scenes drawn from diary entries originally written on a computer use a subdued but slightly more realistic gray ink wash, as well as dialogue and typed-up narration. Most unusually, scenes based on Ariel's handwritten diary entries contain boxed narrative text on lined journal paper, while the visuals are sketchy and at times seem almost unfinished. This approach functions to formally represent Schrag's knowledge that her visual interpretation of a written diary entry is inherently subjective and at best a flawed and incomplete recollection of actual events. Although reminiscent of the famous "epistemological crisis" described by Bechdel in *Fun Home* (141)—because of which the young Alison begins adding a hesitant "I think" to otherwise declarative sentences in her diary—Schrag does not augment the interpretative uncertainty with the accumulation of additional signifiers but instead literalizes her apprehension to fully trust the complicated translation from experience to text to comic by removing visual information from the page. As the narrative at times threatens to dissolve into white space, Schrag's representational strategy is both an attempt to accurately reflect her subjective experience of events and a visual effect signifying the impossibility of doing so. Considered as a natural development from such earlier stylistic experiments as the use of a more realistic style for the dream sequences in *Potential*, Schrag's approach in *Likewise* is therefore far from what critics have often reduced to the unedited ramblings of a teenager.[18] On the contrary, Schrag is in full control of both narrative technique and her ever-changing visual style, to the point where form and content blend together and become difficult to tell apart. But because these shifts are frequent, unannounced, and sometimes very subtle, the result is a book that is a challenging experience on all levels—and not least, perhaps, for Ariel/Schrag herself, who becomes increasingly lost in her own narrative as the comic progresses.

While *Likewise* is a complex book from its very first panel, the dominant storytelling technique for approximately its first half is Ariel's stream-of-consciousness narration, accompanied by images representing either the present day, flashbacks, or imaginary scenarios. On page 221, however, a sudden and decisive shift occurs after Ariel has an especially upsetting conversation with Sally—who is home on a visit from college—about whether she has had sex with a boy she has been dating. As the conversation escalates to the point of heated argument, the present-tense narration and its accompanying images suddenly and without warning switch to a later moment depicting Ariel writing that very sequence on a computer (see fig. 3.11). The next few images show Ariel dutifully recording the details of the

FIG. 3.11. Ariel experiences a crisis of representation, from *Likewise*.

traumatic scene on-screen, until she suddenly changes the topic to describe a beginning crisis of faith in her project: "I'm starting to get really sick of writing this. not cause I'm tired, not cause I've been working on it too long, but cause I'm sick of it and it's going badly. I'm sick of writing it and only thinking about how it's gonna translate into comic form, it's just getting lamer and lamer and the scariest part is that I'm not even really worried about discrediting it cause the whole time I was thinking about how it would be comic translated anyway" (*Likewise* 221). As a consequence of her tendency to envision life as a comic *while* she is living it, Schrag at this point abruptly introduces a new layer concerning the comic's creation into her narrative. In so doing she draws attention to the separation between herself and the character on the page and thereby takes a decisive step in using her art to create emotional distance from the memory of the painful breakup with Sally. The final words of *Likewise*'s part 1 are similarly written on a screen, and read: "Damned to think about Sally for quite some time

FIG. 3.12. Ariel walks away from her computer and into blank space, from *Likewise*.

and time to come. But when you're sick of it you're sick, and I feel like stopping" (*Likewise* 224). At this point, Ariel gets up from her computer and walks away, in a panel that instead of having a right border bleeds into a missing final panel of blank space (see fig. 3.12).

Having metatextually stopped the narrative concerning her obsession with Sally—and discovered the power of storytelling to affect lived experience in the process—Schrag continues the story for twenty unnumbered pages, during which she experiences a crisis of authorship about how to continue recording her life after this decisive break. When part 2 begins, the different methods of recording gradually begin to dominate the storytelling, as Schrag experiments with letting written or tape-recorded material serve as the foundation for a more objective and personally distanced narrative. Part 3 completes the transformation of the story, which is by now solely told through handwritten diary entries, computer-typed first-person narrative, and tape-recorded conversations. This approach indicates both Schrag's obsession with depicting the truth as precisely as possible and her realization that she has been living her life through the comic until she was virtually unable to distinguish between the two. For that reason, it is telling that it is only on the book's last page that the first-person stream-of-consciousness narration from part 1 returns, at exactly the point where the comics project is over and she can again experience a private moment. As an intricately metatextual autobiographical construct, *Likewise* is in this analysis both a conclusion to Schrag's extended project of articulating her increasingly complex sense of self and an indication—through Ariel reclaiming her own voice, independent from the increasingly excessive demands of the narrative—of a new beginning beyond its all-encompassing confines.

In keeping with this end to the *High School Comic Chronicles*, Schrag has subsequently only produced comics work sporadically, and mostly in the form of short stories for various anthologies. Instead, she has worked as a writer for such television shows as *The L Word*, and in 2014 published the nonautobiographical novel *Adam*, which details the experiences of the eponymous heterosexual teenage character as he—to his own surprise—becomes involved with the transgender scene in New York City. It is perhaps curious that the extended and self-guided apprenticeship of making her comics series should result in Schrag all but abandoning the form in her adult career, but as each installment traces a step in her artistic maturation and follows her sexual trajectory from straight to bisexual to lesbian to heartbroken, it is clear that there was always an end in sight. The prolonged narrative thereby also exhibits the melancholia associated with the romantic move from innocence to experience, as the unencumbered and youthful perspective expressed in the early volumes gradually gives way to the self-conscious experimentation of *Likewise*. Importantly, the comics form enables the zine-based project from the beginning and also allows Schrag to simultaneously depict and construct the self-in-process in the dual registers of text and image. Finally, the merging of author and character made possible by both the particularities of the comics' publication history and the fact that their authorial point of view is always rooted in the present allow Schrag to make the discovery that in autobiographical comics life and art can be difficult to tell apart.

As the expansive coming-out story of a lesbian teenager, however, the comics' conflation of life and art takes on a further dimension. Kate Douglas and Anna Poletti have noted that "young women are some of history's most silent subjects" (150), a situation that is further compounded for queer youth, for whom, as Michelle Miller writes, "each of the tasks that make up adolescent development are complicated by ordinary and extraordinary experiences of homophobia" (46). Although Ariel encounters only the occasional moment of explicit homophobia in her relatively sheltered Berkeley environment, Schrag's position in the culture at large is inevitably marginalized because of her gender, age, and sexuality. Seizing upon the subcultural form of the handmade comics zine, however, allows Schrag to engage productively with her specific position and take part in what Douglas and Poletti call "the cultural work that youth-authored life writing can do in terms of asserting young people's voices and creative practices into a variety of public spaces" (226–227). For Schrag, that creative practice is not only a pathway to cultural visibility as a teenage girl but ultimately also the organizing principle through which she makes sense of herself as a lesbian. But where artists like Doucet use the comics form to experiment with the visual representation of women and delineate alternative forms of femininity, gayness does not show on what Dyer calls a "person's person" and must therefore be expressed through other means. As Adrienne Shaw notes in a comparison to visual representations of ethnoracial difference, "race is often, but certainly not always, written on the body and thus requires less discursive space in a media text than sexuality, which so often must be explained" (93). In Schrag's *High School Comic Chronicles*, that extended discursive space consists not only of a series of increasingly lengthy and self-involved autobiographical comics but also of constantly mutating and ever-proliferating narrative perspectives and visual styles. If, as Brian Loftus claims about queer autobiography, "the project of queer is to explode the seamless coherence of the 'I' [and] to reveal its gaps, multiplicities, contradictions, and dependencies" (33), then Schrag's collected autobiographical comics can be understood as inescapably queer in both form and content, and as an expression of the colossal amounts of self-reflection necessary to claim this identity while staying true to the project of documenting the in-progress teenage lesbian self.

4

Staring at Comics

● ● ● ● ● ● ● ● ● ● ● ● ●

Disability and the Body in Al Davison's *The Spiral Cage*

Bodies are everywhere in autobiographical comics. From Julie Doucet's female grotesques to Phoebe Gloeckner's disturbing illustrations of childhood sexual abuse to Ariel Schrag's ever-changing and in-progress queer self, the comics form insists on the visual representation of embodiment in ways that can be either marginalizing or empowering, depending on context and the specific deployment of its overlapping multimodal codes. Compared to the other marginalized identities examined so far in this study, however, disability is perhaps alone in its capacity to persistently arouse visual interest. To be figured as disabled is in key ways to be seen, and to always be the subject of others' visual curiosity. As Rosemarie Garland-Thomson argues, in the culture's "economy of visual difference, those bodies deemed inferior become spectacles of otherness while the unmarked are sheltered in the neutral space of normalcy" (*Extraordinary Bodies* 8). In autobiographical comics about the author's experiences with physical disability, the particular relationship with visual embodiment is therefore inescapable and is often placed front and center for the reader to engage with.

This chapter examines the implications for visual representations of disability in comics autobiography, using as its case study Al Davison's *The Spiral Cage*. A memoir about growing up and living with the developmental congenital disorder spina bifida (a condition that commonly leads to pronounced leg weakness), the book is itself an extended exploration of the particular and attention-grabbing visuality of the disabled body. Noting Davison's constant emphasis on depicting his eyes, as well as his body, I reconfigure Garland-Thomson's concept of the "stare" for the purposes of comics in order to argue that the form allows for the staging of a dynamic exchange of stares with the implied observer that has the potential to help the author elude the objectifying gaze commonly associated with looking at disability.

As both an area of academic inquiry and a field of political struggle, disability has lagged behind other categories of identity, such as race and gender, prompting Tobin Siebers to call it "the final frontier of justifiable human inferiority" (*Disability Aesthetics* 28). Where race and gender have successfully been theorized as cultural constructs naturalizing difference as biological inferiority or deficiency, disability has proven significantly more resistant to cultural resignification and has only recently been subjected to the same ideological critiques.[1] One reason for disability's persistence as an exclusionary category, Siebers explains, is that "it has been extraordinarily difficult to separate disability from the naturalist fallacy that conceives of it as a biological defect more or less resistant to social or cultural intervention" (*Disability Aesthetics* 27). Historically relegated "to hospital hallways, physical therapy tables, and remedial classrooms" (Davis, "Introduction" xv) and conceived of as "a defect or deficit in the individual body that medicine attempts to fix or compensate for" (Couser, "Signifying" 112), disability has traditionally been seen as a medical, and not a social, issue, and one that implies a need for treatment or cure. Doing away with traditional symbolic conceptions of disability as a bodily sign of flawed character or moral failing—a sort of retribution or divine punishment—post-Enlightenment thinking rationalized the problems of disabled people as a biological deficit, and the medical model of disability thereby expresses itself, Garland-Thomson notes, as the intertwining of "the ideology of cure and the mandate for normalcy" ("Disability" 525).[2] As such, the medical model is also related to emerging nineteenth-century ideas of the statistical normal, the result of which was the gradual construction of human difference as pathology, and to the creation of what Robert McRuer (with reference to Adrienne Rich) has called "compulsory able-bodiedness" (89) as the ideology underlying the assumed need and desire for cure.[3] For these reasons, Garland-Thomson argues that the medical model of disability is "a kind of new eugenics that aims to regularize our bodies" ("Disability" 524) through the policing of boundaries and elimination of difference.[4]

Similar to how a historically informed consideration of race reveals it to be a cultural category based on largely visual signifiers, as I explore at length in chapter 5, understanding disability and disablement as a gradually evolving social process rooted in specific discourses of normalization, compensation, and containment allows for a shift that views the disabled figure not as a problem to be solved but instead as an ideological construct. This constructivist view of disability has in the last few decades made a firm critical distinction "between the impaired body and its cultural site" (Couser, *Recovering* 180) in order to move away from the medical model and instead favor a social model that locates disability in society instead of in the individual. One particularly useful intervention is the theorization of the term *impairment* as separate from disability. In this schematic, as Lennard J. Davis explains, "impairment is the physical fact of lacking an arm or a leg. Disability is the social process that turns an impairment into a negative by creating barriers to access" ("End" 232). The social model consequently does not understand disability as a natural state of bodily inferiority, but instead as the result of certain disabling discourses and environments. Following this logic, a person in a wheelchair is not disabled if the lived environment is free of stairs and relies instead on ramps and elevators, and a deaf person is only disabled by a lack of sign language interpreters or the absence of closed captioning.

Although enormously influential and self-evidently useful from the point of view of disability activism, the social model has in recent years been questioned by critics such as G. Thomas Couser, who notes that "unlike other minority conditions manifest in the body, like race and gender, impairment involves disadvantages that are intrinsic, rather than extrinsic, and thus not amenable to discursive or institutional reform" ("Body Language" 5). Similarly, Siebers points out that "some factors affecting disability, such as chronic pain, secondary health effects, and aging, derive from the body" ("Disability and the Theory" 290) and therefore often require medical attention. In response to this theoretical difficulty, Siebers has proposed a "theory of complex embodiment" that "views the economy between social representations and the body not as unidirectional as in the social model, or nonexistent as in the medical model, but as reciprocal" ("Disability and the Theory" 290). As Siebers further argues, "complex embodiment theorizes the body and its representations as mutually transformative. Social representations obviously affect the experience of the body ... but the body possesses the ability to determine its social representation as well" ("Disability and the Theory" 290). As a story told both by and about bodies, then, complex embodiment reimagines disability and its representation as variable and individualized instead of resorting to the totalizing narratives of either the medical or the social model.

Despite these theoretical interventions, representations of disability in literary and visual culture have often relied on the pathologizing and othering perspective of the medical model. As Brenda Jo Brueggemann, Rosemarie Garland-Thomson, and Sharon L. Snyder argue, "disability tends to be figured in cultural representations as an absolute state of otherness that is opposed to a standard, normative body, unmarked by either individual form and function or by the particularities of its history" (2). Literary history, as Garland-Thomson has shown at length, using examples from a wide sample of texts and traditions, is no exception: "From folktales and classical myths to modern and postmodern 'grotesques,' the disabled body is almost always a freakish spectacle presented by the mediating narrative voice. Most disabled characters are enveloped by the otherness that their disability signals in the text" (*Extraordinary Bodies* 10). Employed to denote moral flaws or madness, or as an explanation for a villain's embittered determination to wage war on society, literary representations of disability often adhere to what David Hevey has called "the tragedy principle," which "uses the impairment as a metaphor and a symbol for a socially unacceptable person" and dictates that "fate must be made visible *on the body*" ("Tragedy Principle" 118, 117; emphasis in the original). In its insistence that disability is individual and tragic, literary history has provided few nuanced perspectives on what it might mean to be disabled in and by society. In fact, as Garland-Thomson argues, "Because we often imagine disability solely as tragedy, pathos, inadequacy, abnormality, and unattractiveness, our collective stories not only restrict the lives and govern the bodies of people we think of as disabled but limit the imaginations of those who think of themselves as nondisabled" ("New Disability Studies" 51). In this configuration, stories have the power to help us imagine the lives of others and can create alternative models for human interaction. In the case of autobiographical life writing by disabled people, therefore, they can also provide their tellers with an opportunity to counter objectification by the tragedy principle and assert subjectivity or agency in a marginalizing and ableist society.

Even though life writing has the potential to tell stories about disability that are radically different from those found in nondisabled mainstream culture, the relationship between disability and autobiographical self-representation is somewhat uneasy. On the one hand, as Couser notes, "bodily dysfunction tends to heighten consciousness of self and contingency" (*Recovering* 5), both of which are central preconditions to the project of life writing. In addition to a possible increased sense of introspection, moreover, disability implies narrative. As Couser observes elsewhere, "Whereas the unmarked case—the 'normal' body—can pass without narration, the marked case—the scar, the limp, the missing limb, or the obvious prosthesis—calls for a story" ("Disability" 400). Because most disabilities come with a story, bodily variation typically both inspires and elicits narration, either as a type of origin story or as the answer to the common question of what it is like to be disabled.[5] On the other hand, and despite this apparent relationship and its seeming potential for self-expression, life writing by disabled people has experienced severe limitations due to the genre's historical privileging of narratives of individualism and autonomy. As Couser succinctly states, "the problem of disability autobiography lies in the fact that what Western autobiography has valued (that which distinguishes the individual from others) the medical model of disability has devalued (some deviation from normality in the individual's body)" ("Signifying" 117). In other words, while the literary genre of autobiography has traditionally celebrated deviation from the norm in the form of narratives about exceptional individuals, the medical model has pathologized most examples of somatic variation and thereby discouraged disabled people from writing their life stories, exceptional as they might be.[6] The rise of both the social model and more recent theories attuned to complex embodiment offer a way out of this dilemma, however, by recasting disability at least partially as a discursively constructed political minority identity instead of a pathologized other, and in terms that are affirmative rather than exclusionary and othering. Viewed this way, disability life writing can become a way to tap into that discursive potential and occupy an oppositional speaking position that represents individual and untraditional embodiedness on its own nonmarginalizing terms.

While these critical developments allow for the creation of an alternative to the quantifying and dehumanizing narrative of medical authority, the act of storytelling itself can be similarly generative. If, as Couser suggests, "to have certain conditions is to have one's life written *for* one" ("Disability" 400; emphasis in the original), taking charge of the story can be an act of asserting control over not only the representation of one's circumstances but also the circumstances themselves. Arthur W. Frank, along similar lines, argues that for autobiographers suffering from illness, "telling stories of illness is the attempt, instigated by the body's disease, to give a voice to an experience that medicine cannot describe" and that "the ill person who turns illness into story transforms fate into experience" (18, xi). Like other minority life writing, accordingly, literary self-representation by disabled people is not only a way to challenge and deconstruct stigma but also a crucial venue for exploring and insisting on subjectivity through a self-determined and transformative process that provides unprecedented control of one's own image. In the genre of traditional literary autobiography, however, this image is both tightly controlled and drastically abstracted. Representing one's life verbally therefore allows for an obscuring mediation between author and reader that can be beneficial to inserting the literary self into mainstream nondisabled culture. As Couser suggests, this effect might not be available in visual media: "Because print, unlike photography, effectively masks the body, autobiography serves to deflect the gaze from a body that might otherwise trigger stereotypical responses. It thus removes one impediment to interaction in everyday life—which may remain an obstacle in film, video, and photography. As a verbal rather than visual form, writing may offer a kind of neutral space for self-presentation and the renegotiation of status" (*Recovering* 182). While purely verbal representations of lives that are to a large degree defined by their visual embodiedness can thus help mask the impairment behind the disembodied narrative voice, what is missing from Couser's list of visual media that might impede empathetic responses to disability self-representation is, of course, life writing in the nonmechanical and subjectively representative comics form.

Before examining the implications for self-representation in comics vis-à-vis other visual media, however, it is important to acknowledge the particular status of the visual in many, if certainly not all, conceptualizations of disability.[7] To that effect, Davis has influentially called disability a "specular moment" (*Enforcing* 12), Dale Jacobs and Jay Dolmage refer to it as "a visually overdetermined concept" (76), and Garland-Thomson argues both that "the visual—whether it is looking toward or away—is the major mode that defines disability in modernity" ("Seeing" 340) and that "the history of disabled people in the Western world is in part the history of being on display, of being visually conspicuous while politically and socially erased" ("Politics" 56). Quite literally seen as visibly different curiosities that arouse intense visual interest, disabled people have long been exhibited in such contexts as entertainment (in the form of freak shows), scientific inquiry (such as medical theaters), or a mix of the two (exemplified most famously, perhaps, by Philadelphia's Mütter Museum). Common to these various settings is what Hevey has called the "enfreakment" ("Enfreakment" 367) of disability, either through live display or as captured photographically, as well as the pervasiveness of the belief that disability is worth looking at. But while disability has certainly been highly exploited in its cultural mediation, the heterogeneity of the category and the permeable fluidity of its borders means that it has largely been without the explicit motivations of power and domination that underlie the construction of such categories as race and gender. Instead, the disabled body has been imagined and represented as pure visual spectacle in, as Garland-Thomson explains, "a complex relation between seer and seen, between the opposing subject positions of the intensely embodied, reified, and silenced object and the abstract, unmarked, disembodied normate" (*Extraordinary Bodies* 136). The power inherent in the process of seeing is thus fundamental to the cultural and psychological work of disability since, Garland-Thomson explains, "who we are can shift into focus by staring at who we think we are not" (*Staring* 6). Familiar in some ways because of the concept of the gaze most famously theorized in film studies by Laura Mulvey, what Garland-Thomson has explored at length as "staring" is therefore central both to how we look at disability in general and to our engagement with visual representations thereof.

Differences exist, however, between traditional theories of the gaze and Garland-Thomson's proposition of the stare as a primary mode of looking at disability. As she explains, "The stare is distinct from the gaze, which has been extensively defined as an oppressive act of disciplinary looking that subordinates its victim" (*Staring* 9). Related, of course, to Jacques Lacan's formative conceptualization of the gaze as the projection of a symbolic order, Michel Foucault's examination of the objectifying gaze of medical discourse, and to Franz Fanon's recollection that "the glances of the [colonial] other fixed me there" (82), the gaze can even be said to be constitutive of the social process that creates disability, since, as Davis explains, "a person with an impairment is turned into a disabled person by the Medusa-like gaze of the observer" (*Enforcing* 12). Thus theorized in several different contexts as a regulating one-way process that precludes interaction between the looker and the looked at, the gaze is both a fundamental and formidably powerful component of how we relate to each other visually.

In sharp contrast to these hegemonic models of looking, Garland-Thomson proposes that staring instead "sets in motion an interpersonal relationship" leading to a "dynamic struggle" that "makes things happen between people" (*Staring* 3, 33). In its most basic sense nothing more than "an ocular response to what we don't expect to see," staring "begins as an impulse that curiosity can carry forward into engagement" and continues as "starers inquire, starees lock eyes or flee, and starers advance or retreat; one moves forward and the other moves back" (*Staring* 3–4). Finally, as a "psychologically fraught and socially charged encounter" that is "triggered by the sight of someone who seems unlike us," staring can therefore be "an exploratory expedition into ourselves and outward into new worlds" that differs from the objectifying or colonizing gaze because "its capacity to create meaning is unstable and open-ended" (*Staring* 10, 6, 39). According to Garland-Thomson's model, staring in this way reconfigures the power dynamics of the gaze, opens up the relationship between starer and staree, and has the potential to transform the latter from passive object to active subject.

Notably, the key feature of the stare—what turns a gaze into a stare, so to speak—is the return of the stare by the staree, which sets its social component in motion and allows for possible resignification. While the role of the staree is crucial to the staring encounter, simply locking eyes and passively returning the stare is nevertheless insufficient to resist its objectifying power. In order to achieve the desired effect, Garland-Thomson explains, the returned stare must be elaborately staged: "Starees must insist on recognition as fellow humans by wielding an array of interpersonal techniques that the commonly embodied need not acquire" (*Staring* 94). Central hereto is a stance of confidence so that, staged properly, the "returned stare is not a plea, but rather an assertive outreach toward mutual recognition across difference" (*Staring* 94). Since staring, in this view, is an interpersonal and highly performative exchange that relies on the ability of the staree to produce an appropriate response that will serve to elude disciplinary capture by the attempted gaze, the question arises of whether a similar relationship can be achieved in mediated visual representations like photography and painting, as well as, of course, drawn comics imagery.

Because the stare depends on an interpersonal relationship allowing for dynamic interaction, static visual representations of disabled people would seem to preclude this social component, as the subject is instead frozen in time and space and presented to the viewer's objectifying gaze. Certainly the history of photographing disabled people, for example, has often taken the form of showing the unusual to a curious public that was either unable or too decorous to visit freak shows or other such displays. In this mode, Hevey has argued, disabled people have commonly been photographed to represent "the inconcealable birthmark of fear and chaos," and therefore "the photographic observation of disablement has increasingly become the art of categorization and surveillance" ("Enfreakment" 369, 377). "Enfreaked" by the photographer's lens, Hevey continues, "disabled people, in these photographic representations, are positioned either as meaningful or meaningless bodies" and as such become the "voyeuristic property of the non-disabled gaze" ("Enfreakment" 376, 377). Similarly, Garland-Thomson's examination of what she calls the various "visual rhetorics of disability" leads her to conclude that "None of these rhetorical modes operates in the service of actual disabled people, however. Indeed, almost all of them appropriate the disabled body for the purposes of constructing, instructing, or assuring some aspect of a putatively nondisabled viewer" ("Politics" 58, 59). Accordingly, representations of disabled people run the risk of reducing their subjects to the exteriority of their visible bodies in a conventional taxonomy of established visual rhetorics that invites looking but leaves the production of meaning squarely in the hands and eyes of the observer.

Breaking out of this hegemonic visual mold thus requires a mode of representation that resists objectification and allows the image to interact in some sense with its observer. Garland-Thomson suggests that portraits, if done in a particularly respectful and dignifying mode, "can provide their subjects with an opportunity to deliberately engage their viewers through the conventional poses of traditional portraiture" and that "intense eye-to-eye engagement with the viewer can make a subject seem to reach out of the picture to stare down the viewer" (*Staring* 84–85). While portraits such as the ones discussed by Garland-Thomson of course "show only half of a staring exchange," they nevertheless also "allow us to consider how starees can use comportment, expression, and even costuming to stare back. In other words, these portraits pull the staree out of a live encounter in order to deliberately stage a staree's self-presentation" (*Staring* 86). By privileging eye contact and thoughtful representations of bodily expression, visual depictions of disability can in this way be staged to engage their viewers in something resembling a real-life staring encounter.

Although Garland-Thomson does not address it directly in her book-length study *Staring: How We Look*, it is worth noting that she takes most of her examples of successfully mediated returned stares from the nonmechanical and subjective visual arts of painting and drawing. Examining a series of portraits depicting burn victims and a young woman with Down syndrome, Garland-Thomson argues that by using "the familiar conventions of traditional portraiture—such as realism, texture, color, pose, and likeness—to portray very unconventional subjects" these paintings and drawings "intervene between starees and starers to offer respectful, even beautiful, pictures of people we have not learned to look at in this way" (*Staring* 80, 83). Carefully crafted handmade images of disabled people, Garland-Thomson's analysis suggests, might therefore hold special potential for the respectful depiction of visual differences and the enactment of successfully returned stares, an insight that in combination with staring's dependency on social interaction has significant implications for disability representation in the comics form—and especially autobiographical variations thereof.

Staring at disability in autobiographical comics is a highly complex and visually charged encounter with an author and character who might resist the objectifying gaze and stare back at the observer. As theorists consistently point out, comics is an inescapably subjective form of expression that depends on its interaction with the reader for the production of meaning. Imbued in every panel with the personal signature of their creator, comics visuals present themselves to the reader with a built-in subjectivity that refuses attempts to interpret them as merely objective representations of external reality. To look at comics representations, in other words, is to look at a highly personal creation and to be confronted with an omnipresent subjectivity that is impossible to deny and which can therefore resist passive objectification. In autobiographical comics, the potential for the self-representational character on the page to resist disciplinary capture by the colonizing gaze of the observer is consequently unmistakable. In this view, moreover, the drawings themselves, along with the temporality implied by their handmade creation—as opposed, for example, to the instantaneous freezing of a moment suggested by a snapshot—represent the elaborate staging of what I call a counterstare, which can be both defiantly assertive and welcoming of interpersonal exchange through the relationship established by the effort required to decode the comics page.

In addition, the multimodality, repetitiveness, and fragmented nature of the comics page also challenges easy objectification, allowing for autobiographical characters that are given to changing their appearance from one panel to the next at the same time that they might be staring at the reader— or, alternatively, withholding their counterstare for the moment in order to stage the staring encounter later and on their own terms. As their characters stare back at the reader from any number of possible vantage points, autobiographical comics can thereby influence the power dynamic between observer and observed through the author's skillful deployment of the form's specific visual properties. Where Couser suggests that masking the impaired body through the use of verbal language might be an advantage of traditional prose autobiography when representing disability, the comics form insists instead on putting that very body on visual display, but in a way that can be open to resistance and resignification through the careful composition of its complex semiotic codes. In a discussion of Georgia Webber's *Dumb*, an autobiographical comics series about its author's experience with temporary speech loss, Dolmage and Jacobs take exactly this view when they point specifically to the form's multimodality as "a prosthesis through which [Webber] can not only resist the disability narratives which have been imposed upon her, but also experiment with self-representation of her own identity as someone with a disability" (25–26). In addition to this potential for transformative self-narration, comics' insistence upon showing and materializing the body on the page means that representations are never in danger of succumbing to the potential pitfalls of the social model, in which embodied or medicalized reality is effaced in favor of a purely constructivist approach. As Susan Merrill Squier has argued, with reference to the foundational comics theory of Will Eisner and in a formulation that also brings to mind the gestural mode of the New London Group, because "comics rely on the 'expressive anatomy' of the body," the form "can play a powerful role in DS [disability studies] by framing disability as an experience that may include but also frequently transcends the medical context" (49). As such, the handmade, participatory, and multimodal form of comics allows for an intricate orchestration of the staring encounter that can highlight embodied subjectivity on the staree's own terms. Staring at disability in comics, therefore, is far from the objectifying one-way process familiar from theories of the gaze, but can instead be an unpredictable encounter of open-ended meanings that lets stareable autobiographical characters show and tell the reader how to look at them.

In his autobiographical comic *The Spiral Cage*, Al Davison uses the form in just these ways in order to stage a book-length staring encounter between the drawings of himself and his implied readers. Davison was born in New-castle, England, in 1960, and *The Spiral Cage* is his fragmentary memoir of growing up, being bullied, fighting back, and making peace with his bodily realities as a disabled man in the north of England. Drawn over the course of twenty years, the book was first published as a relatively short 52-page comic in 1988, was expanded with 50 more pages for a new edition in 1990, and finally was published again in a 2003 edition of 124 pages that also includes an additional chapter of various short stories and illustrated dreams, as well as drawings from Davison's sketchbook. Thematically rather than chronologically organized, the book's structure reflects this history, which allows for the gradual incorporation of additional material without disturb-ing the whole. Its five main chapters contain a number of short scenes loosely organized around thematic titles such as "Why Me" and "Push 'n' Shuv," each of which jump around chronologically from earliest childhood to the diegetic present day. The overarching life story presented by Davison, how-ever, is one of gradual acceptance and eventual spiritual overcoming through martial arts and a developing Buddhist practice. Although Davison—writing and drawing in the 1980s and 1990s, at the height of the social model—favors a constructivist approach in which he considers his impairment to be turned into a disability by certain environments and medical discourses, the book's drawings never let the reader forget the particular realities and challenges of Davison's scarred and nonstandard body. To that end the visual style is unconventionally heterogeneous in its combination of a mainly realis-tic register with scenes relying on symbolic flourish and cartoony exaggera-tion, and privileged throughout is a dual visual focus on Davison's masculine yet visibly disabled body and his eyes, which stare back at the reader from almost every page.

The Spiral Cage begins with a title page depicting Al as a child, with his legs in a prominent cast and sitting on a trolley pulled by his sister, who was born with cerebral palsy and whose body seems awkwardly posed (see fig. 4.1). Surrounding them are two cats, along with a number of crude stick figure drawings that float in the air above them. A bright spotlight is shin-ing directly at Al from outside the panel borders and causes his dark shadow

AN AUTOBIOGRAPHY BY

FIG. 4.1. Al and his sister on the title page of *The Spiral Cage*.

to be seen clearly against the brick wall behind him, an effect that in the context of a comic might suggest the Batman signal. Everybody (including the cats) looks directly at the reader with wide-open eyes and insisting stares that make eye contact inevitable. The image is further subtitled "Diary of an Astral Gypsy," and although many of the book's sequences are dated, it in no way conforms to the generic description of a diary as outlined in chapter 3's discussion of Ariel Schrag's high school comics. The rest of the phrase, however, indicates the spiritual and perhaps slightly New Agey direction of Davison's adult life. With a copiously evocative initial image that meets and holds the reader's would-be gaze from the book's very first page, Davison introduces many of his major themes, including the conspicuous visuality of his impaired legs, his family's extensive experience with disability, the objectifying light cast on his condition by outside authorities, his idolization of superheroes, the potential of drawing to help him tell his life story, his decision to return the viewer's stare, and his gradually developing spirituality. In the pages that follow, these themes are woven together in an episodic and impressionistic narrative that is overwhelmingly visual in its approach to depicting disability.

On the very next page, before the narrative proper begins and in a grayed-out tone that suggests nothing so much as a decorative endpaper design, Davison includes an extreme close-up of himself as an infant, lying in a hospital crib. Through the bars of the crib, and dominating the entire top half of the page, a giant eye is watching him. While the owner of the eye is never identified directly, it becomes clear in the context of the first chapter that it represents a sort of depersonalized medical gaze that is determined to quantify Al's impairment and label him as disabled. Commenting on the next page that "First 'they' said I wouldn't live . . then they said I shouldn't live," Davison further inscribes himself as a subject of medical discourse from both infancy and the book's beginning, but also happily notes that "My parents disagreed" (7) with the doctors' assessment.[8] As if the fact that he is alive to write these words is not strong enough proof that his parents were right, Davison lists a number of his achievements on the following page: "Recently I've got into contemporary dance, co-wrote and performed in a play, worked as production artist, and worked on two films. You know . . Your average . . vegetable . . . !" (8). Offering his rather successful life as a counterargument, Davison thereby begins the book by showing how being born with an impairment is akin to being viewed as inferior by a medical gaze eager to quantify and devalue nonstandard bodies.

In a striking sequence early in the chapter, Davison extends this analysis by portraying himself as a fetus in the womb, gradually growing and moving closer to a white light emanating from the bottom right of the panels. As he slowly comes into focus as a recognizable human form, however, it is impossible to identify his lower legs as being affected by spina bifida. When he finally enters the blinding light of the outside world in the page's final panel, the words "It's a boy" (13) appear over his squinting face. In addition to this initial moment of binary sorting, through which Al is both identified and constituted, medical discourse soon after expands its authority and labels him disabled. The next page is dated as occurring the day after his birth and shows a series of X-rays interspersed with commentary from a doctor (see fig. 4.2). Alongside the images showing his skeleton in solid blacks against a white background, the detached medical language explains the images in terse terms while pointing to the problematic areas: "Both femur, fibula, and tibia of both legs are severely distorted . . . such that at the moment we cannot open the legs, we should be able to rectify this to a degree, enough at least for the mother to dress him and change him" (14). Literally penetrated by the gaze of medical technology and with his future quantified by its accompanying verbal discourse, Al is from infancy reduced to a medical "problem" that needs correction. Moreover, while his body is both tested and talked about, it is primarily seen by medical authorities as something aberrant that marks him, according to the doctor, as "literally a 'hopeless case'" (14). In this sequence, Davison thus uses the particularities of the comics form to illustrate the dual ways in which modern medicine objectifies and pathologizes disabled individuals through the use of verbal naming and supposedly objective visual technologies that allow doctors to see inside the bodies of patients.[9] Finally, by letting the sequence follow immediately after the page showing his birth and gender assignment, Davison further suggests that the same type of visually inflected binary social construction that identified him as a boy served to firmly and irrevocably label him as disabled.

Later in the chapter, Davison continues his critique of the medical construction of disability as a permanently disqualifying category. In a full-page panel, Davison draws himself at the age of five, taking his first few steps on wobbly legs while wearing a Batman shirt and a cape (see fig. 4.3). Smiling widely and looking straight ahead, he is framed by a white aura-like light, and the collected visual impression of the image is of someone performing a superheroic feat. As Al says to his mother "Look . . . I can walk!"

Jan 17th 1960.....

SPINA BIFIDA
Dislocation of left hip Caused by Malformation of the lateral surface of the Iliac bone ie. no deep excavation (socket) for the head of the femur to connect with,

we can't tell as of yet if the upper spine is affected, so we have to insert a Valve, in case of fluid pressure on the Brain it will dissolve in a few years if it is not needed. Both femur, fibula, and Tibia of both legs are.....

severly distorted both femur are such that at the moment we cannot open the legs, we should be able to rectify this to a degree, enough at least for the mother to dress him.

and change him etc. His ankles are also fused (the Talus and the two Malleoli) preventing any flexing of the feet.... it is of course unlikely he could flex his feet even without this problem. as in such severe cases as this he will be paralysed from the waist down...

our first job is to cover the open wound at the base of the spine which exposes the lower vertebrae and coccyx. a usual characteristic of spina Bifida, we will graft skin, taken from the shin to cover the wound. two years minimum recovery for this operation

we can't even say he will survive this first operation he is literally a "hopeless case," this not meaning to sound defeatist, but there is little hope. His parents are adamant however to proceed no matter what, against my advice. So we must do what we can,.....

FIG. 4.2. Al is seen by the medical gaze, from *The Spiral Cage*.

FIG. 4.3. Al takes his first steps, from *The Spiral Cage*.

(32), the facing page is a twelve-panel grid showing various responses to the sight of him walking. While every other image is a unique drawing of his parents, friends, and nurses, all of whom are smiling or shedding tears at the happy sight, they are interspersed with the repeated and almost rhythmic image of a doctor professing his disbelief. Aside from the obvious discrepancy in the visual display of emotion—through which Davison subtly argues against the unfeeling detachment of medical objectivity—the repetition of the doctor and his statement also serves to underline the stubborn inability of medical authority to account for human variation even when faced with full-page visual proof of its own fallibility. Compared to the earlier X-ray sequence, moreover, the image allows Davison to use the power of a humanizing full-page drawing to challenge medical notions of his supposed disability and disturb the established visual dynamic of the patient-doctor relationship.

At the bottom of this second page, Davison alludes to the meaning of the book's title when he comments that he was unable, at the time, to understand "what a significant dint I had made in my spiral cage" (33). According to an interview with Davison, the title "came from a feeling of being trapped in a cage that continually changed its perspective, from hospital rooms and walking sticks, callipers, various restrictions that are put on you by society" (qtd. in McIlvenny 115). Despite this early instance of exceeding expectations, Davison's life is still to a large degree circumscribed by disabling societal conditions. While medical discourse was the first to see and declare him disabled, the categorization naturally also influences other aspects of his life. Consequently, in the book's second chapter, entitled "Why Me," Davison explores his trajectory of coming to understand his unusual body and the fact that it will make him a target of an omnipresent gaze that figures him as disabled in public contexts.

In the second chapter's first sequence, Davison shows how his impairment does not necessarily translate to disability. In three strikingly designed and mostly wordless pages, taking place "at home, shortly after my 14th operation" and while "still paralyzed from the waist down" (36), Davison depicts himself as a child of four, wearing a Batman costume and climbing a bookcase using only his arms to reach a book on an upper shelf. As he reaches the shelf, his feet dangling but his eyes determined, he imagines himself as a pirate who boards a ship to snatch a book from the hands of an enemy. As the pirate escapes with the book, jumping overboard, Davison draws himself as similarly falling into the sheets of a bed below, book in hand. Such a climb would be an impressive feat for any child, and the scene indicates that Davison was not held back by what others considered a disability and that he imagined himself to be capable of such typical childhood activities as climbing and physical role playing. In another intricately constructed sequence presenting him as an avid reader in childhood, Davison portrays what is seemingly the first time he comes to consider himself different. Lying in a hospital bed and reading the famous passage from Mary Shelley's *Frankenstein* in which the monster looks at its reflection in a pool, Al sits up and looks at his legs, in a typical scene of immersed childhood reading that is disrupted by its own reflective moment. Interspersing the scene with illustrations of the sorrowful monster as it realizes its true nature, Davison ends the sequence with a close-up of Al's skinny and immobile lower legs, dangling over the bedside. Having just encountered some difficult words in the monster's narration, moreover, Al asks the nurse "What duz despondinse and mortificatshun mean?" (42). The implication is that Al, like the monster, is seeing his body as unusual for the first time, and that he is learning the words for emotions—such as despondence and mortification—that mainstream, nondisabled society will typically expect him to experience as a result of his impairment. Considered in contrast with the bookcase-climbing sequence, the combined effect of Al's question to the nurse, the drawn scenes from *Frankenstein*, and the final close-up is to show how specific cultural discourses serve to usurp and replace organically developed ideas of self in order to position nonstandard embodiment as problematic and in need of correction.

As Al begins school, his body draws renewed attention, and responses by others often take the shape of bullying. Although he is a bright and inquisitive boy—as a sequence in which he challenges a teacher's authority on Christianity demonstrates—Al is routinely called "spacka" or "cripple" by the other kids in school, who seize on his visible difference as a way of increasing their own social standing. Employing the rhetoric of eugenics, for example, a classmate claims that "it's illegal for cripples to do it [have sexual intercourse] . . . It's true 'coz they don't want lotsa, stupid little cripples, been born!!" (49). Underlining his own purported masculinity by grabbing his crotch in the sequence's last panel, the boy shouts, "The way you walk it's obvious y'aint got no bluddy balls" (49), thereby performing manhood in a way that is supposedly in contrast to that of Al, who is assumed to be either asexual or impotent because of his inability to walk without support. Davison in this way portrays a bullying encounter that serves to act as a mediator of insider and outsider status and establish the parameters for what is considered normal in this particular sociocultural milieu. But as the adult Al himself says on the very next page, lying naked in bed and looking very masculine, "Mind you, if 'normal,' means, heartless, mean, narrow minded, etc. then they can keep it" (50). In addition to questioning the value of normalcy as defined throughout his childhood encounters with school bullies, Davison also one-ups the pimpled and weak-chinned antagonist by drawing himself with his adult masculinity on full visual display (see fig. 4.4). By turning away from the reader in the sequence's last panel, and into the embrace of two feminine arms reaching around him, Davison simultaneously marks his body as a site of masculine sexual appeal and disinvites the reader's attention in a subtle act of proactive defiance.

In the next chapter, entitled "Push 'n' Shuv," Davison continues to thematize his increasing refusal to be the passive victim of verbal and physical abuse by both classmates and strangers encountered in public. The chapter's first sequence shows Al retaliating against bullying kids who have been throwing rocks at him. As they call him names like "freak," "cripple," and "crybaby," Al throws a rock directly in the face of one of them, pointing out that "A divn't cry" (62) while scowling at the kids (see fig. 4.5). The incident is the first time the narrative shows Al fighting back against anybody bullying him, and as such represents a key act of resistance. Notably, the scene is visually framed as an encounter of eye contact, with every panel except the last drawn from Al's perspective and with the kids looking directly at him. Seeing the world seeing him as a "freak" or "cripple," Davison pushes back not only by having Al throw the rock but also by changing the perspective in the last panel to that of the kids—who are at this point implied to be occupying the position of the reader—and by meeting their eyes directly in a tense exchange of stares. As an example of an elaborately staged staring encounter supported by the implicit threat of violence, the scene introduces Davison's emerging realization that he need not be a passive victim of interpersonal abuse and cultural disqualification. By collapsing the point of view of the bullies with that of the reader in the final panel, moreover, the encounter exemplifies Davison's use of the comics form to invite the visual attention often commanded by his body in order to subsequently contest it by throwing back a rock or a forceful counterstare at anyone daring to look.

In the chapter's next sequence, Davison more fully invites the stare of the reader by putting his body on explicit display. Dated as taking place in 1988,

FIG. 4.4. A masculine Al turns away from the reader, from *The Spiral Cage*.

FIG. 4.5. Al fights back for the first time, from *The Spiral Cage*.

when Davison was twenty-eight years old, the one-page sequence shifts the focus to Al as an adult man and shows him performing a series of martial arts poses while naked and facing the reader (see fig. 4.6). The top half of the page is composed of two rows of four panels each, separated by a thin black line instead of a traditional gutter. As Al poses his muscular and hairy body, the middle two of the four top images cut his body off just below his crotch, while the comparatively placed images in the second row show only Al's lower body, which is cut off just above the crotch. Across the thin black gutter, the effect is striking. In addition to positioning Al as bigger and stronger, an elongated giant, the composition also creates a doubling of his genitals that accentuates his manhood and virility. While his lower legs carry the obvious marks of spina bifida, the overall impression is of a body in full control of itself, and on display for the admiration of the reader. Moreover, after inviting the reader's visual attention with the top row's presentation of traditional masculinity, the second row's focus on Al's legs—which appear in almost the exact middle of the page—might well provoke a stare at the unexpected sight of such legs being capable of supporting these poses. Responding to this implied stare, Davison immediately follows these body-pose images with a series of four smaller panels showing close-ups of Al's eyes. Changing their expression from pained to angry to focused and wide-eyed, Al's eyes stare back in an encounter that is impossible to ignore and challenges any attempt by the reader to identify his naked body as disabled. After interrupting the would-be disqualifying gaze, Davison concludes the sequence by performing a quickly paced, seven-panel kick directly at the reader in the page's bottom row. In this interpretation, the page in its entirety is thus an elaborately structured staring encounter between Al and the reader that begins by drawing attention to his visually conspicuous body, continues by dynamically staring back in a number of unsettling ways, and ends by delivering a decisive and assertive kick that establishes both his physical ability and his refusal to be seen as disabled.

It is telling that Davison's dignified portrayal of his naked body on this page is performed to almost the opposite effect of, for example, Julie Doucet's oppositional and grotesquely exaggerated unruly female body. As John Berger, among others, has noted, depictions of female nudity in art history have traditionally presented the passive body to the assumed male spectator. Claiming that "nakedness reveals itself. Nudity is placed on display," Berger argues that "a naked body has to be seen as an object in order to become a nude," and that therefore "nudity is a form of dress" applied by

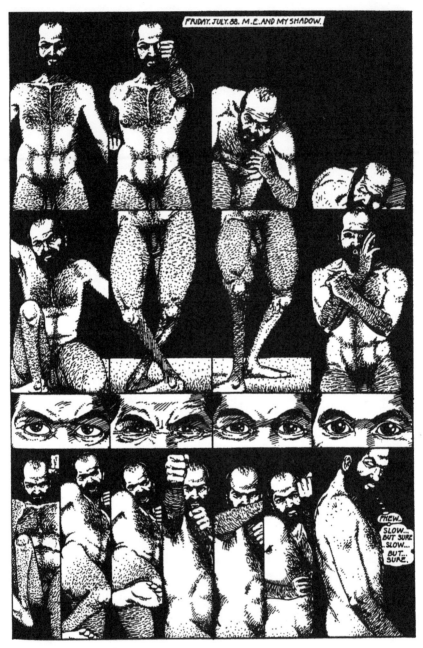

FIG. 4.6. Davison stages a staring encounter between himself and the reader, from *The Spiral Cage*.

the artist (54). While Berger presupposes a distinction between artist and subject that is effaced in self-portraits or other visual autobiographies, the idea that undress is codified differently depending on the intended observer—and, of course, the object's sex and gender—is fundamental to reading and comparing passages of bodily exposure in Doucet's and Davison's comics. Occupying marginalized subject positions and operating in a visual form that privileges seeing, both artists begin from a starting point of expected nudity that they gradually turn into self-possessed nakedness. Playing with our learned conventions of looking at women and the disabled, Doucet and Davison both put their nudity on display, but invite our stare in different ways. While Doucet is opposing the misogynistic tradition of reducing women to passive sexual objects, Davison challenges the objectifying gaze at disability by portraying himself as the literal embodiment of the very things a disabled male body is not supposed to exhibit—namely, self-control, virility, and masculine beauty. As an act of imaginative denuding, this scene thereby functions as Davison's attempt to take control of his body, its representation, and the reader's range of possible responses hereto.

The fact that Davison is able to practice martial arts at this level, of course, makes him rather unusual among people living with spina bifida. Consequently, his impressive display of bodily proficiency at times makes his story resemble the stereotype of the "supercrip." In supercrip narratives, Simi Linton notes, "sheer strength or willpower has brought the person to the point where the disability is no longer a hindrance" (165). As José Alaniz points out, however, "the supercrip, in the eyes of its critics, represents a sort of overachieving, overdetermined self-enfreakment that distracts from the lived daily reality of most disabled people" ("Supercrip" 305). Accordingly, such narratives can have the unfortunate effect of further marginalizing other people unable to perform similarly exceptional tasks. In this vein Couser, speaking directly of disability memoir, writes that while supercrip narratives "may be 'true stories' . . . they are not truly representative lives. This rhetoric tends to remove the stigma of disability from the author, leaving it in place for other individuals with the condition in question." Therefore, he continues, the supercrip scenario "is entirely congruous with the medical paradigm, which locates disability entirely within a 'defective' or 'abnormal' body. Disability is presented primarily as a 'problem' that individuals must overcome; overcoming it is a matter of individual will and determination rather than of social and cultural accommodation" ("Conflicting" 80). By individualizing disability as something that can be overcome with the right attitude,

supercrip narratives, as Wendy L. Chrisman notes, may seem "antitheti-
cal to (or, at least, impede) the idea of viewing disability as a socially constructed site for analysis" (173). In the context of *The Spiral Cage*, this
theoretical problem persists since Davison is no doubt at times both an
impressive and inspirational figure. As Chrisman acknowledges, however,
inspiration can also provide "a vital means to learn, to raise awareness, and
to connect with others" and as such can be "a valuable, rhetorically strate-
gic emotion" (183, 184) similar to how an image of the woman on top can
help reconfigure entrenched ideas about the female body, as was discussed
in chapter 1. It is also important to remember, as Sami Schalk points out,
that "disabled people generally do not always find supercrip representations
to be entirely oppressive or problematic," and also that "we must understand
supercrip as a narrative that produces a stereotype rather than as a static category that a character or person can fully be or embody" (75, 76). Reducing
all inspirational narratives to the maligned supercrip stereotype, in other
words, runs the risk of neglecting individual experience in much the same
way that totalizing cultural discourses tend to view disability as a unified
category of deficiency. Depicting his life in the specific cultural context of
1980s northern England, moreover—that is, well before the term *supercrip*
came into popular use around 1990—Davison's narrative reflects his personal experience with the particular kinds of adversity he faces because of
his impairment, including a masculine culture valuing physical strength and
the ability to fight back.[10] Finally, Davison explicitly drapes the narrative
of overcoming in the visual rhetoric of the superhero, as the many references
to Batman and Superman throughout the comic make clear. In a form
haunted by the spectacle of the superbody—as Alaniz notes, the "entire logic
and *modus operandi*" of superhero comics consists of a "fantastic, quasi-
eugenicist apotheosis of the perfected body" (*Death* 35; emphasis in the
original)—these allusions serve to gently and somewhat ironically undercut claims to exceptionality in scenes detailing relatively ordinary accom-
plishments such as learning to walk. As Davison is well aware, his partial
capacity for overcoming certain limitations does not make him a superhero,
and his display of martial arts proficiency is therefore less an attempt to turn
his condition into a universalizing narrative of overcoming than a specific
and highly personal challenge to the idea that impairment is always equal
to disability.

As a turning point in the narrative—from this point on, Al refuses his
victim status—the martial arts scene is followed by other instances where

he fights back against such antagonists as a group of skinheads and a motorcycle gang. These incidents set him on a course of bodily empowerment and determined self-defense that also includes a dramatic scene in which he breaks his canes with several powerful karate chops. Along with several close-ups of his eyes as he splinters and trashes the canes, the sequence includes five different drawings of his face (see fig. 4.7). Where the first image is grotesquely deformed and returns the stare of the reader, the drawings grow increasingly realistic until the final image of the short sequence, in which Al looks away, withdrawing his attention and looking off to the side with a blissful expression on his face. By destroying his canes, Al has removed one of the most obvious visual clues to his impairment, and the climactic scene serves to suggest that he is now free to withhold his stare and direct his attention elsewhere. As he puts on his sister's sneakers and walks outside without support for the first time, Al turns his back to the reader and appears in framed silhouette against the light of the doorway, in a gesture that symbolizes a measure of self-determination. In combination with his many antagonistic encounters with various assailants, the sequence in this way suggests both that he is ready to be seen on his own terms and that he will fight anyone who dares challenge him.

On the next page, Davison shows the reader what being seen on his own terms might look like. In a full-page drawing, he depicts himself in front of a brick wall, wearing tracksuit pants and a flashy, half-zipped jacket (see fig. 4.8). To his side is a trash can full of broken canes, from which smoke is dramatically (if somewhat incongruously) rising. From the way Al looks directly at the reader with a confident stare, it is clear that he no longer sees himself as a victim because his martial arts practice has given him the skills to resist verbal and physical abuse. In addition, the drawing represents a performance of idealized masculinity inspired by 1980s popular culture and reminiscent of such iconic images as Patrick Swayze on the *Road House* poster or any number of Bruce Springsteen portraits from the era. Stylistically influenced by equal parts action movies and MTV, the glossily drawn portrait privileges traditional notions of bodily prowess and presents Al as a pinup soliciting our admiration. Subtitled "The beginning," it is clear that at least in this one image the act of breaking the canes frees Davison to represent himself as an idealized, hard-hitting, and desirable masculine fantasy.

In the very next sequence, however, Davison explores the limits of this fantasy and its implications for his martial arts practice. Over two pages

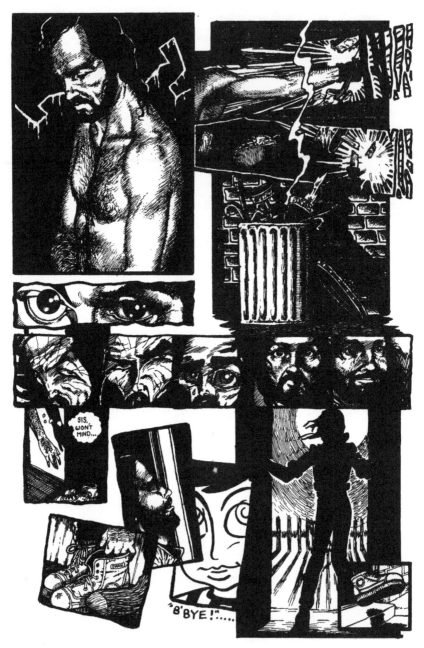

FIG. 4.7. Al breaks his canes and walks out the door, from *The Spiral Cage*.

THE BEGINNING...

FIG. 4.8. Davison draws himself as a masculine fantasy, from *The Spiral Cage*.

consisting of grids that alternate scenes of his many violent encounters with childishly drawn images of cowboys fighting with Indians, Davison says that while the Indians win in the end, "The trick is, to keep winning.. without becoming a cowboy" (80). While it is clear from the sequence that Al is able to defend himself against a group of five skinheads—in one panel he manages to take out two at the same time, one with each arm, comically hitting one of them in the groin in classic cartoon fashion—the implication is that he must find a more peaceful way of dealing with such encounters in order to not become an aggressor himself. Accomplishing this requires a change of perspective on his own impairment, however, and one that is bound up with his increasing understanding that disability is in part a visually determined social construct that marks him as different from the moment others lay eyes on him.

The next sequence documents an encounter that demonstrates how Davison has shifted his perspective on disability away from the medical model that pathologizes his nonstandard body and toward an understanding based in the social model and focused more on perception and interpretation. At an outdoor garden party, another guest asks Al to tell him from a "purely intellectual point of view . . . . What's it like to be .. well disabled?" (81). Al quips that "I'm not that intellectual . . Nor am I disabled . . Sorry . ." and further contests the man's insistence that he "must face up to reality" by noting that "the definition of disability is . . incapable, unable to do, incapacitated . . . lack of ability, etc.. etc." (81). Challenging his interlocutor to a series of physical feats—such a jumping to pick an apple from a tree and bending over backward to reach the ground with his hands—Al proves his point by performing these in a much superior way and consequently asks the man to "Tell me from a purely emotional point of view . . . . How does it feel to be disabled .. ?" (83). By one-upping the man in a display of impressive physical capacity, Al shows how disability is a relative phenomenon depending on context, and does so in a way that in comparison to his violent encounters is playfully nonconfrontational.

Al's realization that he must resist the violence directed at him in peaceful ways is tied both to his martial arts practice and a developing interest in Buddhism. While his introduction to Buddhism comes in the somewhat unpalatable form of a friend suggesting that his spina bifida might be an expression of karma caused by artistic complacency in a past life, Al appreciates the religion's focus on fusing body and spirit through poses, chanting, and meditation. As he becomes increasingly preoccupied with exploring his interior and spiritual life, he also learns to understand that his supposed disability is an imposition made by others with which he can simply refuse to engage. A one-page sequence illustrates how he gradually learns to deflect the aggression of others through nonviolent means and the practice of self-control as empowered by Buddhist chanting. Taking place over two weeks, the sequence consists of four rows of panels, each depicting similar encounters in an Indian restaurant. Verbally taunted and physically attacked, Al responds in the first three encounters by violently fighting back, which causes the assailants to move away. Each row, significantly, concludes with an image of Al chanting while putting his palms together in front of his chest, and it is clear from his facial expression and the look in his eyes that he is struggling with uniting his peaceful Buddhist practice with his capacity for violence. Conversely, in the final encounter, instead of retaliating when an attacker challenges him to "See how hard y' really are," Al simply says "No" and walks away (84). The final row's concluding image shows him chanting with a peaceful look on his face, as he has overcome his instinctual response of fighting back when assaulted. As Davison's increasing introspection in this way intertwines with a growing self-confidence and a determination to not let his impairment define him as disabled in the eyes of others, the book's preoccupation with looking and staring takes on an increasingly spiritual tone.

The most important texts for Davison's Buddhist practice are the various writings of Nichiren Daishonin, to the point where they become something of an intertext to *The Spiral Cage*. In addition to providing the epigraph to four of the book's five chapters—with, for example, such inspirational commentary as the reminder that "Even one extra day of life is worth more than ten million ryu of gold" (9)—Nichiren's writings also play an important part in the way Davison's developing mastery of his body relates to both visuality and the comics form itself. While Nichiren's philosophical ideas are scattered throughout the book, a passage regarding the necessity of "polishing your mirror" is especially prominent. Excerpted from "On Attaining Buddhahood," the passage is used both in an opening section and as the inspiration for the book's concluding sequence, in which Davison illustrates the story of a young boy who performs the arduous task of polishing an ever-dirty mirror. As the boy grows older, the mirror becomes increasingly tarnished and he eventually begins to focus on the easy parts—with the result that he quickly loses sight of himself. Finding a clean cloth, however, the boy resumes his work of diligently polishing the mirror, and as it grows brighter his life begins to shine again. Davison finishes the book by quoting directly from Nichiren: "Even a tarnished mirror will shine like a jewel if it is polished," and one should therefore "Arouse deep faith and polish your mirror night and day" (124). The parable's implications for his life are unmistakable: polishing the mirror of both spirit and body is fundamental to his project of overcoming the social limitations and antagonistic encounters he experiences as a result of his impairment.

In addition to the straightforward spiritual lesson that Davison must face adversity and polish both his body and spirit in order to achieve enlightenment and avoid losing sight of himself, however, the special role played by the mirror in the allegory is important to the comic's overall emphasis on visualization and embodiment. As such, drawings of mirrors are central to the visual design of *The Spiral Cage*, and appear with regularity throughout the comic—often in panels showing Davison looking at himself with disbelief. Building from Lacan's influential account of the primal stare at the self in the mirror stage, Garland-Thomson has argued about the peculiarity of regarding a reflection of ourselves that "the person in the mirror . . . is not the person we experience ourselves to be; rather, that person is the one others see" (*Staring* 51). While looking at the self holds the potential to be a profoundly othering experience, Garland-Thomson notes elsewhere that in the context of disability, "the picture of ourselves as disabled is an image fraught with a tangle of anxiety, distance, and identification" ("Politics" 57). In an especially striking sequence in chapter 3 of *The Spiral Cage* Davison experiences just such a complicated response to seeing his own reflection. On a page that highlights his thin and scarred legs, Al catches a glimpse of himself in the bathroom mirror as he gets out of bed on a Saturday morning, and reacts first with curiosity and then with horror (see fig. 4.9). As Al is caught off guard by the same visual representation that identifies him as disabled to others, the image contrasts starkly with his own self-perception and triggers a series of recollections of "conflicting voices" that speak about his impairment and eventually cause him to collapse in front of the mirror. As a staring encounter with himself in which the only possible outcome is a stalemate, the look into the mirror allows Al/Davison temporary and troubled access to the viewing position of the starer and the psychological process that marks him as a cultural outsider because of his appearance. The stare into the mirror thereby also becomes a stare into the flip side of disability, in which Davison sees himself through the surrounding tarnish of its culturally imposed identity. In this way, polishing

FIG. 4.9. Al sees himself in the mirror, from *The Spiral Cage*.

the mirror to remove the tarnish means that he must gradually eliminate the objectifying and disabling gaze of medical authority in order to
reveal the brightly shining reflection underneath. The subjective mirror
of the comics form is therefore a profound act of literal re-vision that allows
Davison to control and polish his visual reflection in opposition to conventional notions of disability. Further, through Davison's many elaborately
staged staring encounters, as well as through the book's many depictions of
eyes and the act of looking, his representation itself becomes a kind of distorted funhouse mirror for the nondisabled observer, whose sense of self
and body might suddenly be thrown into question by the confrontation
with a dynamic counterstare that resists reassuring objectification and
unsettles straightforward conceptions of embodiment.

In *The Spiral Cage* Davison stares back at the reader from almost every
page in a way that both invites identification and confronts the reader with
a radically embodied subjectivity. Whereas the previous chapters have
argued that Julie Doucet resists objectifying capture by the would-be male
gaze through a performance in form and content of grotesque and unruly
femininity, that Phoebe Gloeckner uses fragmented comics imagery to show
(and work through) the trauma associated with concealed sexual abuse to
both herself and the reader, and that Ariel Schrag portrays her unseen but
in-progress sexuality through a queer and excessive approach to style, Davison employs the multimodal visuality of comics to perform an extended
staring encounter that engages with various disabling discourses. Although
the autobiographical characters of the other artists discussed in these pages
look out from the page from time to time and let their eyes meet those of
the viewer, Davison is alone in his continued insistence upon using the
form as a vehicle for the potential reconfiguration of the interpersonal
relationship between author and reader of autobiographical comics. Putting his body on display for the reader's attention, Davison's many intricately structured images repeatedly challenge the very nature of that
attention through the orchestration of an assertive counterstare that complicates and resists ableist mainstream society's visual representations of
disability as characterized by the various tropes of enfreakment. As the
comic refuses the reader's attempted colonizing gaze and instead returns
the attention as an assertive stare, the dynamically interactive relationship
enabled by the hand-drawn and multimodal comics form serves as affirmation of the argument that disability is literally in the eyes of the beholder.

5

Stereotyping
the Self

● ● ● ● ● ● ● ● ● ● ● ● ●

Toufic El Rassi's *Arab in America*

In his 2007 comics memoir entitled *Arab in America*, Lebanese-born artist and educator Toufic El Rassi consistently and without much variation depicts himself as a visual stereotype of an Arab man, complete with pronounced Semitic features and thick black facial hair. Throughout the comic, the numerous self-portraits also insist on his hair being identically styled and his eyebrows similarly arched. In addition, most drawings of Toufic show him with the same facial expression and in three-quarter profile. So invariable is this stereotyped self-portrait that El Rassi even uses it across the several different time periods depicted in the book, ranging from his childhood to the present day. As such, the book's many depictions of Toufic as an adult man in his late twenties use the same exact visual model as, for example, an eighth grade classroom scene, in which his teacher is also depicted as jokingly saying that if the Islamic forces had won the Battle of

FIG. 5.1. Toufic in eighth grade, but drawn as an adult man, from *Arab in America*.

Tours, "we would all be Arabs. Can you imagine? Ha ha ha!" (37) (see fig. 5.1). Such casually racist remarks from teachers, neighbors, friends, and politicians fill the pages of *Arab in America*, in which El Rassi's repetitive insistence upon portraying himself as a distinctly Arab stereotype illustrates both how he is seen by others (and perhaps has come to see himself) and how easily individual specificity is turned into general stereotype in comics art.

Where the other artists discussed in this book often insist on portraying themselves as unruly and multiple, in strategies that allow them to challenge or elude hegemonic notions of identity and insist on being seen by the reader on their own terms, El Rassi's self-portrait instead opts for identification with a stereotype that has often been used to marginalize or exclude him. As I have argued throughout, the comics form's sequential nature makes it exceptionally well equipped for the task of representing marginalized selves, because no single image is ever made to stand in for the totality of identity. In other words, by visually performing changing and often confrontational selves throughout the pages of their comics, artists can take control of representation and insist on establishing new ways of experiencing and seeing subjectivities and/or bodies marked by the various cultural discourses of gender, trauma, homosexuality, and disability. While representations of such identities in comics are to various extents defined by their relationships with established visual frameworks ranging from the hypervisuality of disability to the lack of bodily indicators for gayness, El Rassi's self-conscious use of an unchanging stereotype highlights how the depiction of ethnoracial difference stands out from this company because of its association with an especially virulent and derogatory visual tradition that has often been directly employed in the service of domination and exploitation.

As a cultural form, comics has been involved in the visual stereotyping of nonwhite people since its inception and, especially in the United States, such representations have been used to establish and uphold boundaries between masters and slaves, old immigrants and new, and friends and enemies. So entrenched is the relationship between comics art and stereotype that it has often been theorized as a foundational building block of the form itself. Frances Gateward and John Jennings, for example, have argued that "comics traffic in stereotypes and fixity. It is one of the attributes at the heart of how the medium deals with representation" (2). Jeet Heer, bringing a similar point to bear specifically on the topic of race, sharply but perhaps slightly hyperbolically notes that "at its root cartooning is a matter of black and white" (251). As the example of El Rassi shows, the form's reliance on such marginalizing visual codes poses a question of self-representation for authors of autobiographical comics who are visually marked as ethnoracially different. Asking, along with El Rassi, what it means to draw oneself in a cultural form that only recognizes and knows that self as injurious stereotype, this chapter concludes the present volume by taking a deeper dive into several of the issues underlying the previous chapters, including comics' visual reliance upon various exclusionary representational schemes rooted in cultural attempts at distinguishing insiders from outsiders.

El Rassi's comic is a book-length exploration of the limitations of comics art to depict the ethnoracial other, as well as an examination of the power of such representations to preclude the expression of individual subjectivity in interpersonal encounters. Told from the highly politicized point of view of an Arab man living in post-9/11 America, the book is a meditation on El Rassi's particular cultural position. Born in Beirut in 1978 to a

Lebanese and Egyptian family, El Rassi and his family immigrated to the United States in 1979 in order to escape the Lebanese Civil War. After growing up in the Chicago area, El Rassi graduated from DePaul University with a bachelor's degree in communications and a master's degree in modern Middle Eastern history. In addition, El Rassi holds a master's degree from the School of the Art Institute of Chicago, where he also teaches painting and drawing. El Rassi's first comic, *Arab in America* is a fragmented account of being visibly and recognizably Arab in the United States. Part personal memoir and part history of the representation of Arabs in American popular and political culture, the comic also educates its readers about such topics as the large Christian minority in Lebanon and the differences between the often but not always overlapping categories of Arab ethnicity and Muslim religion. Throughout the book, El Rassi's narrative voice exhibits a mix of resignation and bemusement at the continued failure of American culture to both correctly identify his ethnicity and to recognize his individual subjectivity.

As the title suggests, El Rassi portrays an opposition between his Arab heritage and the surrounding American culture, and the book's cover introduces this theme through its densely suggestive visuals (see fig. 5.2). The cover image shows half of Toufic's face in front of an American flag. The flag, however, drawn vertically and upside down, has many more stars than the customary fifty, and the stripes also greatly outnumber the official thirteen representing the original states in the union. Thematically complex, the image is simultaneously a humorous undermining of the flag's authority, a sly reminder that the United States is greatly more culturally plural than typically acknowledged or imagined, and a critique of the country's incorporation of many other states into its de facto "empire." In addition, the thinness of the red-and-white stripes also suggests prison bars, which, in combination with the worried look on Toufic's face—his eyebrow is arched and his mouth is slightly open—indicates both the hostility of American society to people who look like him and his fundamental exclusion from it. Toufic himself is drawn with much thicker lines than the flag itself, a strategy that gives prominence to his Semitic features and represents them as standing out from the inconspicuous white norm of America. The title of the comic itself, moreover, is written as *ARAB in america*, and the uneven use of capital letters thereby underscores his position as an Arab man in a society that refuses to let him blend in and claim an American identity, despite the fact that he has lived in the United States for almost his entire

FIG. 5.2. Toufic in front of too many stars and stripes on the cover of *Arab in America*.

life. His Arab identity is further accentuated through the golden yellow color filling in the uppercase word "ARAB," which in contrast to the grayness of the lowercase "america" also indicates the vibrancy of Arab culture compared to the dull melting pot of mainstream American society. Finally, El Rassi's name in the Roman alphabet is accompanied by his first name written in Arabic script, underlining once again his intercultural position and the fact that his name belongs to two different and incompatible visual and cultural idioms. Crucially, neither the title nor the cover drawing identifies him as Arab American, but instead stresses his position as someone who is identifiably and perilously other. This position, the comic argues both thematically and through its highly charged visuals, is supported by the culture's pervasive stereotypical imagery of Arabs and Muslims, which serves to reinforce ethnoracial categories and negate expressions of individual subjectivity for Arabs in America. Through his highly stylized use of the comics form to depict himself as an unchanging stereotype, El Rassi both implicates the form itself in this marginalizing process and finds new ways to reappropriate and destabilize such deeply ingrained images. Comics, as El Rassi is well aware, is far from an innocent bystander in the history of establishing and reinforcing the various codes that make up racist visual stereotypes, as the form's long relationship with such imagery bears witness to. This relationship lies at the very center of especially the more cartoony variations of comics art, and is entangled with our way of perceiving the world, our sense of self, and the formation of racist ideologies themselves.

Stereotyping, in its most basic form, is nothing more than a helpful cognitive process that works by reducing the complexity of the world through simplification and generalization. While seemingly innocuous, stereotypes nevertheless have the potential to deny individuality by ignoring differences and instead grouping objects or people in categories based on certain distinguishing attributes or characteristics. In this view, stereotyping is a reductive process of categorization based on superficial difference, and because "types are always formed in relation to some purpose at hand," John Heeren argues, "it is this immediate interest that determines which traits will be equalized and what 'individuality' will be ignored" (51). While stereotypes can in principle be either positive or negative, they therefore also have an intrinsic relationship with subjectivity, power, and ideology. Walter Lippmann, who first introduced the concept into the social sciences in 1922, makes a similar point:

A pattern of stereotypes is not neutral. It is not merely a way of substituting order for the great blooming, buzzing confusion of reality. It is not merely a short cut. It is all these things and something more. It is the guarantee of our self-respect; it is the projection upon the world of our own sense of our own value, our own position and our own rights. The stereotypes are, therefore, highly charged with the feelings that are attached to them. They are the fortress of our tradition, and behind its defenses we can continue to feel ourselves safe in the position we occupy. (63–64)

Lippmann makes clear that in addition to functioning as a cognitive ordering process and a mental shortcut, stereotypes are intricately bound up with both our sense of self and our experience of the world around us. By stereotyping our surroundings, including various social groups, we thereby create a sense of order in the world—an order that is always an expression of our own values and beliefs.

By processing complex information through a practice of simplification and generalization and then projecting it back onto the world as an expression of consensus, the stereotyping of people becomes a demonstration of values that serves to establish boundaries between insiders and outsiders in a given society. As Richard Dyer argues, "Stereotypes proclaim, 'This is what everyone—you, me and us—thinks members of such-and-such a social group are like'" (14). Dyer claims that it is this feature that is "the most important function of the stereotype: to maintain sharp boundary definitions, to define clearly where the pale ends and thus who is clearly within and who clearly beyond it" (16). The creation of a stereotype in this way implies that every person belonging to the outsider group in question must share some fundamental trait which serves to demarcate them as different from the self—and, by extension, the insider group to which the self is in turn stereotyped as belonging. In this view, stereotyping is a highly divisive practice, and one that is deeply invested in identity formation and a psychological need to establish difference between the self and others.[1] As Judith Butler argues, the "exclusionary matrix by which subjects are formed thus requires the simultaneous production of a domain of abject beings, those who are not yet 'subjects,' but who form the constitutive outside to the domain of the subject" (*Bodies* xiii). This outside can be constructed by the act of stereotyping, and it is through the designation of the abject other that subjectivity is in turn produced and insider status attained and confirmed. In this view, the formation of the subject depends on the construction of difference between the self and others through the creation of stereotypical representations of social categories, such as for example race.

Historically, stereotypes of race have contributed to the ideological work of racism by pretending to stand in for reality and through the encouragement of the pretense that racial difference is real and definable. As such, the social construction of race is a projection of a set of fictions onto others with the intent of making them sufficiently different so as to be less threatening to the self's sense of identity and social group affiliation. In a phrase that explicitly suggests the imaginative nature of the conceptual work needed for the creation and preservation of racial difference and hierarchy, Wahneema Lubiano has likened this process of hegemonic assignment of identity to "being mugged by a metaphor" (64). In the absence of biological difference, racism as an ideologically inflected social construct thereby creates difference by employing largely visual signifiers to categorize subjects as either insiders or outsiders.[2] In visual systems of representation, these differences are often expressed in terms of binary oppositions that further simplify and stereotype the other as inferior and abject to the self. Because representations teach us how to see the world, what we see—and how we see it—is therefore inflected by the various hegemonic discourses of difference made operative in a specific context. In this vein, Michael D. Harris argues that "images help ideological constructions like race take form in the physical world. They construct, confirm, and affirm identity. When associated with power, images can impose and reiterate social and conceptual models on others" (14). Over time, different forms of representation have acquired their own sets of visual or verbal shorthand, in which a few stereotyped traits can be made to signify character, and the long history of racial stereotypes in the comics form is among the many "regimes of visuality" (Wallace 344) that has served to establish and enforce boundaries by way of minimizing individual difference while exaggerating group difference.

Since the beginning of mass media newspaper comic strips in the late nineteenth century, comics have developed and worked with a set of visual codes that allows the form to communicate efficiently and immediately through stereotypical representation of the world. Moreover, the stereotypes that often constitute the physiognomic representation of people in the comics form are intimately related to the development of caricature in the late sixteenth century.[3] In a foundational work on caricature, art historian E. H. Gombrich discusses how the modern history of the visual arts is in some respects a move away from the "circumspect and even heavy technique" (331) of naturalism and toward a more pronounced reliance on simplicity, with the discovery that "once the requisite mental set was established among the beholders, the careful observation of all clues was not only redundant but something of a hindrance" (332).[4] Stereotypical visual caricature, in this view, is a shortcut to meaning employed by the pictorial artist in order to communicate clearly, directly, and unambiguously. Gombrich's analysis of this "emancipation from the study of nature" leads him to note that it "was first tried out in the licensed precincts of humor and elucidated in the experiments of Töpffer" (356). Rodolphe Töpffer was a Swiss schoolteacher and caricaturist whose humorous pictorial narratives from the 1820s and 1830s are often considered the first examples of comics art. The experiments Gombrich refers to are a series of drawings contained in Töpffer's theoretical *Essai de physiognomonie* from 1845. While Töpffer was dismissive of the contemporary scientific practice of phrenology, he was intensely interested in how character and personality could be conveyed in drawing through the use of stereotypes and caricature. As such, the *Essai* includes many examples of how slight variations in nose, chin, and other facial and bodily features contribute to the impression of difference in character. In short, Töpffer believed that cartooning could be a way of exposing the "soul" of an individual through the distillation of traits into caricatured stereotype, and he therefore experimented with reducing the human face and figure to its essentials, in order to show that a few well-placed or exaggerated elements can suggest personality.[5] This idea is familiar from both contemporary comics theory and commentary by practitioners, and is one that has unmistakable implications for the depiction of race in the form.

Perhaps the most influential theory regarding this kind of iconic abstraction is Scott McCloud's ideas about what he calls "amplification through simplification" (30). McCloud's central tenet is that we are prone to seeing ourselves in any shape that resembles the human form or facial expressions, and that "by stripping down an image to its essential 'meaning,' an artist can amplify that meaning in a way that realistic art can't" (30). Comics art, McCloud believes, relies on simplified iconic abstraction and thus depends on reductionist and stereotyped imagery in order to communicate simply and without contradiction. Similarly, Will Eisner points out that "the stereotype is a fact of life in the comics medium" and argues that the need to communicate quickly (as compared, he notes, to the relatively slow pace of film) "makes necessary the simplification of images into repeatable symbols.

Ergo, stereotypes" (*Graphic Storytelling* 17).[6] Likewise, Art Spiegelman contends that "since cartoons are a visual sign language, the stereotype is the basic building block of all cartoon art" (*Comix* 99). Eisner calls this reliance on simplified stereotype "an accursed necessity" (*Graphic Storytelling* 17), and Spiegelman—in an essay about the cartoons depicting Muhammad that appeared in the Danish newspaper *Jyllands-Posten* in 2005 and caused an international controversy with reverberations that are still ongoing—is similarly frustrated with this inevitability of the form: "Cartoon language is mostly limited to deploying a handful of recognizable visual symbols and clichés. It makes use of the discredited pseudo-scientific principles of physiognomy to portray character through a few physical attributes and facial expressions" ("Drawing" 45).[7] Drawn cartoon images thus, as Marc Singer has cogently put it, "rely upon visually codified representations in which characters are continually reduced to their appearances" (107). The idea that personality and character can be portrayed through the abbreviated and stereotyped visual shorthand of cartoon imagery is one that is strikingly similar to the systems of representation used to construct and justify human racial exclusion, a predicament that is central to much of the work making up the visual history of the comics form.

In a North American context, cartoon imagery in either comics or related forms has historically been associated with ethnic and racist stereotypes, to the point where one tradition is often inseparable from the other. As acclaimed cartoonist Chris Ware notes about contemporary comics, "its strongest roots are . . . in an arcane system of 19th century physiognomy and racial caricature" (8). Elsewhere Ware comments specifically about the form's reliance on racial and ethnic caricature, writing that "a great part of the 'visual rush' of comics is at least partially, if not almost entirely, founded in racial caricature. If you look at many early comic strips, they're endemically 'ethnic.' Abie the Agent is obviously a Jewish caricature. Happy Hooligan is an Irish caricature. And black caricatures obviously go back to the minstrel days and earlier. Even Mickey Mouse" (qtd. in Juno 41). Compared to today's much more uniformly white strips, early newspaper strips like those mentioned by Ware were relatively ethnoracially varied but traded almost without exception in noxious caricature and stereotype.[8] Tied to an exclusionary logic of representing unfamiliar people in an attempt to ensure, as Henry B. Wonham has argued, that "ethnic identities remain fixed and discernible in the bewildering flux of multiethnic society" (26), these early comics art stereotypes largely followed immigration patterns and in addition to African Americans therefore included representations of such groups as the Chinese, Irish, and Italians. Even a cursory examination of early comics such as R. F. Outcault's famous *Hogan's Alley* (home of the Yellow Kid and commonly considered to be the first newspaper comic) or the classic *Little Nemo* strips by Winsor McKay reveals a strong reliance on racial and ethnic caricature that insists on visually codifying boundaries between population groups—a tendency that is even more prevalent in such half-forgotten early strips as *Darktown Comics, The Gallus Coon, Pore Lil Mose,* and *Sambo and His Funny Noises.*[9] So entrenched were the various stereotypes that Frederick Burr Opper, the creator of *Happy Hooligan,* could write about "caricature country" in 1901:

> Colored people and Germans form no small part of the population of Caricature Country. The negroes spend much of their time getting kicked by mules, while the Germans, all of whom have large spectacles and big pipes, fall down a good deal and may be identified by the words, "Vas iss," coming out of their mouths. There is also a sprinkling of Chinamen, who are always having their pigtails tied to things; and a few Italians, mostly women, who have wonderful adventures while carrying enormous bundles on their heads. The Hebrew residents of Caricature Country, formerly numerous and amusing, have thinned out of late years, it is hard to say why. This is also true of the Irish dwellers, who at one time formed a large percentage of the population. (778)

The reason for the gradual disappearance of the Irish and Jews from the comics pages, as Opper was probably well aware despite his assumed naiveté (he was, after all, the creator of a strip lampooning the former), was most likely that the increased social status of those groups made them more difficult to ridicule and marginalize in a humor strip.[10] In this way, Opper's comment bears witness to the social power of the early comic strips to make known and exclude an ever-changing immigrant proletariat. As Wonham argues, such early ethnoracial caricatures "served to delineate the boundaries of legitimate citizenship for a culture unsure of its claim to authority. By denying sentient personhood to others, the caricaturist shored up the embattled bourgeois self, restoring confidence in the unstable margins of a vaguely discernible 'American' identity" (31). The history of comics art stereotyping is therefore also the visual history of the shifting social status of different ethnoracial groups in American society and beyond. At times, however, the form has been used as a vehicle for outright racial propaganda intended to portray the inferiority of other peoples and to uphold existing hierarchies. As Bradford W. Wright argues, for example, the popular jungle comics genre of the 1930s "showed the reductionist comic book style at its ugliest . . . and posed justification for Western colonial domination and white supremacy enforced through violence" (36–37). Similarly, with the birth of the comic book superhero coinciding with World War II, stereotypical representations of Germans and Japanese dominated the war, and spy stories portrayed heroic and square-jawed white Americans fighting the racialized enemy both abroad and in the form of fifth columns operating within the nation's borders. To borrow a phrase from Michael A. Chaney, ethnoracial comics art stereotyping has in this way historically functioned to reduce the visibly other to a "generic truncation" (*Fugitive* 6) that eliminates individuality and clearly marks its subjects as amusing outsiders or outright enemies.

Portraying the ethnoracial other in a humorous or demeaning way as deformed and intellectually inferior, however, is part of a larger tradition of comedy in America. As Menachem Feuer explains, "ethnic bodies and faces have been the mainstay of comedy since the minstrel show and Vaudeville. To be sure, expressions of the comic body, found in the exaggeration and caricature of physiognomy, speech, and gesture show an overlapping of entertainment and racism, and have constituted the signs of ethnicity" (88). Comics imagery stands out in this history, however, because of its ability to distill, distort, and standardize visual identity into basic and often hugely exaggerated stereotypical forms that are presumed to function as expressions of character. Such nineteenth-century cartoon staples as the black Sambo stereotype and the simian Irishman in turn reconfigure, fix, and iconize identity in a way that a live stage or musical performance cannot. Because the aesthetic program of caricature, as Wonham shows, understands its function "in terms of 'penetration' and 'exposure'" and claims "a unique capacity to lay bare the 'essence' of the human subject" (9), comics art is in an exceptionally troublesome position in terms of depicting ethnoracial difference neutrally and respectfully.

If, as these considerations of comics form and history suggest, comics communicate in a visual language that is dependent on the stereotyped externalization of presumed interiority and are therefore inflected with the same principles as those that uphold hegemonic racist hierarchies, a pertinent question is whether the form is almost by default a tool of racist ideology and a vehicle for marginalization. Historically, commentators on comics have often pointed to what they perceive as the potential of the highly visual form to transmit harmful and unchallenged cultural messages of ethnoracial difference. Fredric Wertham, for example, much like his concerns about the possible homosexual subtext of certain comics (which I discussed in chapter 3), believed that comics art has the potential to instill "false stereotypes of race prejudice" (105) in unsuspecting and impressionable children. This view became a central argument in Wertham's *Seduction of the Innocent*, in which he also claimed that comic books "expose children's minds to an endless stream of prejudice-producing images" that might lead to outright "race hatred" (100). From reading comic books, Wertham further observed, children learn that

> there are two kinds of people: on the one hand is the tall, blond, regular-featured man sometimes disguised as a superman . . . and the pretty young blonde girl with the super-breast. On the other hand are the inferior people: natives, primitives, savages, "ape men," Negroes, Jews, Indians, Italians, Slavs, Chinese and Japanese, immigrants of every description, people with irregular features, swarthy skins, physical deformities, Oriental features . . . The brunt of this imputed inferiority in whole groups of people is directed against colored people and "foreign born." (101)

Wertham was so persuasive in his argument that children internalize ethnoracial categories from the caricatured stereotypes of the foreign other found in comic books that the Comics Code of 1954 included a clause stipulating that "Ridicule or attack on any religious or racial group is never permissible" (qtd. in Nyberg 167). In the same way that Wertham's influence on the code helped to effectually ban the portrayal of (intended or otherwise) homosexual themes, a much more positive outcome was the attempt to limit the damaging racial stereotypes that had for so long been part of the comics form's stock-in-trade. Viewed in a certain light, the inclusion of this clause therefore also functioned as something of an implicit acknowledgment by the industry-backed code that comics both relied on such damaging visual stereotypes and had the potential to contribute to the visual codification and marginalization of certain ethnoracial groups.

The question of how to use a visual language that both formally and historically relies on reductive visual shorthand to represent race is especially vexing for authors of autobiographical comics. Writing generally about the representation of African Americans in comics, Rebecca Wanzo argues that "the phenotypic excesses of caricature produce challenges for creators of black characters, who recognize that blacks are always already stereotyped when their bodies are represented" (97). Similarly, bell hooks notes in the broader context of visual culture at large that "creating counter-hegemonic images of blackness that resist the stereotypes and challenge the artistic imagination is not a simple task . . . since there is no body of images, no tradition to draw on" (96). Although both Wanzo and hooks focus their analyses on images of African Americans, the challenge for all groups that have historically been marginalized in and by comics art is to find a visual language adequate to the task of portraying difference on their own terms. For creators of autobiographical comics, the stakes of this challenge are especially high, since personal identity and the expression of subjectivity are both on the line. As David Palumbo-Liu puts it, to be personally associated with an already existing stereotypical representation is akin to "stepping into a narrative-in-progress, of being cast in a role that has been worked out and placed into the realm of a naturalized assumption" (767). But while the seriality and multimodality of comics offer certain opportunities for the radical depiction of femininity in the comics of Julie Doucet, for example, and enable Al Davison's transformative insistence upon depicting his visibly different body, El Rassi's engagement with the "narrative-in-progress" of Arab stereotypes throughout *Arab in America* is one of direct and confrontational appropriation—a strategy that in turn allows him to reflect on the form's complicity in constructing and empowering such stereotypes, as well as on their potentially productive possibilities.

Although for historical reasons not as ubiquitous as stereotypes of African Americans, depictions of Arabs in American visual culture similarly tend to rely on exclusionary and derogatory stereotypes. But where offensive African American stereotypes have in recent decades become significantly less acceptable in the culture, this has not been the case for both Arabs and Arab Americans. As Shelley Slade recognizes, "Arabs remain one of the few ethnic groups who can still be slandered with impunity in America" (143).[11] In *Arab in America*, El Rassi himself similarly notes that "Americans tend to dislike Arabs or people who are mistaken for Arabs. In fact I think racism against Arabs is one of the few prejudices that is not only tolerated but sometimes actively encouraged" (29). In the comic, El Rassi examines many such examples from popular culture, ranging from war films depicting conflict in the Middle East, like *Courage under Fire* and *Rules of*

Engagement, to the Star Wars villain Jabba the Hut, "who lounges in his lair with his harem of slave girls" and "even smokes a water pipe" (45). In comic books, as Jack G. Shaheen has noted after examining several hundred examples, representations of Arab characters are equally disparaging, and typically fall into the three categories of "the repulsive terrorist, the sinister sheikh or the rapacious bandit." Visually, too, Arabs are negatively stereotyped, Shaheen notes, and are drawn with features that are "frequently bestial, demonized and dehumanized" and faces dripping with "hatred and fanaticism" ("Arab Images" 123). Given a tradition of representation—in comics and in the culture at large—that is both thematically and visually hostile, El Rassi could perhaps be expected to attempt evasion of such imaginary capture through formal experimentation. Instead of attempting resignification through sequential unruliness or visual fluidity, however, El Rassi's choice to autobiographically align himself with injurious imagery means that the reader is repeatedly and incessantly confronted with the marginalizing power of such stereotypes on nearly every page.

In the same way that the original meaning of the word *stereotype* refers to a mold from which identical printings can be made, the Arab stereotype employed by El Rassi is consistent throughout the comic, where it is used to illustrate the extent to which it has become an almost inescapable way of seeing Arabs in American society and visual culture. In addition to its Semitic features, El Rassi's autobiographical portrayal of himself as an Arab stereotype relies on the thick lines delineating his face and hair. Combined with the heavy blacks of his eyes, eyebrows, and beard, these make him stand out on the page when compared to other characters, who are often drawn with markedly lighter lines and less shading. In the classroom scene mentioned above, for example, the drawing of El Rassi is significantly more visually pronounced than the background characters' thin outline and the relatively indistinct impression made by the sketchy face and vacant eyes of the teacher. In images such as these El Rassi uses the form to illustrate both how his dark features make him stand out and how America sees him only according to a preformed stereotype. Early in the narrative, El Rassi describes how he first experienced the feeling of being conspicuously and visually Arab in his mostly white environment when he watched a videotape of an eighth grade school performance and noticed that "in sharp contrast to the angelic white faces arrayed in the chorus, the dark splotch on the grainy tape was me" (6). Here El Rassi's comic brings to mind W. E. B. DuBois's concept of the "double-consciousness" of African Americans, which produces a "sense

FIG. 5.3. El Rassi meditates on how we are viewed by others, from *Arab in America*.

of always looking at one's self through the eyes of others" (3). In this way, the pages of *Arab in America* work analogously to the video recording, and the comic represents El Rassi's book-length engagement with what it feels like to stand out and be visually different from white mainstream culture. As El Rassi notes, "Who we are is in large part determined by how we are viewed by others and apparently, 'scary' or threatening is how most Americans see me" (76). This point is expressed above an image of Toufic in an art gallery, where he is looking at a painting of a grotesquely deformed face that, in this context, appears to mirror and reflect his otherwise nonthreatening appearance back to him through the disfiguring eyes of white American culture (see fig. 5.3). Informed by an awareness of the power of visuals to distort through stereotyping, El Rassi's drawing shows how his individual subjectivity is both warped and denied by preformed imagery imposed upon him by the culture, and the comic as a whole consequently sets out to explore this issue.

FIG. 5.4. A cartoon displayed by El Rassi's high school teacher, from *Arab in America*.

The close relationship between El Rassi's self-portraits and the Arab stereotype is further made clear in a number of drawings directly commenting on such representations. After noting that one of his high school teachers had a cartoon pinned to the wall behind his desk, El Rassi draws his recollection of it (see fig. 5.4). The drawing shows an American soldier threatening an Arab man with a machine gun in order to take his oil, and while the cartoon in this context reverses the stereotype of violence (in a way presumably not intended by the teacher), it also points to the similarity between the drawing of the oil sheikh and El Rassi's self-portrait. Exhibiting similar facial hair, eyebrows, eyes, and nose, and drawn in the same three-quarter profile, the sheikh is only by a slight degree more caricatured than Toufic himself. In another set of drawings appearing later in the narrative, El Rassi similarly and purposefully mobilizes noxious Arab stereotypes at their worst, and in ways that explicitly call to mind Shaheen's examples of the sinister sheikh-bandit-terrorist (see fig. 5.5). As such, the four drawings depict stereotypes of Arabs as "inveterate liars, greedy schemers," "oversexed maniacs with multiple wives," "crazed religious fanatics," and "stupid savages" (39). Compared to the teacher's cartoon, it is evident that once again the effect has been achieved through only a slight further exaggeration of certain features. The weight of a few lines and the curve of the nose in these drawings make all the difference, and the three levels of stereotype—from Toufic to oil sheikh to sword-wielding oversexed religious fanatic—thereby

FIG. 5.5. Common stereotypes of Arabs, from *Arab in America*.

illustrate the easy slippage between the more realistically drawn self-portraits and the ready-made comics stereotypes whose shadows they struggle to escape. For racialized faces in comics, El Rassi suggests, even a realistic self-portrait carries the potential to be read negatively because of its implicit relationship with an extended history and visual tradition of stereotyped caricature in the form.

Throughout the comic El Rassi further explores how the culture's many derogatory stereotypes of Arabs both precede him and ultimately exclude him from being accepted as an American. Doing so, he uses both images and explanatory narration to show that his association with such stereotypes means that he has been variously identified in interpersonal encounters as, for example, a "street thug," an "uneducated immigrant," and a "sexual pervert who wants nothing more than to molest your daughter" (77) (see fig. 5.6). In these images El Rassi simply adds his stereotyped face to drawings depicting these characters and thereby demonstrates how easily such representations of Arabs are accepted by visual culture, even in the context of an autobiographical narrative from the point of view of someone who does not otherwise embody any of those stereotypes. Unsurprisingly, however, El Rassi's most commonly encountered Arab stereotype is that of Muslim terrorist, as associated especially and most notably with the events of September 11, 2001. In a full-page image that appears to be a drawn copy of a front page of the *Chicago Tribune* depicting the faces of the suspected terrorists from September 11, El Rassi inserts his own face among the others, and asks: "Could the average American distinguish me from a Muslim terrorist? I saw the photos of the hijackers and the fact is . . . they looked like me, and the images appeared everywhere" (19) (see fig. 5.7). While the cartoon portraits on the *Tribune*'s front page are copied from photographs, they resemble classic stereotypes in that they minimize individual difference while exaggerating common traits like dark eyes, heavy eyebrows, prominent facial hair, and long and distinctive noses. As seen through the equalizing art of black and white cartooning, El Rassi himself blends perfectly into this company, and it is only through the context of the narrative as provided by the rest of the comic that we can recognize his face as standing out from these terrorist-labeled portraits. Lacking both this context and an interest in looking beyond the stereotype, white America at large sees him only through the distorting prism of the media-disseminated stereotype of the Muslim terrorist.

FIG. 5.6. El Rassi adds his own face to common stereotypes of Arabs, from *Arab in America*.

FIG. 5.7. Toufic in the company of the 9/11 hijackers, from *Arab in America*.

FIG. 5.8. Toufic and a more religious friend, from *Arab in America*.

Continuing his exploration of the affinity between his own appearance and such stereotypes, on the following page El Rassi provides close-ups of the face, eyes, and mouth of Mohamed Atta, one of the lead hijackers, and comments that "his menacing, grimacing photo must have been a godsend for the media which did not pass up any opportunity to display the photogragh [*sic*] on every news report" (20). In these images El Rassi searches for the visual traits that finger someone as a terrorist in the semiotic game of tag that constitutes popular discourse on Arabs in post-9/11 America, and concludes that stereotypical regimes of seeing—such as, for example, certain styles of comics imagery—have obliterated the culture's ability to perceive individual difference when contemplating Arab faces. Similarly, in a further example of how the stereotypic signs of Islamic fundamentalism and terrorism can overwhelm individual subjectivity, El Rassi draws himself and a friend in two juxtaposed panels (see fig. 5.8). While El Rassi is relatively irreligious, the friend, Ahmed, is unashamed and even confrontational about his Muslim faith, and wears a full beard and a taqiyah on his head. With the drawings mirroring each other, however, the resemblance between the two men is striking, and illustrates how a small amount of facial hair and a cap can amplify identification with the fundamentalist/ terrorist stereotype. The implication is that mainstream society and media discourse are largely both unable and unwilling to differentiate between the two appearances, and that El Rassi's in many ways average American disposition is therefore easily subsumed into a different category and associated with Muslim terrorism.

In scenes such as this, El Rassi thus visually—in real life as well as in comics art—steps into the well-established "narrative-in-progress" of the Arab terrorist constructed by stereotyped representations in popular media. According to Evelyn Alsultany, the stereotype of the Arab as terrorist solidified with the events of the 1972 Munich Olympics and the Iran hostage crisis of 1979, the latter of which was also, she argues, "an important moment in conflating Arab, Muslim, and Middle Eastern identities" (9).[12] Examples of such conflation in popular culture are numerous, and include people speaking Arabic on the streets of Pakistan in the film *Zero Dark Thirty* and the comic book character the Joker wearing a traditional Arab headdress when appointed as the Iranian ambassador to the UN in the classic Batman story *A Death in the Family*. Such a conflation of ethnic, religious, and political identities has been key, Alsultany argues, in establishing an Arab/Muslim "look" that enables both a general marginalization and such specific phenomena as the widespread racial stereotyping and profiling experienced by people of numerous different ethnoracial backgrounds after September 11, 2001 (9–10). In *Arab in America*'s most striking example of such conflation, El Rassi rides the subway next to a man wearing what appears to be a Sikh turban and who is reading a Hindi newspaper. Such ethnic, linguistic, and cultural subtlety, however, is lost on two young men who enter the car and immediately start verbally abusing the newspaper-reading man by calling him "Osama" and asking him: "You gonna blow us up?" (84). The combination of turban and facial hair, along with a dark complexion, here serves to metonymically stereotype the man as a terrorist, indistinguishable from popularized images of what was at the time the world's most wanted man in the same way that El Rassi looked similar to the 9/11 hijackers on the *Tribune*'s front page. Adding another layer of conflation, El Rassi repeatedly draws himself looking similar to the verbally abused man and even juxtaposes these panels on the page (see fig. 5.9). As well as providing the suggestion that he could as easily have been the object of the verbal attack, El Rassi's deconstructive deployment of such images once again draws attention to the difference-obliterating potential of the Arab/Muslim stereotype from the point of view of white America.

In addition to being a product of carelessness and ignorance, however, such conflation of course also serves an ideological purpose. As Alsultany

FIG. 5.9. Toufic is juxtaposed to a man who is verbally abused because of his appearance, from *Arab in America*.

argues, "projecting all Muslims as one very particular type: fanatical, misogynistic, anti-American" constructs an opposition between enlightened subjects and primitive objects: "With this conflation established, it is easy to conceptualize the United States as the inverse of everything that is 'Arab/Muslim': The United States is thus a land of equality and democracy, culturally diverse and civilized, a land of progressive men and liberated women" (9). The Arab/Muslim world is in this way constructed stereotypically as the outside to the enlightened and civilized West—as the abject other that ensures the formation of the American self. Similarly, the establishment of difference can also be a shortcut to acceptance for groups marginalized by mainstream culture. In the same way that groups such as the Irish and Italians gradually became assimilated into white American society through a juxtaposition to other and more visibly different groups, the construction of the conflated Arab/Muslim/terrorist stereotype allows for easy scapegoating and subsequent attainment of insider status through the designation of an abject and un-American other.

In *Arab in America* El Rassi depicts an encounter that functions in just this way. The scene begins with him declaring: "Most Americans don't know what an Arab is. In the week after the [September 11, 2001] attacks, I took comfort being in Chicago's diverse neighborhoods" (16). After a man asks him in Spanish whether he has a light, Toufic first replies that he does not speak Spanish and then, after the request is repeated in English, lights the man's cigarette. Noting that "being ambiguous to Americans can also be a problem" (16), Toufic is then asked by the man if he is Pakistani. Unthinkingly, he first agrees to this interpellation, but as El Rassi points out, "I immediately knew he meant to say Palestinian since the 2 nationalities are often confused since they sound similar" (17). The man subsequently asks: "You a terrorist motherfucker?" (17), and despite Toufic's protestations maintains that "Yes you are. I saw your fuckin' ass on TV" (17). The aggressive man eventually calls for his friends to join the confrontation, and although Toufic escapes unharmed the scene illustrates how various national, ethnic, and political identities are conflated into one—namely the "terrorist motherfucker"—in post-9/11 America. Moreover, the encounter demonstrates the unstable nature of ethnoracial categories of inclusion and exclusion. By first addressing Toufic in Spanish, the man apparently presumes a Latino heritage. When an opportunity arises to instead identify and stereotype Toufic as Pakistani/Palestinian, the man immediately calls him a terrorist and thereby certifies his own inclusion as an insider defending America by identifying its enemies. Although the man was himself initially marked as an outsider by his use of Spanish (in the context of the wider culture, at least, although perhaps not in this specific neighborhood), the mobilization of the conflated Arab/Muslim/terrorist stereotype—supported as it is by pundits calling for the racial profiling of Arabs, the official policy of the War on Terror, and the military invasion of Arab/Muslim countries, all in the name of national security—allows him to temporarily identify with official society and assert relative interpersonal power. By drawing himself as corresponding in key ways with the conflated and popularly imagined "look" of the Arab terrorist, El Rassi thus willingly contributes to this misidentification in order to point to the difficulty of escaping the association with this stereotype in a society that continually treats him as an outsider because of his appearance and ethnic background.

Since El Rassi is marked visually as an outsider in America, he feels deprived of identity and a sense of belonging. Noting that "After being ashamed and rejected in the U.S. for so long many Muslims and Arabs find ways to deal with being alienated" (75), El Rassi then outlines his own personal crisis: "I had no idea who I was. American? Arab? I spoke English perfectly and grew up here in the midst of this culture but I did not belong here and I knew that" (75). To illustrate his inability to blend in, El Rassi depicts himself as occupying two different visual identities recognized by American society. The first of these is Rambo, a symbol of extreme American masculinity as well as bodily and technological superiority. Next to the Rambo posters, however, El Rassi appears as almost the inverse of this representation, with a worried look and weak, slouching shoulders (see fig. 5.10). Transposing his stereotyped face onto Rambo's body in the next panel further illustrates the point. Here the odd-looking drawing demonstrates that the stereotyped face of the Arab/Muslim is not as easily associated with idealized American heroism as it is with the aforementioned street thugs and terrorists. In a further example of the comic's use of pointed imagery to draw attention to the visual contrasts between the Arab stereotype and culturally accepted American identities, El Rassi's second attempt to occupy such a position is his cultivation, during his teenage tears, of "a punk-hippie look" inspired by an Iranian friend "who went out of his way to conceal his ethnicity" (69). As evidenced by both the humorous drawing and El Rassi's dry observation that this experiment "didn't work out" (69), the comic makes clear that not even the otherwise leveling effect of belonging to an oppositional and highly visible subculture is able to make him a recognizable insider in an already oppositional culture. Unable to identify with either mainstream or alternative positions, El Rassi is the ultimate outsider in American society, a position he finally both welcomes and explores through his insistence upon drawing himself as a largely unchanging stereotype in the pages of *Arab in America*.

El Rassi's strategy of self-representation thereby departs significantly both from those of the other artists discussed in this study and most scholarly arguments concerning the potential of serialized comics imagery to subvert or destabilize ethnoracial stereotypes. As Jared Gardner notes, "A single-panel cartoon gag of an ethnic or racial stereotype is contained by its frame . . . it is static and resists ambiguity, directing the reader to very specific ways of reading." Gardner adds that "Reading that same image in sequential comics becomes, inevitably, a more complicated and unruly enterprise" ("Same Difference" 136). Similarly, Derek Parker Royal emphasizes the form's spatialization of time and argues that "where readers see the character development across panels, comics can underscore the fluidity of ethnic identity" (10). While both Gardner and Royal are therefore optimistic about the potential of the serial form to oppose or otherwise destabilize racial stereotypes, both arguments assume that the desired outcome is a certain fluidity of visual representation. But where Ariel Schrag, for example, uses the full visual potential of the form to represent herself in multiple and variable ways throughout her extended high school narrative—which is also, to a large degree, *thematically* about her changing and in-progress queer self—the

I SHOULD MENTION THAT I DIDN'T ALWAYS FEEL THIS WAY; DURING THE 1980s, ACTION STAR SYLVESTER STALLONE MADE A SERIES OF VERY POPULAR FILMS THAT CAPTURED MY IMAGINATION. I WAS SUCH A BIG FAN OF RAMBO THAT THE WALLS OF MY ROOM WERE ADORNED BY THE MOVIE POSTERS.

AS A BOY, I REALLY WANTED TO "SERVE MY COUNTRY" AND BE A SOLDIER BUT THE GULF WAR CHANGED ALL THAT FOR ME. THE PROSPECT (IN FACT THE LIKELIHOOD) THAT I WOULD BE KILLING FELLOW ARABS ONE DAY JUST DID NOT APPEAL TO ME.

FIG. 5.10. El Rassi considers the heroism of Rambo, from *Arab in America*.

performance of the autobiographical self as constantly in flux might at times run counter to the project of realistically representing lived experience. For artists of color like El Rassi, the visual depiction of the self as fluid and lacking in stability might also go against certain cultural or social attachments at the same time that it does little to redress the fundamental injustice of treating people who look a certain way differently. In other words, compared to Schrag's queering and stylistically experimental use of the comics form, people whose bodies are visibly different might have significantly more to lose by letting go of visual specificity and consistency. In the examples of Doucet and Davison, it is therefore also the very insistence upon the specific nature of their embodiment (as, respectively, a woman and a man living with a visible impairment) that both gives rise to the visual power of their comics and provides them with occasions for resisting dominant cultural narratives about what it means to look a certain way. For Arabs and other ethnoracial outsiders in America, however, that same insistence may lead to injurious stereotyping that can be difficult to unfix serially or multimodally.

When considering the specifics of ethnoracial representation in autobiographical comics, it is also worth remembering that theories about the ability of seriality to potentially undo fixed representations rely upon versions of McCloud's concept of closure, which leaves much of the meaning making to the imagination of the reader. While an artist's skilled pen might guide resistant readings and help form radical interpretations of some visual identities, however, the virulence and extended history of racist stereotypes mean that they may be less open to reconfiguration than other categories. After hundreds of years of stereotyped imagery working to visually distill certain groups to a derogatory and iconic essence, those representations have become so deeply embedded in the culture that they are exceptionally difficult to unsettle. Consider, for example, the critical debate about the representation of African American characters in the comics of Robert Crumb. As Corey Creekmur notes about such images, using the notorious example of Crumb's character Angelfood McSpade, "While the sort of hip reader underground artists imagined themselves to be might find them ironic and satiric, a conservative reader might find them reassuring" (29). Consequently, Creekmur concludes about Crumb's comics that "Insofar as their reception seems to persistently allow for both responses (as well as others, perhaps), we may have to admit that both meanings are always allowed by images that draw upon a fraught and volatile history of representation" (30). In such highly charged images, therefore, which also include the various representations of Arabs discussed by El Rassi, seriality and repetition run the risk of merely restating ideologically troublesome visual stereotypes in a replication of the process that enabled their marginalizing powers in the first place.

Because the constant repetition of stereotypes is central to their power—as Homi Bhabha explains, a stereotype "vacillates between what is always 'in place,' already known, and something that must be anxiously repeated" (66)—the serial nature of comics imagery means that even if characters take on an increased humanity through narrative, each new visual iteration will always be in danger of succumbing to (and serving as an expression of) the same racism that informs its underlying model. For creators of autobiographical comics like El Rassi, this issue is especially troubling, since the symbolic power of the stereotype to subsume all expressions of individuality and subjectivity under its totalizing and hegemonic system of representation means that there is very little opportunity to perform it differently to subversive effect. Instead, variations of the self may simply become variations of the stereotype.

For El Rassi, finding himself in a marginalizing culture that is largely unable to see past the Arab stereotype—and using a visual language that similarly relies, in Gombrich's phrase, on "the absence of contradictory clues" (336) for its effects—the way out of this predicament is not through serial fluidity but instead through defiant appropriation of the very codes that serve to exclude him. Regarding such appropriation of racist imagery, Bridget R. Cooks has asked: "How are images of the racialized spectacle (specifically by artists who are socially constructed as spectacle) able to make successful interrogations of their own construction? In what ways can images of spectacle be used to support a reading that challenges the social order's dominant racial meaning?" (70). In this formulation, Cooks's equation of racial stereotype with spectacle brings to mind chapter 1's discussion of how women artists can turn the spectacle of femininity on its head. Although important differences exist, of course, between the representation of women and the racial other in comics, Kerry Soper has drawn on the same body of Bakhtinian theory concerning carnival and the grotesque to suggest that minstrelsy and the wearing of certain masks—such as blackface by black performers—can constitute a "playful exploration of the freedom of being the other, of inverting societal roles, of incorporating subcultures into the dominant culture, or of using the license of the mask to disrupt (albeit temporarily) the rules of the dominant social order" (262). Much like how the unruly visual language of the comics form allows Doucet to perform a series of alternative expressions of femininity, the wearing of the unchanging mask of ethnoracial stereotype may therefore give rise to subversive expressions of subjectivity in autobiographical comics. In this view, by putting on a mask and fully inhabiting the stereotype, El Rassi trades destabilization for reappropriation in a book-length portrayal of himself that takes much of its subversive power from the direct redeployment of representations originally intended to degrade and exclude him. At the same time, the very act of observing El Rassi self-consciously depicting himself as an injurious Arab stereotype draws attention to the ideological work of such representations in ways that stereotypical representations of Arabs by others do not. Although Harris cautions about such approaches that "Turning derogatory images in on themselves or inverting them to destabilize their meanings is not as effective as the performance of speech has been in undermining terms" (221), the ability of comics to supplement such images with verbal elements like dialogue and narration gives the form a potential advantage over purely visual cultural forms. While racist stereotypes, in this analysis, might never be entirely subverted or neutralized, their amplified redeployment by the very people they are meant to ridicule may, in combination with the verbal elements of the comics form, at least enable a critical engagement with such representations for as long as it takes to read—or draw—a comic.

By insisting on visual self-representation based in stereotype, El Rassi's comic does not constitute an attempt to reconfigure personal identity in order to achieve insider status. Instead, *Arab in America* functions as an appropriation of the Arab stereotype through an insistence upon those markers that serve to exclude him, in a process that also has implications for the formation of his own subjectivity in the context of visual autobiography. As Ann Miller argues, authors of autobiographical comics "may fetishize a particular manifestation of selfhood, a kind of scale model, and make it stand for totality" (250–251), and El Rassi's defiantly persistent use of the derogatory stereotype may therefore also suggest a certain fondness for it in the absence of the ability to unfix it from hegemonic cultural discourses. About the potential for such "injurious interpellations" to become a "site of radical reoccupation and resignification," Butler argues that "called by an injurious name, I come into social being, and because I have a certain inevitable attachment to my existence, because a certain narcissism takes hold of any term that confers existence, I am led to embrace the terms that injure me because they constitute me socially" (*Psychic Life* 104). In this view, and in the context of the comic, El Rassi's relationship with the Arab/Muslim stereotype is paradoxical because it serves to exclude him at the same time that it constitutes him as a cultural subject. In other words, the stereotype, though marginalizing, provides a place of identification and a subject position to inhabit.[13] Butler further claims that "only by occupying—being occupied by—that injurious term can I resist and oppose it, recasting the power that constitutes me as the power I oppose" (*Psychic Life* 104). In these terms, the stereotype inhabited autobiographically by El Rassi is not only constitutive of subjectivity in its ability to name him but also serves as the primary location for the oppositional rearticulation of its power. By giving voice *to* the stereotype, therefore, El Rassi is simultaneously voiced *by* the stereotype, in a visual performance of marginality that temporarily, at least, empowers him rhetorically.

For El Rassi, the strategy of representing himself from the point of view of hegemonic visual discourse, and as virtually indistinguishable from the conflating stereotype of the Arab/Muslim terrorist, finds perfect expression in the comics form, which has historically depended on exactly such visual shorthand. The result is an exploration of the power of visual stereotype to marginalize and exclude, as well as the facility with which it can preempt the construction of subjectivity in interpersonal encounters. Where Doucet, in her self-portrait as Medusa, proclaims an unruly and grotesquely excessive visual identity that provides a direct challenge to the reader's expectations of how a woman should look and act, the measured art and unvarying nature of El Rassi's autobiographical deconstruction of the stereotype forces introspection upon the reader through its identification of the sympathetic author with derogatory imagery literally drawn from the same representational system as injurious racial profiling. Through its subversive deployment of harmful and deindividualizing racist stereotypes, *Arab in America* thereby uses the comics form to expose the mechanism behind anti-Arab prejudice while also providing an opportunity for El Rassi to embrace the drawn stereotype in order to assert subjectivity as an Arab man in a marginalizing and hostile culture.

Conclusion

● ● ● ● ● ● ● ● ● ● ● ● ●

Making an Issue of Representation

An early sequence in Al Davison's *The Spiral Cage* takes place when the author is a child of about four. Hospitalized, Al meets a man who has suffered acute facial damage in a car accident. Observing the man's bandages, behind which only his eyes are visible, Al exclaims, "You're the Invisible . . man!!. Awn't you . . ." (55), a case of mistaken identity the man at first agrees to. After some initial jokes about avoiding men in dark glasses and big hats, the two become friends, but it is only when the man leaves the hospital that Al sees his face, which is severely scarred. In the context of the book, the episode suggests that people's appearances do not always correspond to their subjective experience of themselves and that how we see them is as much a result of our particular culturalization as it is of "objective" external reality. But the idea of the invisible man is also an apt metaphor for the comics autobiographer, who puts on a drawn cloak of visibility in order to be seen by the reader-observer. From this vantage point, autobiography functions as the disguise put on by the author to mask the lack of a stable referent underneath, a perspective that also suggests the role of life writing itself in the formation of identity. As Davison says elsewhere in the book, in a contemplative passage in which he draws himself looking at an earlier version of his comics memoir, "Funny things autobiographies . . You start out to record events in your life . . And the process, becomes an event in itself. Capable of transforming your perceptions of those previous events and even your life, itself . ." (115).

Simultaneously draping and shaping the self with the drawn character on the page, the comics autobiographer gives concrete form to slippery identity in a process that itself turns into a life event and thereby may come to play a significant role in the formation of selfhood and subjectivity going forward. For autobiographers like Davison and the others discussed in this book—all of whom are writing and drawing against visual traditions and social contexts that marginalize certain perspectives—this reflective engagement with depicting the self in comics form allows them to literally draw themselves into cultural visibility through the making of marks on a blank page. Crucially, the comics form's capacity for externalizing and structuring the experienced self onto the page in highly personal visual terms means that artists are brought face-to-face with their own subjectivities in an encounter that might not only influence how they shape and view their past selves but also creates new opportunities for self-representation in the present.

As these artists make clear, the representation of the self in the visual comics form is an inherently political undertaking, especially when it comes to bodies and subjectivities that are socially marginalized. In conventional comics traditions, this particularity of the form is typically suppressed or effaced, as bodies are made subject to both hegemonic cultural narratives and stylistic principles embracing unity and homogeneity. In a consideration of the tendency of mainstream superhero comics to provide an "illusion of change" by recasting established characters (who are almost always white, straight, and able-bodied men) in ways that may be considered diverse or progressive, Zak Roman and Ryan Lizardi conclude that "any time American superhero comics implement these kinds of conspicuous changes, the gay, feminine, or racially diverse iteration is almost always ephemeral, and also is frequently overtly subjugated" (19). Similarly, Ellen Kirkpatrick notes about the superhero genre's traditional approach to depicting the human body that it commonly "features all manner of material transformations and yet remains obsessed with rigidly and obviously gendered bodies" (126).

Noting the striking paradox of "so much stability in the face of so much flux," Kirkpatrick argues that in superhero comics, "gender norms and stability are performed and reperformed to such an extent that, through repetition, they become not only ubiquitous and 'naturalized' but also, I suggest, unseen, and by being unseen, they become unassailable and untouchable" (126). Kirkpatrick's argument thereby draws attention to the ability of the comics form to naturalize the power structures inherent in both its own visual language and, by extension, visual culture more broadly conceived. In this view, certain traditions of comics art function as potentially reactionary forces that anxiously suppress difference in the service of bodily and cultural containment or exclusion.

In the pages of this book I have discussed how the history of comics imagery is in many ways a history of exactly this type of cultural exclusion, whether in the form of, for example, the long tradition of ethnoracial stereotype or the privileging of conventionally feminine and explicitly sexualized female bodies in mainstream comics. Despite their many innovations and immense influence upon later generations of comics creators, including those considered in this volume, artists associated with the underground comix movement often also defaulted to misogynistic or racist imagery that served to reproduce various marginalizing and exclusionary cultural scripts. Most infamously, underground pioneer Robert Crumb's many comics and illustrations depicting his various sexual fantasies almost always involve the domination and humiliation of women, who are further objectified by Crumb's exaggeration of physical features such as breasts, legs, and buttocks. Similarly, Crumb's depictions of nonwhite characters often reduce those bodies to a set of signifiers that place them in a lineage of racist stereotype and caricature. While the underground revolution did much to establish comics as a form capable of telling individual and personal stories in words and pictures, it also somewhat unwittingly demonstrated just how intimately bound up comics imagery is with a long history of visual marginalization and how easy it can be for artists to slip into certain established but injurious representative traditions. From this perspective, the central issue that has animated this book's examination of autobiographical comics is the question of how to affirmatively represent a culturally marginalized self in a form that on the one hand privileges strategies of visual containment and homogeneity and on the other has traditionally relied on stereotypical shorthand and cartoony caricature for its effects.

In seeking to answer that question I have examined five artists whose life and work exist in different ways on the cultural and stylistic margins—that is, in addition to their creating comics from and about underrepresented perspectives, their artwork typically refuses to conform to conventional ideas about what "good" or "appropriate" comics art is supposed to look like. Throughout, I have focused my analysis on the particular opportunities the comics form provides to these artists in terms of challenging conventional representational schemes, especially in comparison with other forms of autobiography, such as prose and photography, and have argued that the hand-drawn aesthetics and multimodal mixing of visual and verbal elements provide a unique set of features with which to experiment with self-expression. Perhaps the key attribute of all comics representation is that it takes place in a fundamentally visual idiom, and therefore not only tells us about but also insists on *showing* bodies. By outlining how specific artists employ the visuality of comics to depict bodies in often novel and sometimes radical ways, I have demonstrated that the form can engage critically with notions of identity constructed visually through—and hegemonically imposed by—various cultural processes of exclusion and marginalization. I have shown that in combination with the heightened subjectivity implied by the individual creator's stylistic imprint as expressed in drawn imagery, the very same formal features that sometimes function to exclude certain perspectives can be turned on their heads and used to open up a space for individual expression, subversive experimentation, and more inclusive modes of representing difference.

Because the mechanisms that produce cultural exclusion and marginality are different for each of the artists discussed in this book, their approaches to using comics for self-expression are as heterogeneous as the lives they depict. Common to all, however, is an adventurous approach to form that takes advantage of the specific properties of comics to tell new stories in novel ways. As such, the artists examined here often experiment with the limits of comics imagery in ways that push the form in unexpected directions and which may therefore have the potential to unsettle established ways of representing and seeing bodies. In their different ways, these artists employ the comics form's narrative and visual potential to delineate and rephrase marginalized identities as subjective representations on the page in order to explore what can happen when the self is not only abstracted in language but also visualized in stylized images.

In the comics of Julie Doucet and Phoebe Gloeckner these experiments in autobiography consistently engage with the ways in which women's bodies and subjectivities are represented in both comics and the broader visual culture. Challenging masculine ideas of feminine decorum, as well as expectations concerning how women are expected to appear, Doucet and Gloeckner both use the comics form to oppose cultural frameworks that marginalize women's experiences. But while Doucet employs a rough and unruly visual style that actively asks readers to modify their conceptions of femininity, Gloeckner's more traditionally beautiful drawings invite the eye to look at and engage with scenarios of childhood sexual abuse that are commonly hidden from view. Similarly, where Doucet takes a punk-infused oppositional stance rooted in grotesque fantasy and in one instance even depicts the imagined castration of a male reader, Gloeckner's approach is both less overtly confrontational and more self-reflective as she employs the distinctive spatiotemporal features of comics to depict, sort through, and narrate her personal trauma. As two strikingly different examples of artists using the form to represent various aspects of female experience, the work of Doucet and Gloeckner together suggests how autobiographical comics can provide new and subjective perspectives that may upend certain cultural assumptions or visual conventions.

Compared to Doucet and Gloeckner's direct engagements with established ways of looking at and depicting women in both comics and the culture at large, the work of Ariel Schrag is concerned with using the form to catalog a life and a subjectivity undergoing rapid development. To that end, Schrag plays with the form's capacity for serial open-endedness to create a real-time narrative of her personal and artistic development from (mostly) heterosexual teenage high schooler to mature and experimental lesbian artist in full control of her work. Especially in *Likewise*, the concluding volume of her extended autobiographical project, Schrag experiments with form in ways that would be impressive for any comics artist but are especially so for someone who has just graduated high school. Writing against cultural traditions that devalue and often directly dismiss youthful perspectives, Schrag's experiments are never superficially gratuitous, but are employed in the service of her gradual queering of both herself and the extended comics autobiography. Similar in some respects to Doucet's idiosyncratic stylistic innovations and to Gloeckner's use of comics to simultaneously stage, examine, and present her past life for both herself and the reader, Schrag writes herself into a small but growing comics tradition at the same time that her work illustrates the potential of autobiographical comics to represent and make sense of open-ended lives and fluid identities.

For Al Davison, in contrast, the ability of comics to let him insist on a relatively stable visual identity far outweighs the potential benefits of serial fluidity, and he instead works to assert cultural visibility in the face of the social and medical discourses that have marginalized him because of his impairment. Similarly, where Doucet employs the form to present alternative femininities, Davison instead uses his comics autobiography to depict himself as precisely the type of masculine ideal he has been prevented from identifying with by ableist discourses that insist on seeing him as a cripple. Much like Doucet, however, Davison fully exploits the form's capacity for portraying bodily stances signifying strength and power, and also uses—in ways that are reminiscent of Gloeckner's intricate spatial grammar in crucial sequences—its structural and relational features to create expertly paced and laid-out pages that perform a virtual karate kick in the direction of the reader's attempted gaze. Although all of the artists considered in this study draw themselves addressing and looking at the reader, it is Davison who most consistently uses the form's visuality to stage what I have theorized as a counterstare, through which he is able to assert a measure of subjectivity and recalibrate the power balance between himself and anyone daring to look. The result is a comic that both invites attention and actively resists it, in a complex reading experience enabled by Davison's clever deployment of a wide range of formal features.

In the company of such bodily mutability and formal experimentation, Toufic El Rassi stands out because of his unvarying insistence upon depicting himself as an Arab stereotype throughout his comics memoir. Whereas the others draw themselves in ways that are often unpredictable, defiant, or even aggressively confrontational, El Rassi engages with the specific and virulent history of representing the ethnoracial other in comics and related forms by appropriating the very stereotype that is used to exclude him. Compared to Doucet, for example, who turns misogynistic traditions associated with women's bodies on their head through inversion and parodic excess, El Rassi patiently and soberly works to deconstruct the Arab stereotype by forcing the reader to consider both its historical prominence and contemporary ubiquity. Compared to Schrag's use of comics to destabilize and develop her visual appearance through formal play and open-ended seriality, El Rassi is unable to locate a space for experimenting with visible fluidity in the context of a visual culture that has so thoroughly colonized his

Arab features that it is incapable of reading his face as anything other than belonging to a "Muslim terrorist." As such, El Rassi's somewhat resigned memoir also points to certain limitations of the form itself, as it is always in conversation with other visual traditions that may at times threaten to overwhelm or otherwise impede attempts to reconfigure visual identity on the page. In this view, while the skilled comics artist might work to manipulate formal features and restate visual appearance in terms that are respectful and affirmative, such attempts are always at risk of going astray and playing into the hands of the very same marginalizing discourses they seek to oppose. As argued throughout this book, the artists whose work I examine largely escape such entrapment in their efforts to find new visual languages for depicting marginalized identities, but much of the form's disruptive potential stems directly from the ability of individual artists to manipulate the fluctuating give and take between established visual traditions and more diverse models of representation.

In sum, these artists use the comics form's many different and overlapping multimodal codes to make, in Christophe Menu's phrase, an "issue of representation" (qtd. in Groensteen, *Comics* 98) in ways that may in turn be experimental, messy, and excessive but never straightforward or predictable. Compared to the slickly drawn and brightly colored world of most mainstream comics, the visual styles of which are typically meant to allow for relatively unproblematic forward momentum through the narrative, the black-and-white comics of Doucet, Gloeckner, Schrag, Davison, and El Rassi bear the unmistakable stylistic imprint of their creators. As the personal and often volatile expressions of individual subjectivities, these confrontational and sometimes willfully difficult comics betray a lineage that goes back to the world of 1960s and 1970s underground comix at the same time that they point to more inclusive futures of the form. Indebted to the underground comix revolution in both form and content, these artists believe in the use of comics for personal expression and the depiction of subjective experience. But where the cartoonists behind the underground movement were overwhelmingly white, male, straight, and able-bodied, the artists I consider here approach the blank comics page with new and diverse perspectives that together challenge the traditions and assumptions of the form. By drawing in and from the margins and inserting their own lives into comics history, they push against established narrative conventions and visual traditions, and in the process invent new ways of seeing and being seen in comics.

In this book I have argued that the comics form contains an essentially infinite potential for drawing and representing lives that are multiple in every sense of the word. Writing and drawing in the 1980s, 1990s, and 2000s, the artists I discuss sit near the midpoint of the last half century's worth of alternative comics, and as such have already become part of the form's storied history, which new generations of artists must engage with in terms of both influence and opposition. As indicated by the last decade's explosion of autobiographical comics depicting a multitude of different experiences, a further revolution is well underway, a development that underscores this book's argument that the comics form is particularly well equipped to serve as a place to experimentally engage with and work out the various complex interfaces between the self and the world.

Acknowledgments

While my name alone appears on this book's cover, its writing would not have been possible without an extensive scholarly and personal network. For offering their valuable suggestions on the manuscript in its early stages, I am grateful to Sean Carney, Charles Hatfield, and Robert Schwartzwald. Charles, especially, has been extraordinarily generous with his input over the years, and the book is much stronger for it. As the book neared completion, I benefited tremendously from the expert comments of Michael Chaney and Dale Jacobs, both of whom helped me steer the manuscript in better directions. For their last-minute help with working through some structural issues, as well as for their friendship, Colin Beineke and Christina Maria Koch deserve an enormous thank-you.

I owe a special debt of gratitude to Bart Beaty and Nick Sousanis, who warmly welcomed me into their tiny bubble of comics studies when I was a postdoctoral scholar at the University of Calgary. Since we first met at a conference when I was a graduate student, Bart has been a mentor and a friend, and his constant support and generosity have been invaluable. As a fellow recent transplant to Calgary, Nick provided not only friendship but also some of the most stimulating conversations about comics I have ever had. Coteaching a course with him was a privilege that has profoundly impacted the way I approach comics in both my teaching and research. In Calgary, my many conversations with David Sigler helped shape the final form of the book, and I am thankful also for his friendship.

At the University of East Anglia I have benefited from the support of many colleagues in both the School of Art, Media and American Studies and beyond. Nick Grant, especially, has listened patiently to me talking about comics and has been a friend from the beginning, as have Hilary Emmett, Ross Hair, and Emma Long. A thank-you is also due to my fellow comics scholars across UEA—Rayna Denison, B. J. Epstein, Richard Hand, Miriam Kent, Ben Little, and Rachel Mizsei-Ward—for their conversations and support of this project. My students, too, at UEA as well as at the University of Calgary and OCAD University in Toronto, have provided often brilliant insights that helped give shape to my thoughts about comics.

Others who have been instrumental to the development of the ideas contained in this book, either through specific conversations or because they offered encouragement at crucial moments, include José Alaniz, Jonathan Crago, Corey Creekmur, Jared Gardner, Leigh Gilmore, Josh Kopin, Andrew Kunka, Ann Miller, Biz Nijdam, Tahneer Oksman, Ben Novotny Owen, Natalie Pendergast, Barbara Postema, Roger Sabin, and Susan Squier. I am thankful also to the scholars associated with the Nordic Network for Comics Research and the Canadian Society for the Study of Comics, who provided a professional context for my early work and confirmed to me that these ideas were worth pursuing.

A few friends have had an outsize impact on my academic career so far, including first and foremost Ole Birk Laursen, my oldest scholarly friend and recent coeditor. Without our regular conversations over the last almost twenty years, this book would not have happened. Similarly, J. F. Bernard has been a friend and a colleague for a decade, and I doubt I would have made it to this stage without his unfailing good humor. While living in Montreal, I met with a small community of people every month for almost six years to talk about comics. To members of that group—especially Claudine Gélinas Faucher, Matt Jones, Maude Lapierre, Jade Menni, Matthew Mongrain, Toni Pape, Alison Pearce, Julian Peters, Sara Smith, and Ben Lee Taylor—I owe much of any ability I have to think and write about comics. Special thanks also go to Melissa Bull, one of the best minds, readers, and editors I know; although we have been on separate paths for a while now, her support during the writing of most of this book made all the difference in bringing it to completion. Finally, Kim Davies provided feedback and encouragement during the final stretch of preparing the manuscript for publication, and her company made the process much less arduous.

I also want to extend an extra special thank you to Julie Doucet for her generous permission to use the image that appears on the cover, which so perfectly speaks to many of the ideas presented in this book. Reading *Dirty Plotte* for the first time was a formative experience that inspired me to study comics academically, and I am thrilled to have the book represented with a drawing from her pen. My brother Lasse provided expert last-minute help with getting the book's many images into publishable shape. Earlier versions of chapters 1 and 2 have appeared in the *Journal of Graphic Novels and Comics* and *South Central Review*; I am grateful for their permission to reprint elements from those articles as part of this book.

Finally, the support of my family has been unwavering since I first started talking about studying comics, and I owe everything to them: Dorde, Kurt, Henrik, Lasse, Nanna, Valdemar, and Wilfred. Thank you.

Notes

Introduction

1   While autobiography and memoir constitute two different genres within the larger form of life writing (along with, of course, several other modes), such taxonomic differentiation has only minor and very occasional bearing upon my central discussion of self-representation in comics. In this study, I therefore generally use the terms *autobiography* and *autobiographical* to refer to most instances of life writing.

2   See Bruss, *Autobiographical Acts* and "Eye for I"; Eakin, "Breaking" and *Touching*; and Smith.

3   See Jacobs, *Graphic Encounters*, "More," and "Multimodal Constructions."

Chapter 1   Female Grotesques

1   It is worth noting that historical exceptions to this view also exist, such as the large female readership of romance comics around the middle of the last century (which were, however, almost exclusively created by men). For a discussion of the female readership of midcentury comics, including the impact of the Comics Code, see Sabin.

2   The book collections of Doucet's comics work from *Dirty Plotte* include *Lève ta jambe mon poisson est mort!* (1993), *My Most Secret Desire* (1995; new expanded edition 2006), and *My New York Diary* (1999; revised edition 2004), all published by Drawn & Quarterly. Most recently, francophone Montreal publisher L'Oie de Cravan published a bilingual collection of Doucet's early mini-comics as *Fantastic Plotte!* in 2013, in chronological order and complete with the original covers.

3   This story is reprinted in *Lève ta jambe mon poisson est mort!* Neither the individual comic books nor the various collected volumes of Doucet's work have pagination. Because the run of *Dirty Plotte* serialized by Drawn &

Quarterly is long out of print (as are, of course, the mini-comics), in this chapter I instead refer to the book collection reprinting the story discussed in the text.

4   Fitting with Doucet's informal use of the English language throughout, her French, as in this example, is often unaccented.

5   "Heavy Flow," reprinted in *Lève ta jambe mon poisson est mort!* In order to avoid confusion, here and throughout this study I refer to the author of the work in question by last name and the autobiographical character by first name.

6   "Dirty Plotte vs. Super Clean Plotte," reprinted in *Lève ta jambe mon poisson est mort!*

7   "My Conscience Is Bugging Me," reprinted in *Lève ta jambe mon poisson est mort!*

8   "Dogs Are Really Man's Best Friend," reprinted in *Lève ta jambe mon poisson est mort!*

9   These stories are reprinted in both the mini-comic and Drawn & Quarterly versions of *Dirty Plotte*, as well as in *Lève ta jambe mon poisson est mort!*

10 Although many of the stories originally published in the mini-comics were translated (by Doucet herself) into English for both the Drawn & Quarterly run of *Dirty Plotte* and her first book collection, published with the French title *Lève ta jambe mon poisson est mort!*, they retain several French phrases and exclamations throughout. Her second collection, *My Most Secret Desire*, is entirely in English. In this context it is worth noting that Doucet has also been published in mostly unilingual French, in various collections by L'Association in France.

11 The passages occur, respectively, in an untitled story and in "Charming Periods," both of which are reprinted in *Lève ta jambe mon poisson est mort!*

12 In an interview with PictureBox publisher Dan Nadel, Doucet said about her decision to quit comics: "I got completely sick of it. I was drawing comics all the time and didn't have the time or energy to do anything else. That got to me in the end. I never made enough money from comics to be able to take a break and do something else. Now I just can't stand comics. I'm not interested anymore" (47). Elsewhere Doucet has explained how she gradually soured on the male-dominated world of comics: "I was very much at ease in the most part, me being more comfortable with men than with women, at the time. I felt I was at the right place. It's later that I started to not relate with those guys anymore. They were not much interested in anything else than comics and that killed me" (Køhlert n.p.).

Chapter 2 Working It Through

1   The two most notable cases of Gloeckner's work causing controversy are the confiscation, in 2000, of *A Child's Life* at the French border and its ban from the public library system of Stockton, California. For a discussion of Gloeckner's work in relation to censorship, see Chute, *Graphic Women* 77–78.

2   Gloeckner discusses the source and particular textual arrangement of the *Diary* in Atkinson 18.

3   The term *scriptotherapy* has an unclear genealogy, but is in literary studies mainly associated with Henke. For authoritative overviews of the scientific literature on scriptotherapy, see Riordan, as well as Smyth and Greenberg.

4   For a reading of the image that connects it to Marcel Duchamp's famous installation *Étant Donnés*, on which it is clearly based, see Chute, *Graphic Women* 71–72.

5   In this formulation, Whitehead is explicitly drawing on Caruth.

6   Regarding Gloeckner's awareness of her own trauma, she mentions in an interview with Juno that she spent the entirety of a ten-thousand-dollar trust fund on psychiatrist bills in the years after the relationship with her mother's boyfriend. After she wrote him a letter explaining that he owed her the money because he was at least partly responsible, he sent her an entirety of five hundred dollars over the course of a year. See Juno 154.

Chapter 3   Queer as Style

1   While Schrag's comics elicited some interest at the Alternative Press Expo, it was not until she mailed a self-published copy of *Definition* along with a submission cover letter to Slave Labor Graphics that she secured publication, but on the condition that she clean up some of the lettering. For marketing purposes, Slave Labor Graphics wanted to begin with *Definition*, the more "mature" work (Schrag, message to the author, January 20, 2014).

2   In the scant critical attention to Schrag, this publication history has often been misrepresented as having initially occurred entirely (with the obvious exception of *Likewise*) while Schrag was still a high school student. The information imparted here comes from personal correspondence with Schrag, October 27, 2013.

3   The exception, once again, is *Likewise*, which took Schrag eight years to ink and which was therefore completed when she was well into her twenties. The book was, however, written the year after Schrag's graduation from high school in 1998, and as such retains its teenage perspective.

4   Today, of course, the role of zines has been largely supplanted by various online platforms and social networks, such as Instagram, Tumblr, and YouTube, as well as the now all but deceased MySpace. Something of an intermediary between analog and digital youth culture, the latter seemed (in its early incarnations, at least) directly inspired by zine culture in the ability of users to experiment with altering its visual presentation instead of adhering to predetermined layouts (as exemplified most strikingly by Facebook's orderly sameness and corporate blue color scheme).

5   For a discussion of riot grrrl zines, see Garrison.

6   While Schrag eventually published her work with Slave Labor Graphics and Simon & Schuster, one only needs to imagine the limited commercial market for a rudimentarily drawn comic by a fifteen-year-old girl to understand that the genesis and initial appearance of the project is clearly based in contemporary zine culture. Moreover, her published work with Slave Labor Graphics was never subject to the kind of censorship that limited the syndication potential of Bechdel's similarly queer-themed *Dykes to Watch Out For*, for example.

7 Although the distinction is sometimes difficult to maintain, especially as the series progresses, I will refer to the author as Schrag and the character as Ariel in my discussion of the books.

8 In the case of Chester Brown's *Louis Riel*, for example, Brown became increasingly influenced by the style of Harold Gray's *Little Orphan Annie* strip as he worked on the book's initial serialization from 1999 to 2003. Because his character design changed accordingly, he redrew many early panels for the collected one-volume edition published in 2003.

9 Due to *Awkward* and *Definition* being collected in a single volume, page numbers are not continuous throughout but are instead reset at the beginning of *Definition*, keeping each book's original pagination. Page references in my discussion of these two comics are contextual to the installment under consideration. Throughout the four volumes, Schrag sometimes dispenses with capitalization and punctuation, and I reproduce her words here and elsewhere without correction.

10 Before its publication as a collected volume, *Potential* was the first of the four books to be serialized (in six issues, with each issue having its own cover). None of these are reprinted in the 2008 Simon & Schuster edition, which reuses the cover image of the collected Slave Labor Graphics edition from 2000. The original covers all feature drawings humorously translating biological principles to Ariel's life and have such subtitles as "Unit One: The Cell" and "Unit Two: The Gene."

11 The book in question is the third edition of *Biology* by Neil A. Campbell, published in 1993. Although it is never mentioned by name or author and only appears as a rudimentary drawing in *Potential*, the likeness is perfectly rendered and clearly intentional.

12 Fredric Wertham is a polarizing figure in twentieth-century cultural criticism. Born in Germany and trained as a psychologist in Germany, France, and the United Kingdom, he came to the United States in 1922 to work and teach at the Johns Hopkins Hospital and School of Medicine. Influenced by the Frankfurt School of social theory, the topic of much of Wertham's work was the influence of culture and the mass media on children, especially regarding violence, prejudice, and various forms of juvenile delinquency (Nyberg 87–89). Additionally, Wertham was a staunch supporter of racial equality, and his writings were used as evidence in the landmark Supreme Court case *Brown v. Board of Education*. Beginning in the 1930s, Wertham worked at Harlem's Lafargue Clinic, the only psychiatric center in New York City that welcomed black patients. It was during his time at the Lafargue Clinic that Wertham conducted the many interviews with children that would form the empirical basis of *Seduction of the Innocent*'s condemnation of comic books. Historically Wertham has been viewed as a negative figure largely responsible for the Comic Book Scare of the early 1950s and the resulting Senate hearings leading to the establishment of the first Comics Code in 1954. In recent years, several revisionist studies have provided a more nuanced portrait of Wertham in attempts to rehabilitate his popular image somewhat (see Beaty; Nyberg; and Wright). After Wertham's papers were made public in 2010, however, an article by Carol L. Tilley argued that Wertham had systematically "manipulated, overstated, compromised, and fabricated evidence—especially that

evidence he attributed to personal clinical research with young people—for rhetorical gain" (383).

13 Whether Bechdel intended the similarity or not, it is clear that she is intimately familiar with Schrag's work from her endorsement printed on the cover of all three volumes of the Simon & Schuster editions, in which she calls the comics "A scathing and meticulously documented autobiographical triumph."

14 The early parts of *Likewise* were serialized by Slave Labor Graphics in three issues from 2003 to 2004, all of which feature interior scenes from Schrag's house on the cover, with no people present.

15 See, for example, the review of the series by Kristian Williams, who claims about *Likewise* that "the style changes frequently, sometimes for no apparent reason. It feels like Schrag just periodically got bored with what she was doing, and decided to try something else, often mid-page" (n.p.). For a similar response, see Clough. In addition to their needlessly dismissive tone, such responses reveal the culture's blindness to the fact that a teenage girl could produce a thematically and formally intricate literary work, especially when compared to the more entrenched idea of the "boy genius."

16 While *Definition* runs eighty-four numbered pages, it concludes with both a blank page and a page including a three-panel coda, bringing its total to eighty-six pages.

17 So dedicated is Schrag to portraying only events from the school year that aside from a one-panel flashback in *Potential* to a family trip to France taken the summer between her sophomore and junior years, this short sequence is the only time in the entire series that a scene is set during summer—which, of course, is when Schrag was habitually occupied with writing and drawing each year's book.

18 For example, Ng Suat Tong, a long-time reviewer for the *Comics Journal*, calls Schrag's work "a poorly edited journal" and states that "Quite simply put, these are comics which contain little in the way of beauty of form or language" (n.p.). A similarly inattentive and dismissive reading of Schrag's complex stylistic choices as nothing more than the result of a kind of artistic laziness is put forth by Elisabeth El Refaie, who says about *Potential* that "Schrag's choice of drawing style has less to do with their visual modality in relation to the other panels and more to do with practical considerations, such as the fact that realistic drawings require more investment in terms of time and effort than do the more cartoonish images that fill most of the 224 pages of the book" (158).

Chapter 4 Staring at Comics

1 As an example of the relationship between disability and other marginalized identity categories, all of which depend on systems that naturalize inferiority in the service of oppression or violence, consider how pseudoscientific schemes such as phrenology have been employed in attempts to establish exclusionary categories of race based on an appeal to biology in a process that equates certain observable visual markers with natural inferiority. Chapter 5 examines the implications of these insights for the representation of ethnoracial

difference in autobiographical comics. According to Sharon L. Snyder and David T. Mitchell, moreover, disability can be considered the "master trope of human disqualification" (127), and Siebers argues that "beneath the troping of blackness as inbuilt inferiority, for example, lies the troping of disability as inferior. Beneath the troping of femininity as biological deficiency lies the troping of disability as deficiency" (*Disability Aesthetics* 24).

2   Regarding the symbolic conception of disability, Tom Shakespeare mentions the idea of karma (197), and Couser indicates that "in the Old Testament being blind, deaf, crippled, sick, or diseased is a sign of having done something to incur God's disfavor; sin brings on disability. The New Testament characterizes people with disabilities as cursed or possessed by evil" (*Recovering* 181).

3   Firmly rooting the "problem" of disability in the individual body, this mandate for normalcy can be traced, as Davis has shown, to the appearance of the concept of the "normal" in the period 1840–1860. Associated with Belgian statistician Adolphe Quetelet's idea of "l'homme moyen," or the average man, the concept gradually supplanted notions of the "ideal," especially as concerning bodily variation. The result, Davis argues, was that instead of a "culture with an ideal form of the body, [in which] all members of the population are below the ideal," the concept of normalcy created instead a statistical view of the normed population, where "the new ideal of ranked order is powered by the imperative of the norm, and then is supplemented by the notion of progress, human perfectibility, and the elimination of deviance, to create a dominating, hegemonic vision of what the human body should be" ("Constructing" 4, 8). Influential in the openly mainstream eugenics movement of the turn of the century, this "imperative of the norm" also underlies several other ideological theories of the time, Davis argues, such as psychoanalysis, industrial capitalism, and Marxism, all of which aim to eliminate the abnormal in the service of standardized normalcy ("Constructing" 6–10).

4   An important reason for the success of the medical model is the personal and social anxiety experienced by the nondisabled when confronted with the presence of the disabled. Much like the social construction of race is intimately bound up with a psychological desire to distinguish between ourselves and an abject outside, as described in chapter 5, our culture's idealization of the body and its demands that we control it creates a dichotomy wherein "the disabled are made 'the other,' who symbolize failure of control and the threat of pain, limitation, dependency, and death" (Wendell 63). Instead of internalizing what Sander L. Gilman has called the "fear of collapse" (*Disease* 1), we project it outward in order to localize and domesticate it, and the result is the creation of the category of disability as embodied by those who we perceive as having already succumbed to collapse or disintegration. Compared to categories such as race and gender, however, the borders that separate the nondisabled from the disabled are significantly more fluid and permeable, and they are therefore perhaps even more threatening and in greater need of policing. As Siebers observes, "I know as a white man that I will not wake up in the morning as a black woman, but I could wake up a quadriplegic" (*Disability Theory* 5). Since all humans are subject to becoming disabled at any time, especially if we live long enough, disability is therefore both a universal

and foundational category of human identity, but one that is regularly individualized and pathologized in the service of preserving the self as whole and uncontaminated.

5 As Siebers emphasizes, only 15 percent of disabled people are born with their impairments ("Disability in Theory" 176).

6 The complications produced by the particular cultural history of autobiography is only part of three interrelated obstacles that Couser, in a different context, outlines as possibly impacting the accessibility of life writing for disabled people. They include "having a life, writing a life, and publishing a life" ("Conflicting" 78).

7 One unfortunate drawback of the social model is its reliance on physical and visible bodily variation as the preferred prism through which to approach disability. As several critics have noted, what Alaniz calls the "ocularcentric 'disability as visuality' thesis" ("Chris Ware" 515) has either excluded or not sufficiently accounted for disabilities such as epilepsy, deafness, and autism, which, as Sarah Birge cautions, "do not disappear with the alteration of the disabled person's environment" (n.p.). So prevailing is the equation of disability with visuality, Alaniz points out, that popular representations of mental disorders such as autism or Asperger's syndrome "go out of their way to limn the disabled as visually marked through tics, odd walks, stony expressions, 'adorable' quirks, etc." ("Chris Ware" 515).

8 *The Spiral Cage* includes many instances of untraditional spelling, grammar, capitalization, and punctuation, such as Davison's habit of using two periods to indicate a pause. In order to maintain fidelity to the work's idiosyncrasies, I reproduce the text as published throughout this discussion.

9 As Couser, in a passage worth quoting at length, has noted about medical science's historical privileging of the visual,

> In the seventeenth century the testimony of the patient, in the form of a narrative elicited by the physician, was the main basis for diagnosis. But since then a whole array of diagnostic tools—the laryngoscope, ophthalmoscope, microscope, fluoroscope, endoscope, x-ray, the medical laboratory, and various electronic scanning devices—have offered increasingly detailed and "objective" evidence of the body's internal workings. The effect has been to extend the range and domain of the medical gaze and to efface the skin as an obstacle to vision and thus to diagnosis. (The common suffix *scope* is symptomatic of the privileging of vision as the preeminent sense for diagnosis. Significantly, the term *stethoscope* refers to a tool for listening as though it were a device for seeing: its root meaning is "I see the chest.") (*Recovering* 21–22)

10 Alaniz notes that the term *supercrip* "came into popular use around the time of the passage of the ADA [Americans with Disabilities Act] in 1990" (*Death* 31), and although Schalk locates a few instances in the 1970s and 1980s, she notes that "the term seems to have gained much scholarly currency since the late 1990s" (74).

Chapter 5 Stereotyping the Self

1 As Sander L. Gilman argues about the implications of stereotypes for identity formation, "stereotyping is a universal means of coping with anxieties

engendered by our inability to control the world" (*Difference* 12). As a clearly defined schematic that is imposed upon a complex and often confusing reality, stereotypes therefore "perpetuate a needed sense of difference between the 'self' and the 'object,' which becomes the 'Other'" (*Difference* 18).

2　Regarding the role of the visual in the construction of racial difference, Sandra Oh notes that "although theories of blood have also played a role in the way that Americans define and are defined by race, racial designation continues to rely largely on certain bodily markers" (132). Similarly, Eleanor Ty argues that "what generates the classification and ordering of things is still predominantly appearance or the scopic drive. Though thinking about race has shifted and changed over history, to a large extent, visibility is still the basis for discourses about difference" (8).

3　According to E. H. Gombrich, "the word and the institution of caricature date only from the last years of the sixteenth century, and the inventors of the art were not the pictorial propagandists who existed in one form or another for centuries before, but those most sophisticated and refined of artists, the brothers Carracci" (343).

4　Gombrich traces this development to the invention of caricature and links it to such diverse pictorial forms as expressionism, cubism, and newspaper cartooning, among others.

5　In similar terms Annibale Carracci, one of the brothers who according to Gombrich (343) gave his name to the art of caricature, believed that the skilled artist could strive to "grasp the perfect deformity, and thus reveal the very essence of a personality. A good caricature, like every work of art, is more true to life than reality itself" (qtd. in Nicholas K. Robinson 1).

6　Eisner further speculates that comics art stereotypes are often based on animals such as lions, foxes, snakes, and owls, because "in the early experience with animal life, people learned which facial configurations and postures were either threatening or friendly. It was important for survival to recognize instantly which animal was dangerous" (*Graphic Storytelling* 20).

7　In January 2015 the controversial use of cartoon imagery to depict the prophet Muhammad again led to violence when Saïd and Chérif Kouachi forced their way into the Paris editorial offices of the French weekly newspaper *Charlie Hebdo*, where they opened fire and killed twelve staff members, wounding several others.

8　Regarding the gradual disappearance of black characters from newspaper comic strips, Heer notes that
> Paradoxically, the Civil Rights agitation of the 1940s did not just lead to the disappearance of offensive stereotypes, but to a larger ethnic cleansing of the comics. With publishers and cartoonists afraid to offend Black readers, characters like Ebony White—the cringe-making sidekick to Will Eisner's The Spirit—disappeared. But they were not replaced, except in a few cases, by non-racist Black characters (who might have offended racist White readers). Instead the comics sections of the 1950s became very lily-white, with far fewer non-White characters than before. (255–256)

9　For discussions of these and other early comics featuring explicit racist stereotypes, see Appel; Goulart; and Nelson. For a more extensive engagement, see Gordon, who provides detailed context and lengthy close readings of several such strips.

10 For a visual history of the changing representation of the Irish in American comics art, see Appel and Appel, as well as Soper.

11 See also Ayish (80) and Shaheen (*Guilty* 143).

12 While there is significant overlap between these three categories, there is no necessary or direct relationship between what are, respectively, ethnic, religious, and geographic classifications. The most common misapprehension, perhaps, is the notion that Iranians are Arabs, when in fact they are Persians. El Rassi himself points this out by noting, in an image in which he jokingly portrays himself as sitting on a camel, "I suppose what is most confusing for people is that one could be a Muslim (a religion) but not necessarily be an Arab (an ethnicity). For example Turks, Iranians, and Pakistanis are not Arabs but are mostly Muslims" (64).

13 As several commentators have noted, the early history of newspaper comic strips might have provided a similar point of identification for their urban and largely immigrant readership. Davis-McElligatt, for example, speculates about such immigrant readers that "far from being offended by the racial (and what one might now call racist) caricatures, they instead felt as though these comics were written about their experiences and presented in a format they could all easily comprehend" (137). For similar arguments, see Appel (14); Hajdu (10–11); and Soper (272).

Bibliography

Akhtar, Salman. *Comprehensive Dictionary of Psychoanalysis*. Karnac, 2009.

Alaniz, José. "Chris Ware and 'Autistic Realism.'" *International Journal of Comic Art*, vol. 13, no. 1, 2011, pp. 514–528.

———. *Death, Disability, and the Superhero: The Silver Age and Beyond*. University Press of Mississippi, 2014.

———. "Supercrip: Disability and the Marvel Silver Age Superhero." *International Journal of Comic Art*, vol. 6, no. 2, 2004, pp. 304–324.

Alsultany, Evelyn. *Arabs and Muslims in the Media: Race and Representation after 9/11*. New York University Press, 2012.

Appel, John, and Selma Appel. *Pat-Riots to Patriots: American Irish in Caricature and Comic Art*. Michigan State University Museum, 1990.

Appel, John J. "Ethnicity in Cartoon Art." *Cartoons and Ethnicity*. The Ohio State University Libraries, 1992, pp. 13–48.

Atkinson, Nathalie. "My Not-So-Secret Identity: The Fact and Fiction of Phoebe Gloeckner." *Broken Pencil*, vol. 22, 2003, pp. 17–19.

Ault, Donald. "'Cutting Up' Again Part II: Lacan on Barks on Lacan." *Comics & Culture: Analytical and Theoretical Approaches to Comics*, edited by Anne Magnussen and Hans-Christian Christiansen, Museum Tusculanum Press, 2000, pp. 123–140.

Ayish, Nader. "Stereotypes, Popular Culture, and High School Curricula: How Arab American Muslim High School Students Perceive and Cope with Being the 'Other.'" *Arabs in the Americas: Interdisciplinary Essays on the Arab Diaspora*, edited by Darcy A. Zabel, Peter Lang, 2006, pp. 79–116.

Baetens, Jan. "Revealing Traces: A New Theory of Graphic Enunciation." *The Language of Comics: Word and Image*, edited by Robin Varnum and Christina T. Gibbons, University Press of Mississippi, 2001, pp. 145–155.

Baetens, Jan, and Hugo Frey. *The Graphic Novel: An Introduction*. Cambridge University Press, 2015.

Bakhtin, Mikhail. *Rabelais and His World*. Indiana University Press, 1984.

Beaty, Bart. *Fredric Wertham and the Critique of Mass Culture*. University Press of Mississippi, 2005.

Bechdel, Alison. *Fun Home*. Houghton Mifflin, 2006.

Berger, John. *Ways of Seeing*. Penguin, 2008.

Bhabha, Homi K. *The Location of Culture*. Routledge, 1994.

Birge, Sarah. "No Life Lessons Here: Comics, Autism, and Empathetic Scholarship." *Disability Studies Quarterly*, vol. 30, no. 1, 2010, n.p.

Booker, M. Keith. *Techniques of Subversion in Modern Literature: Transgression, Abjection and the Carnivalesque*. University of Florida Press, 1991.

Breuer, Josef, and Sigmund Freud. *Studies on Hysteria*. Basic Books, 1957.

Brophy, Sarah, and Janice Hladki. "Visual Autobiography in the Frame: Critical Embodiment and Cultural Pedagogy." *Embodied Politics in Visual Autobiography*, edited by Sarah Brophy and Janice Hladki, University of Toronto Press, 2014, pp. 3–28.

Brueggemann, Brenda Jo, et al. "Introduction: Integrating Disability into Teaching and Scholarship." *Disability Studies: Enabling the Humanities*, edited by Sharon L. Snyder et al., Modern Language Association, 2002, pp. 1–12.

Bruss, Elizabeth. *Autobiographical Acts: The Changing Situation of a Literary Genre*. Johns Hopkins University Press, 1976.

———. "Eye for I: Making and Unmaking Autobiography in Film." *Autobiography: Essays Theoretical and Critical*, edited by James Olney, Princeton University Press, 1980, pp. 296–320.

Butler, Judith. *Bodies That Matter: On the Discursive Limits of "Sex."* Routledge, 1993.

———. *Gender Trouble: Feminism and the Subversion of Identity*. Routledge, 2006.

———. *The Psychic Life of Power: Theories in Subjection*. Stanford University Press, 1997.

Cardell, Kylie. *Dear World: Contemporary Uses of the Diary*. University of Wisconsin Press, 2014.

Cardell, Kylie, and Kate Douglas. "Telling Tales: Autobiographies of Childhood and Youth." *Prose Studies*, vol. 35, no. 1, 2013, pp. 1–6.

Caruth, Cathy. "Introduction." *Trauma: Explorations in Memory*, edited by Cathy Caruth, Johns Hopkins University Press, 1995, pp. 3–12.

———. *Unclaimed Experience: Trauma, Narrative, and History*. Johns Hopkins University Press, 1996.

Cates, Isaac. "The Diary Comic." *Graphic Subjects: Critical Essays on Autobiography and Graphic Novels*, edited by Michael A. Chaney, University of Wisconsin Press, 2011, pp. 209–226.

Chaney, Michael A. *Fugitive Vision: Slave Image and Black Identity in Antebellum Narrative*. Indiana University Press, 2008.

———. *Reading Lessons in Seeing: Mirrors, Masks, and Mazes in the Autobiographical Graphic Novel*. University Press of Mississippi, 2016.

Chase, Alisia. "You Must Look at the Personal Clutter: Diaristic Indulgence, Female Adolescence, and Feminist Autobiography." *Drawing from Life: Memory and Subjectivity in Comic Art*, edited by Jane Tolmie, University Press of Mississippi, 2013, pp. 207–240.

Chrisman, Wendy L. "A Reflection on Inspiration: A Recuperative Call for Emotion in Disability Studies." *Journal of Literary & Cultural Disability Studies*, vol. 5, no. 2, 2011, pp. 173–184.

Chute, Hillary L. *Graphic Women: Life Narrative and Contemporary Comics*. Columbia University Press, 2010.

————. *Why Comics? From Underground to Everywhere.* HarperCollins, 2017.

Cioffi, Frank L. "Disturbing Comics: The Disjunction of Word and Image in the Comics of Andrzej Mleczko, Ben Katchor, R. Crumb, and Art Spiegelman." *The Language of Comics: Word and Image,* edited by Robin Varnum and Christina T. Gibbons, University Press of Mississippi, 2001, pp. 97–122.

Cixous, Hélène. "The Laugh of the Medusa." *Signs: Journal of Women in Culture and Society,* vol. 1, no. 4, 1976, pp. 875–893.

Clough, Rob. "Self-Portrait of the Artist: *Likewise.*" *High-Low,* May 14, 2009, highlow-comics.blogspot.com/2009/05/self-portrait-of-artist-likewise.html.

Cohen, Barry M., and Anne Mills. "Skin/Paper/Bark: Body Image, Trauma and the Diagnostic Drawing Series." *Splintered Reflections: Images of the Body in Trauma,* edited by Jean Goodwin and Reina Attias, Basic Books, 1999, pp. 203–211.

The Comics Journal, vol. 162, 1993.

Cooks, Bridget R. "See Me Now." *Camera Obscura: Feminism, Culture, and Media Studies,* vol. 12, no. 3, 1995, pp. 66–83.

Cope, Bill, and Mary Kalantzis. "Introduction: Multiliteracies: The Beginnings of an Idea." *Multiliteracies: Literacy Learning and the Design of Social Futures,* edited by Bill Cope and Mary Kalantzis, Routledge, 2000, pp. 3–8.

Couser, G. Thomas. "Body Language: Illness, Disability, and Life Writing." *Life Writing,* vol. 13, no. 1, 2016, pp. 3–10.

————. "Conflicting Paradigms: The Rhetorics of Disability Memoir." *Embodied Rhetorics: Disability in Language and Culture,* edited by James C. Wilson and Cynthia Lewiecki-Wilson, Southern Illinois University Press, 2001, pp. 78–91.

————. "Disability, Life Narrative, and Representation." *The Disability Studies Reader,* edited by Lennard J. Davis, 2nd ed., Routledge, 2006, pp. 399–401.

————. *Recovering Bodies: Illness, Disability, and Life Writing.* University of Wisconsin Press, 1997.

————. "Signifying Bodies: Life Writing and Disability Studies." *Disability Studies: Enabling the Humanities,* edited by Sharon L. Snyder et al., Modern Language Association, 2002, pp. 109–117.

Creekmur, Corey K. "Multiculturalism Meets the Counterculture: Representing Racial Difference in Robert Crumb's Underground Comix." *Representing Multiculturalism in Comics and Graphic Novels,* edited by Carolene Ayaka and Ian Hague, Routledge, 2015, pp. 19–33.

Davis, Lennard J. "Constructing Normalcy: The Bell Curve, the Novel, and the Invention of the Disabled Body in the Nineteenth Century." *The Disability Studies Reader,* edited by Lennard J. Davis, 2nd ed., Routledge, 2006, pp. 3–16.

————. "The End of Identity Politics and the Beginning of Dismodernism: On Disability as an Unstable Category." *The Disability Studies Reader,* edited by Lennard J. Davis, 2nd ed., Routledge, 2006, pp. 231–242.

————. *Enforcing Normalcy: Disability, Deafness, and the Body.* Verso, 1995.

————. "Introduction." *The Disability Studies Reader,* edited by Lennard J. Davis, 2nd ed., Routledge, 2006, pp. xv–xviii.

Davis-McElligatt, Joanna. "Confronting the Intersections of Race, Immigration, and Representation in Chris Ware's Comics." *The Comics of Chris Ware: Drawing Is a Way of Thinking,* edited by David M. Ball and Martha B. Kuhlman, University Press of Mississippi, 2010, pp. 135–145.

Davison, Al. *The Spiral Cage.* Active Images, 2003.

Dolmage, Jay, and Dale Jacobs. "Mutable Articulations: Disability Rhetorics and the Comics Medium." *Disability in Comic Books and Graphic Narratives*, edited by Chris Foss et al., Palgrave Macmillan, 2016, pp. 14–28.

Doucet, Julie. *365 Days*. Drawn & Quarterly, 2007.

———. *Carpet Sweeper Tales*. Drawn & Quarterly, 2016.

———. *Elle-Humour*. PictureBox, 2006.

———. *Fantastic Plotte!* L'Oie de Cravan, 2013.

———. *J comme je: essais d'autobiographie*. Seuil, 2005.

———. *Lady Pep*. Drawn & Quarterly, 2004.

———. *Lève ta jambe mon poisson est mort!* Drawn & Quarterly, 1993.

———. *Long Time Relationship*. Drawn & Quarterly, 2001.

———. *The Madame Paul Affair*. Drawn & Quarterly, 2000.

———. *My Most Secret Desire*. Drawn & Quarterly, 2006.

———. *My New York Diary*. Drawn & Quarterly, 2004.

Doucet, Julie, and Michel Gondry. *My New New York Diary*. PictureBox, 2010.

Douglas, Kate, and Anna Poletti. *Life Narratives and Youth Culture: Representation, Agency and Participation*. Palgrave Macmillan, 2016.

DuBois, W. E. B. *The Souls of Black Folk*. Washington Square Press, 1970.

Dyer, Richard. *The Matter of Images: Essays on Representation*. 2nd ed., Routledge, 2002.

Eagleton, Terry. *Walter Benjamin: Or Towards a Revolutionary Criticism*. Verso, 1981.

Eakin, Paul John. "Breaking Rules: The Consequences of Self-Narration." *Biography*, vol. 24, no. 1, 2001, pp. 113–127.

———. *Touching the World: Reference in Autobiography*. Princeton University Press, 1992.

Eisner, Will. *Comics & Sequential Art*. Poorhouse Press, 1985.

———. *Graphic Storytelling*. Poorhouse Press, 1996.

El Rassi, Toufic. *Arab in America*. Last Gasp, 2007.

El Refaie, Elisabeth. *Autobiographical Comics: Life Writing in Pictures*. University Press of Mississippi, 2012.

Erni, John Nguyet. "Eternal Excesses: Toward a Queer Mode of Articulation in Social Theory." *American Literary History*, vol. 8, no. 3, 1996, pp. 566–581.

Fanon, Frantz. *Black Skin, White Masks*. Pluto Press, 2008.

Fawaz, Ramzi. *The New Mutants: Superheroes and the Radical Imagination of American Comics*. New York University Press, 2016.

Feuer, Menachem. "Every*body* Is a Star: The Affirmation of Freaks and Schlemiels through Caricature in the Comics of Drew and Josh Friedman." *MELUS*, vol. 32, no. 3, 2007, pp. 75–101.

Frank, Arthur W. *The Wounded Storyteller: Body, Illness, and Ethics*. University of Chicago Press, 1995.

Freiwald, Bina Toledo. "Social Trauma and Serial Autobiography: Healing and Beyond." *Unfitting Stories: Narrative Approaches to Disease, Disability, and Trauma*, edited by Valerie Raoul et al., Wilfrid Laurier University Press, 2007, pp. 227–235.

Freud, Sigmund. *The Interpretation of Dreams*. Basic Books, 2010.

———. *Introductory Lectures on Psychoanalysis*. W. W. Norton, 1989.

Gardner, Jared. "Autography's Biography, 1972–2007." *Biography*, vol. 31, no. 1, 2008, pp. 1–26.

———. "Same Difference: Graphic Alterity in the Work of Gene Luen Yang, Adrian Tomine, and Derek Kirk Kim." *Multicultural Comics: From Zap to Blue Beetle*, edited by Frederick Luis Aldama, University of Texas Press, 2010, pp. 132–147.

Garland-Thomson, Rosemarie. "Disability and Representation." *PMLA*, vol. 120, no. 2, 2005, pp. 522–527.

———. *Extraordinary Bodies: Figuring Physical Disability in American Culture and Literature.* Columbia University Press, 1997.

———. "The New Disability Studies: Inclusion or Tolerance?" *ADFL Bulletin*, vol. 31, no. 1, 1999, pp. 49–53.

———. "The Politics of Staring: Visual Rhetorics of Disability in Popular Photography." *Disability Studies: Enabling the Humanities*, edited by Sharon L. Snyder et al., Modern Language Association, 2002, pp. 56–75.

———. "Seeing the Disabled: Visual Rhetorics of Disability in Popular Photography." *The New Disability History: American Perspectives*, edited by Paul K. Longmore and Lauri Umansky, New York University Press, 2001, pp. 335–374.

———. *Staring: How We Look.* Oxford University Press, 2009.

Garrison, Ednie Kaeh. "U.S. Feminism—Grrrl Style! Youth (Sub)Cultures and the Technologics of the Third Wave." *Feminist Studies*, vol. 26, no. 1, 2000, pp. 141–170.

Gateward, Frances, and John Jennings. "Introduction: The Sweeter the Christmas." *The Blacker the Ink: Constructions of Black Identity in Comics and Sequential Art*, edited by Frances Gateward and John Jennings, Rutgers University Press, 2015, pp. 1–15.

Gibbs, Alan. *Contemporary American Trauma Narratives.* Edinburgh University Press, 2014.

Gilman, Sander L. *Difference and Pathology: Stereotypes of Sexuality, Race, and Madness.* Cornell University Press, 1985.

———. *Disease and Representation: Images of Illness from Madness to AIDS.* Cornell University Press, 1988.

Gilmore, Leigh. *Autobiographics: A Feminist Theory of Women's Self-Representation.* Cornell University Press, 1994.

———. *The Limits of Autobiography: Trauma and Testimony.* Cornell University Press, 2002.

———. "Witnessing *Persepolis*: Comics, Trauma, and Childhood Testimony." *Graphic Subjects: Critical Essays on Autobiography and Graphic Novels*, edited by Michael A. Chaney, University of Wisconsin Press, 2011, pp. 157–163.

Giroux, Henry A. "Teenage Sexuality, Body Politics, and the Pedagogy of Display." *Youth Culture: Identity in a Postmodern World*, edited by Jonathon S. Epstein, Blackwell, 1998, pp. 24–55.

Gloeckner, Phoebe. "Autobiography: The Process Negates the Term." *Graphic Subjects: Critical Essays on Autobiography and Graphic Novels*, edited by Michael A. Chaney, University of Wisconsin Press, 2011, pp. 178–179.

———. *A Child's Life and Other Stories.* Frog, 2000.

———. *The Diary of a Teenage Girl.* Frog, 2002.

Gombrich, E. H. *Art and Illusion: A Study in the Psychology of Pictorial Representation.* Princeton University Press, 2000.

Gordon, Ian. *Comic Strips and Consumer Culture, 1890–1945.* Smithsonian Institution Press, 1998.

Goulart, Ron. *The Funnies: 100 Years of American Comic Strips.* Adams Publishing, 1995.

Groensteen, Thierry. *Comics and Narration.* University Press of Mississippi, 2013.

———. *The System of Comics.* University Press of Mississippi, 2007.

Grosz, Elizabeth. "Notes Towards a Corporeal Feminism." *Australian Feminist Studies*, vol. 5, 1987, pp. 1–16.

Groth, Gary. "Interview: Phoebe Gloeckner." *The Comics Journal*, vol. 261, 2004, pp. 78–123.

Hajdu, David. *The Ten-Cent Plague: The Great Comic-Book Scare and How It Changed America*. Farrar, Straus and Giroux, 2008.

Harris, Michael D. *Colored Pictures: Race and Visual Representation*. University of North Carolina Press, 2003.

Hartsock, Nancy. "Foucault on Power: A Theory for Women?" *Feminism/Postmodernism*, edited by Linda J. Nicholson, Routledge, 1990, pp. 157–175.

Hatfield, Charles. *Alternative Comics: An Emerging Literature*. University Press of Mississippi, 2005.

Heer, Jeet. "Afterword: Race and Comics." *Black Comics: Politics of Race and Representation*, edited by Sheena C. Howard and Ronald L. Jackson II, Bloomsbury, 2013, pp. 251–256.

Heeren, John. "Alfred Schutz and the Sociology of Common-Sense Knowledge." *Understanding Everyday Life: Towards the Reconstruction of Sociological Knowledge*, edited by Jack D. Douglas, Aldine Publishing, 1970, pp. 45–56.

Henke, Suzette A. *Shattered Subjects: Trauma and Testimony in Women's Life Writing*. St. Martin's Press, 2000.

Herman, Judith Lewis. *Trauma and Recovery*. Basic Books, 1997.

Hevey, David. "The Enfreakment of Photography." *The Disability Studies Reader*, edited by Lennard J. Davis, 2nd ed., Routledge, 2006, pp. 367–378.

———. "The Tragedy Principle: Strategies for Change in the Representation of Disabled People." *Disabling Barriers—Enabling Environments*, edited by John Swain et al., Sage-Open University Press, 1993, pp. 116–121.

Hipchen, Emily, and Ricia Anne Chansky. "Looking Forward: The Futures of Auto/Biography Studies." *a/b: Auto/Biography Studies*, vol. 32, no. 2, 2017, pp. 139–157.

hooks, bell. *Art on My Mind: Visual Politics*. The New Press, 1995.

Hutcheon, Linda. "Modern Parody and Bakhtin." *Rethinking Bakhtin: Extensions and Challenges*, edited by Gary Saul Morson and Caryl Emerson, Northwestern University Press, 1989, pp. 87–103.

Jacobs, Dale. *Graphic Encounters: Comics and the Sponsorship of Multimodal Literacy*. Bloomsbury Academic, 2013.

———. "More than Words: Comics as a Means of Teaching Multiple Literacies." *The English Journal*, vol. 96, no. 3, 2007, pp. 19–25.

———. "Multimodal Constructions of Self: Autobiographical Comics and the Case of Joe Matt's *Peepshow*." *Biography*, vol. 31, no. 1, 2008, pp. 59–84.

Jacobs, Dale, and Jay Dolmage. "Difficult Articulations: Comics Autobiography, Trauma, and Disability." *The Future of Text and Image: Collected Essays on Literary and Visual Conjunctures*, edited by Ofra Amihay and Lauren Walsh, Cambridge Scholars Publishing, 2012, pp. 69–89.

Joiner, Whitney. "Not Your Mother's Comic Book." *Salon*, March 15, 2003, www.salon.com/2003/03/15/gloeckner/.

Juno, Andrea. *Dangerous Drawings: Interviews with Comix & Graphix Artists*. Juno Books, 1997.

Kaplan, E. Ann. *Trauma Culture: The Politics of Terror and Loss in Media and Literature*. Rutgers University Press, 2005.

Karlyn, Kathleen Rowe. *Unruly Girls, Unrepentant Mothers: Redefining Feminism on the Screen*. University of Texas Press, 2011.

Kearney, Mary Celeste. *Girls Make Media*. Routledge, 2006.

Kirkpatrick, Ellen. "TransFormers: 'Identity' Compromised." *Cinema Journal*, vol. 55, no. 1, 2015, pp. 124–1133.

Køhlert, Frederik Byrn. "Words into Pictures: An Interview with Julie Doucet." *Lemonhound*, February 19, 2013, lemonhound.com/2013/02/19/words-into-pictures-an-interview-with-julie-doucet.

Kress, Gunther. "Multimodality." *Multiliteracies: Literacy Learning and the Design of Social Futures*, edited by Bill Cope and Mary Kalantzis, Routledge, 2000, pp. 179–199.

LaCapra, Dominick. *Writing History, Writing Trauma*. Johns Hopkins University Press, 2014.

Laub, Dori. "Truth and Testimony: The Process and the Struggle." *Trauma: Explorations in Memory*, edited by Cathy Caruth, Johns Hopkins University Press, 1995, pp. 61–75.

Lejeune, Philippe. "How Do Diaries End?" *Biography*, vol. 24, no. 1, 2001, pp. 99–112.

———. *On Autobiography*. University of Minnesota Press, 1989.

———. *On Diary*. University of Hawaii Press, 2009.

Leys, Ruth. *Trauma: A Genealogy*. University of Chicago Press, 2000.

Lim, Shirley Geok-lin. "Semiotics, Experience, and the Material Self: An Inquiry into the Subject of the Contemporary Asian Woman Writer." *Women, Autobiography, Theory: A Reader*, edited by Sidonie Smith and Julia Watson, University of Wisconsin Press, 1998, pp. 441–452.

Linton, Simi. "Reassigning Meaning." *The Disability Studies Reader*, edited by Lennard J. Davis, 2nd ed., Routledge, 2006, pp. 161–172.

Lionnet, Françoise. *Autobiographical Voices: Race, Gender, Self-Portraiture*. Cornell University Press, 1989.

Lippmann, Walter. *Public Opinion*. Free Press, 1997.

Loftus, Brian. "Speaking Silence: The Strategies and Structures of Queer Autobiography." *College Literature*, vol. 24, no. 1, 1997, pp. 28–44.

Lubiano, Wahneema. "Like Being Mugged by a Metaphor: Multiculturalism and State Narratives." *Mapping Multiculturalism*, edited by Avery F. Gordon and Christopher Newfield, University of Minnesota Press, 1996, pp. 64–75.

Lynch, Claire. "Ante-Autobiography and the Archive of Childhood." *Prose Studies*, vol. 35, no. 1, 2013, pp. 97–112.

Marshall, Elizabeth, and Leigh Gilmore. "Girlhood in the Gutter: Feminist Graphic Knowledge and the Visualization of Sexual Precarity." *Women's Studies Quarterly*, vol. 43, no. 1 & 2, 2015, pp. 95–114.

McCloud, Scott. *Understanding Comics: The Invisible Art*. Harper, 1994.

McDonnell, Jane Taylor. *Living to Tell the Tale: A Guide to Writing Memoir*. Penguin, 1998.

McIlvenny, Paul. "The Disabled Male Body 'Writes/Draws Back': Graphic Fictions of Masculinity and the Body in the Autobiographical Comic *The Spiral Cage*." *Revealing Male Bodies*, edited by Nancy Tuana et al., Indiana University Press, 2002, pp. 100–124.

McNally, Richard J. *Remembering Trauma*. Belknap Press of Harvard University Press, 2003.

McRuer, Robert. "Compulsory Able-Bodiedness and Queer/Disabled Existence." *Disability Studies: Enabling the Humanities*, edited by Sharon L. Snyder et al., Modern Language Association, 2002, pp. 88–99.

Mikkonen, Kai. "Subjectivity and Style in Graphic Narratives." *From Comic Strips to Graphic Novels: Contributions to the Theory and History of Graphic Narrative*, edited by Daniel Stein and Jan-Noël Thon, de Gruyter, 2013, pp. 101–123.

Miller, Ann. "Autobiography in *Bande Dessinée*." *Textual and Visual Selves: Photography, Film, and Comic Art in French Autobiography*, edited by Natalie Edwards et al., University of Nebraska Press, 2011, pp. 235–262.

Miller, Ann, and Murray Pratt. "Transgressive Bodies in the work of Julie Doucet, Fabrice Neaud and Jean-Christophe Menu: Towards a Theory of the 'AutobioBD.'" *Belphégor*, vol. IV, no. 1, 2004, n.p.

Miller, Michelle. "Theorizing 'The Plunge': (Queer) Girls' Adolescence, Risk, and Subjectivity in *Blue Is the Warmest Color*." *Girlhood Studies*, vol. 10, no. 1, 2017, pp. 39–54.

Moore-Gilbert, Bart. *Postcolonial Life-Writing: Culture, Politics and Self-Representation*. Routledge, 2009.

Mulvey, Laura. "Visual Pleasure and Narrative Cinema." *Film Theory and Criticism*, edited by Leo Braudy and Marshall Cohen, 6th ed., Oxford University Press, 2004, pp. 837–848.

Munford, Rebecca. "'Wake Up and Smell the Lipgloss': Gender, Generation and the (A)politics of Girl Power." *Third Wave Feminism: A Critical Exploration*, edited by Stacy Gillis et al., Palgrave Macmillan, 2004, pp. 142–153.

Nadel, Dan. "A Good Life: The Julie Doucet Interview." *The Drama*, vol. 7, 2006, pp. 44–52.

Nelson, Angela M. "Studying Black Comic Strips: Popular Art and Discourses of Race." *Black Comics: Politics of Race and Representation*, edited by Sheena C. Howard and Ronald L. Jackson II, Bloomsbury, 2013, pp. 97–110.

Nyberg, Amy Kiste. *Seal of Approval: The History of the Comics Code*. University Press of Mississippi, 1998.

Oh, Sandra. "Sight Unseen: Adrian Tomine's *Optic Nerve* and the Politics of Recognition." *MELUS*, vol. 32, no. 3, 2007, pp. 129–151.

Opper, Frederick Burr. "Caricature Country and Its Inhabitants." *Independent*, vol. 53, 1901, pp. 778–781.

Palumbo-Liu, David. "Assumed Identities." *New Literary History*, vol. 31, no. 4, 2000, pp. 765–780.

Poletti, Anna. *Intimate Ephemera: Reading Young Lives in Australian Zine Culture*. Melbourne University Press, 2008.

Reilly, Maura. "Cindy Sherman's *Untitled Film Stills*: Reproductive or Transgressive Mimicry? (1977–81)." *Women Making Art: Women in the Visual, Literary and Performing Arts since 1960*, edited by Deborah Johnson and Wendy Oliver, Peter Lang, 2001, pp. 117–140.

Rich, Adrienne. "Compulsory Heterosexuality and Lesbian Existence." *Feminism and Sexuality: A Reader*, edited by Stevi Jackson and Sue Scott, Columbia University Press, 1996, pp. 130–143.

Riordan, Richard J. "Scriptotherapy: Therapeutic Writing as a Counseling Adjunct." *Journal of Counseling & Development*, vol. 74, 1996, pp. 263–269.

Robbins, Trina. "Babes & Women." *The Complete Wimmen's Comix*, vol. 1, Fantagraphics, 2016, pp. vii–xiii.

Robinson, Nicholas K. *Edmund Burke: A Life in Caricature*. Yale University Press, 1996.

Robinson, Paul. *Gay Lives: Homosexual Autobiography from John Addington Symonds to Paul Monette*. University of Chicago Press, 1999.

Roman, Zak, and Ryan Lizardi. "'If She Be Worthy': The Illusion of Change in American Superhero Comics." *Inks: The Journal of the Comics Studies Society*, vol. 2, no. 1, 2018, pp. 18–37.

Rowanchild, Anira. "'My Mind on Paper': Anne Lister and the Construction of Lesbian Identity." *Representing Lives: Women and Auto/Biography*, edited by Alison Donnell and Pauline Polkey, Macmillan, 2000, pp. 199–207.

Rowe, Kathleen. *The Unruly Woman: Gender and the Genres of Laughter*. University of Texas Press, 1995.

Royal, Derek Parker. "Introduction: Coloring America: Multi-Ethnic Engagements with Graphic Narrative." *MELUS*, vol. 32, no. 3, 2007, pp. 7–22.

Russo, Mary. "Female Grotesques: Carnival and Theory." *Feminist Studies, Critical Studies*, edited by Teresa de Lauretis, Indiana University Press, 1986, pp. 213–229.

Sabin, Roger. *Comics, Comix & Graphic Novels: A History of Comic Art*. Phaidon, 2001.

Said, Edward W. *Out of Place: A Memoir*. Granta, 2000.

Samanci, Özge. "Lynda Barry's Humor: At the Juncture of Private and Public, Invitation and Dissemination, Childish and Professional." *International Journal of Comic Art*, vol. 8, no. 2, 2006, pp. 181–199.

Schalk, Sami. "Reevaluating the Supercrip." *Journal of Literary & Cultural Disability Studies*, vol. 10, no. 1, 2016, pp. 71–86.

Schrag, Ariel. *The High School Comic Chronicles of Ariel Schrag: Awkward and Definition*. Simon & Schuster, 2008.

———. *The High School Comic Chronicles of Ariel Schrag: Likewise*. Simon & Schuster, 2009.

———. *The High School Comic Chronicles of Ariel Schrag: Potential*. Simon & Schuster, 2008.

———. Message to the author, October 27, 2013. E-mail.

———. Message to the author, January 27, 2014. E-mail.

Schulz, Gabby. "Di(e)ary Comic." *Gabby's Playhouse*, August 7, 2012, www.gabbysplayhouse.com/more-bits/.

Sedgwick, Eve Kosofsky. *Tendencies*. Routledge, 1994.

Sewell, Edward H., Jr. "Queer Characters in Comic Strips." *Comics & Ideology*, edited by Matthew P. McAllister et al., Peter Lang, 2001, pp. 251–274.

Shaheen, Jack G. "Arab Images in American Comic Books." *Journal of Popular Culture*, vol. 28, no. 1, 1994, pp. 123–133.

———. *Guilty: Hollywood's Verdict on Arabs after 9/11*. Olive Branch Press, 2008.

Shakespeare, Tom. "The Social Model of Disability." *The Disability Studies Reader*, edited by Lennard J. Davis, 2nd ed., Routledge, 2006, pp. 197–204.

Shaw, Adrienne. "Women on Women: Lesbian Identity, Lesbian Community, and Lesbian Comics." *Journal of Lesbian Studies*, vol. 13, no. 1, 2009, pp. 88–97.

Shelton, Jama. "Redefining Realities through Self-Representational Performance." *Queer Youth Cultures*, edited by Susan Driver, State University of New York Press, 2008, pp. 69–86.

Siebers, Tobin. *Disability Aesthetics*. University of Michigan Press, 2010.

———. "Disability and the Theory of Complex Embodiment—For Identity Politics in a New Register." *The Disability Studies Reader*, edited by Lennard J. Davis, 4th ed., Routledge, 2013, pp. 278–297.

———. "Disability in Theory: From Social Constructionism to the New Realism of the Body." *The Disability Studies Reader*, edited by Lennard J. Davis, 2nd ed., Routledge, 2006, pp. 173–183.

———. *Disability Theory*. University of Michigan Press, 2008.

Silverman, Kaja. *The Threshold of the Visible World*. Routledge, 1996.

Singer, Marc. "'Black Skins' and White Masks: Comic Books and the Secret of Race." *African American Review*, vol. 36, no. 1, 2002, pp. 107–119.

Slade, Shelley. "The Image of the Arab in America: Analysis of a Poll on American Attitudes." *Middle East Journal*, vol. 35, no. 2, 1981, pp. 143–162.

Smith, Sidonie. "Performativity, Autobiographical Practice, Resistance." *a/b: Auto/Biography Studies*, vol. 10, no. 1, 1995, pp. 17–33.

Smith, Sidonie, and Julia Watson. *Reading Autobiography: A Guide for Interpreting Life Narratives*. 2nd ed., University of Minnesota Press, 2010.

Smyth, Joshua M., and Melanie A. Greenberg. "Scriptotherapy: The Effects of Writing about Traumatic Events." *Psychodynamic Perspectives on Sickness and Health*, edited by Paul Raphael Duberstein and Joseph M. Masling, American Psychological Association, 2000, pp. 121–163.

Snyder, Sharon L., and David T. Mitchell. *Cultural Locations of Disability*. University of Chicago Press, 2006.

Soper, Kerry. "From Swarthy Ape to Sympathetic Everyman and Subversive Trickster: The Development of Irish Caricature in American Comic Strips between 1890 and 1920." *Journal of American Studies*, vol. 39, no. 2, 2005, pp. 257–296.

Spiegelman, Art. *Comix, Essays, Graphics and Scraps (From Maus to Now to Maus to Now)*. Raw Books & Graphics, 1999.

———. "Drawing Blood: Outrageous Cartoons and the Art of Outrage." *Harper's*, June 2006, pp. 43–52.

Squier, Susan Merrill. "The Uses of Graphic Medicine for Engaged Scholarship." *Graphic Medicine Manifesto*, edited by MK Czerwiec et al., The Pennsylvania State University Press, 2015, pp. 41–66.

Stallybrass, Peter, and Allon White. *The Politics and Poetics of Transgression*. Cornell University Press, 1986.

Stamant, Nicole. *Serial Memoir: Archiving American Lives*. Palgrave Macmillan, 2014.

Tensuan, Theresa M. "Up from Surgery: The Politics of Self-Representation in Women's Graphic Memoirs of Illness." *Graphic Subjects: Critical Essays on Autobiography and Graphic Novels*, edited by Michael A. Chaney, University of Wisconsin Press, 2011, pp. 180–194.

Tilley, Carol L. "Seducing the Innocent: Fredric Wertham and the Falsifications That Helped Condemn Comics." *Information & Culture*, vol. 47, no. 4, 2012, pp. 383–413.

Tong, Ng Suat. "In Search of 'It': A Response to a Review of *Potential*." *Hooded Utilitarian*, February 22, 2010, www.hoodedutilitarian.com/2010/02/in-search-of-it-a-response-to-a-review-of-potential/.

Ty, Eleanor. *The Politics of the Visible in Asian North American Narratives*. University of Toronto Press, 2004.

van der Kolk, Bessel A., and Onno van der Hart. "The Intrusive Past: The Flexibility of Memory and the Engraving of Trauma." *Trauma: Explorations in Memory*, edited by Cathy Caruth, Johns Hopkins University Press, 1995, pp. 158–182.

Wallace, Michele. "Afterword: 'Why Are There No Great Black Artists?' The Problem of Visuality in African-American Culture." *Black Popular Culture*, edited by Gina Dent, Bay Press, 1992, pp. 333–346.

Wanzo, Rebecca. "Black Nationalism, Bunrako, and Beyond: Articulating Black Heroism through Cultural Fusion and Comics." *Multicultural Comics: From Zap to Blue Beetle*, edited by Frederick Luis Aldama, University of Texas Press, 2010, pp. 93–104.

Ware, Chris. *The Acme Novelty Library Annual Report to Shareholders and Rainy Day Saturday Afternoon Fun Book*. Pantheon, 2005.

Watson, Julia. "Autographic Disclosures and Genealogies of Desire in Alison Bechdel's *Fun Home*." *Biography*, vol. 31, no. 1, 2008, pp. 27–58.

Watson, Julia, and Sidonie Smith. "Introduction: Mapping Women's Self-Representation at Visual/Textual Interfaces." *Interfaces: Women, Autobiography, Image, Performance*, edited by Sidonie Smith and Julia Watson, University of Michigan Press, 2002, pp. 1–46.

Wendell, Susan. "Toward a Feminist Theory of Disability." *Feminist Perspectives in Medical Ethics*, edited by Helen Bequaert Holmes and Laura M. Purdy, Indiana University Press, 1992, pp. 63–81.

Wertham, Fredric. *Seduction of the Innocent*. Clarke, Irwin & Company, 1954.

Whitehead, Anne. *Trauma Fiction*. Edinburgh University Press, 2004.

Whitlock, Gillian. *Soft Weapons: Autobiography in Transit*. University of Chicago Press, 2007.

Williams, Kristian. "The High School Comic Chronicles of Ariel Schrag by Ariel Schrag." *Verbicide*, January 29, 2010, www.verbicidemagazine.com/2010/01/29/the-high-school -comic-chronicles-of-ariel-schrag-by-ariel-schrag/.

Wonham, Henry B. *Playing the Races: Ethnic Caricature and American Literary Realism*. Oxford University Press, 2004.

Wright, Bradford W. *Comic Book Nation: The Transformation of Youth Culture in America*. Johns Hopkins University Press, 2001.

Index

Italicized page numbers indicate illustrations.

About the Author

FREDERIK BYRN KØHLERT is Lecturer in the School of Art, Media and American Studies at the University of East Anglia. He is also the author of *The Chicago Literary Experience: Writing the City, 1893–1953*.